THE

BUDDHA

AND THE

BADASS

ALSO BY VISHEN LAKHIANI

The Code of the Extraordinary Mind

THE
BUDDHA
AND THE
BADASS

THE SECRET SPIRITUAL ART OF

SUCCEEDING AT WORK

VISHEN LAKHIANI

RODALE
NEW YORK

All rights reserved.
Published in the United States by Rodale Books, an imprint of Random House,
a division of Penguin Random House LLC, New York.
rodalebooks.com

RODALE and the Plant colophon are registered trademarks of Penguin Random House LLC.

Library of Congress Cataloging-in-Publication Data
Names: Lakhiani, Vishen, author.
Title: The buddha and the badass : the secret spiritual art of succeeding at work / Vishen Lakhiani.
Description: First edition. | New York : Rodale, [2020] | Includes bibliographical references and index.
Identifiers: LCCN 2019058910 (print) | LCCN 2019058911 (ebook) | ISBN 9781984823397 (hardcover) |
ISBN 9781984823403 (epub)
Subjects: LCSH: Self-actualization (Psychology) | Self-realization. | Work.
Classification: LCC BF637.S4 L322 2020 (print) | LCC BF637.S4 (ebook) | DDC 158.1—dc23
LC record available at https://lccn.loc.gov/2019058910
LC ebook record available at https://lccn.loc.gov/2019058911

ISBN 978-1-9848-2339-7
Ebook ISBN 978-1-9848-2340-3
International Edition ISBN 978-0-593-13816-8

Printed in the United States of America

Book design by Meighan Cavanaugh
Cover design and photo-illustration: Tanya Tesoro
Cover photographs: Shutterstock

10 9 8 7

First Edition

To Hayden and Eve. First and foremost.

And to my family, Kristina, Roope, Liubov, Mohan, Virgo.

For my team at Mindvalley
and all the amazing authors and students across the world
who we live to serve.

CONTENTS

PART I

BECOMING MAGNETIC: GO INWARD TO ATTRACT OUTWARD

PART II

FINDING YOUR POWER: THE FOUR ELEMENTS THAT TRANSFORM WORK AND AMPLIFY RESULTS

PART III

BECOMING A VISIONARY: MERGING THE BUDDHA AND THE BADASS TO CHANGE THE WORLD

BEFORE YOU BEGIN . . .

Know that this book may challenge some of your deeply held beliefs about life.

I always write about a topic with the intention to disrupt. In other words, to wedge new ideas into your mind in between the normal stream of thoughts you run on autopilot. Awareness sets you free. New ideas that you *never even had an inkling of* are gateways to becoming a bigger, better, more powerful version of yourself. And that benefits not just yourself, but also your family, your community, and the world.

My friend the great philosopher Ken Wilber popularized the importance of worldviews in his work on integral theory. You can simplify his work and determine that the readers of this book will fall in one of the four following worldview categories. Depending on your worldviews certain aspects of this book will appeal to you and others might affront you.

You could be a rationalist. In which case you'll love the business ideas in this book but scoff when I speak of the magic of the mind, intuition, or listening to your soul.

You could be a traditionalist. In which case you'll love anything that reminds you of your spiritual beliefs but may feel threatened when I talk about questioning culture and traditional rules.

Or you could be a green, which means you might also be a spiritual junkie, and you'll love the talk of magic but maybe dread the sections on taking action and running a business.

Finally, you might be viewing this from the integral level. This means you are open minded and can integrate all these worldviews without feeling your ego is threatened, by picking and choosing what resonates with you. This is the most productive way to read this book.

That's because this is not a traditional book on entrepreneurship or business. The world is changing fast. When I started out teaching meditation in 2003, I had to hide my career from friends. Today meditation companies have valuations of over a billion. And today when I meet with the upper echelon of people in government, sports, Hollywood, Silicon Valley, and business, they privately share their deep spiritual beliefs and how they no longer see their work and their career from a strict material point of view.

Many have gone on record to publicly share this. My appreciation to the R&B star Miguel who spoke in *Billboard* magazine about using my 6-Phase Meditation before his concerts (more on this in Chapter 5). And to Tony Gonzalez, the famous football star, for doing the same in countless interviews. Also to Bianca Andreescu who, after beating Serena Williams in the US Open at the age of nineteen, endorsed my work and book to the press as a tool she used. Billionaires and game-changing entrepreneurs are talking about some of the controversial ideas from this book in private. And my goal is to make this conversation more public. Because now is the time.

And so this book is designed to disrupt the way you see the world and to give you the tools to shift the world through cognitive changes in your mind. In short, it creates a transformation. Once you see the patterns this book unveils, you cannot "unsee" them.

Depending on your worldview, you will either love this book or hate this book. That's by design. It's because we grow through discomfort or insight. But never through apathy.

You may have found this book in the business section at a bookstore. Though, honestly, I don't know if it truly belongs in that section. Indeed, this book is about the way we work today—because the way we work is utterly broken. But let me warn you that this book is not about business in any conventional sense. It's about transforming the way you work from the inside out—and how that internal change can ripple out to change the world.

So, what *is* this book? It's about the mastery of your work and your life, whether you're launching a start-up, at the helm of a major organization, or only starting your first job. It's for someone who's pouring their energy into a job that doesn't feed their soul or conversely for someone who has an incredible vision for their company but can't figure out how to expand it to a world-changing level.

My first book, *The Code of the Extraordinary Mind,* accidentally became a bible for athletes across the world because it explored performance. This book explores teamwork, running a business, and making a dent in the Universe. I'd like it to be a bible for changing the nature of work.

Disrupting the Brules (Bullsh*t Rules)

If you know me already, you understand that's what I'm about. We all live by a set of rules that are conditioned into us. These beliefs are firehosed into our psyches by our parents, teachers, culture, governments, and the media. In *The Code of the Extraordinary Mind,* I created a name for these beliefs: BRULES. It stands for "bullshit rules."

They are all around us. And when we don't question them, they trap us. They can rob us of a fuller version of life that we could be tapping into. Now it's time to disrupt your long-held brules around work. Why? Well, because if you're the average person in the developed world, you spend 70 percent of your waking hours there. And if you're the average person, you're also miserable at your job because of these brules—which is simply not an acceptable state of affairs for your one shot at life. More on that later.

Now, I'm not a business consultant. But I was once a struggling entrepreneur with a penchant for questioning rules. As I experimented with disrupting some of the traditional brules on how work was meant to function, I created a business, workplace, and life that is beyond extraordinary.

My research lab was my own life and company. And I've codified everything I've learned here into *how-to* steps. I've learned that when work is tuned to what we're passionate about, it ceases to be work.

What you must understand is that no matter your station, you possess incredible unique powers that you must learn to use. Hard work and hustle as a path to success are a modern myth. Inside you is a spirit and a soul that many of us refuse to unleash into the domain of work. But this is a brule. When we bring an awakened mind to work, magic happens.

Now let's go deep about that word *magic*. Some of the ideas I share in this book are in the realm of the spiritual. In other words, they cannot (yet) be proven by science. I will speak of the soul, intuition, synchronicity, and *bending reality*. Keep an open mind. If you think these ideas are BS, remember that men like Steve Jobs, whom we see as one of the greatest creators and CEOs of all time, embraced them.

If these ideas really don't resonate with you, hand this book over to someone who may benefit. Because getting these ideas into practice matters. We need to fix work. We are operating inside old obsolete models. According to Gallup, 85 percent of workers hate their job. Most people are living their lives doing work they *don't love*, to earn money to afford to live lives they *don't love*. Far worse, they lie to themselves about it. They pretend they semi-enjoy what they do to earn a paycheck. An alien species watching planet Earth would think, *What is wrong with these creatures?*

From a global perspective that means around 5,369 people across the world die every hour, every day, without having fulfilled their highest potential and experienced their deepest joy. Most of us put off our own happiness and dreams until tomorrow in an attempt to just stay afloat today. But that's a catastrophic mistake. The inescapable truth is this: Time. Runs. Out.

If you're reading this book, I would wager you have incredible aspirations. You dream of writing books, building successful companies, running for office, or making a difference in your community. So don't waste your time. It's your most precious commodity.

When it comes to work, it's time to discard whatever doesn't empower you. This is your companion guide.

How This Book Was Written

Like my first book, *The Code of the Extraordinary Mind,* this book has some unique learning methodologies embedded in it. My company, Mindvalley, specializes in human transformation and so I care about making learning stick. These are the methods that ensure that these ideas will stay with you and take root in your life.

EXERCISES

I share tools, techniques, thought experiments, and exercises throughout the book, and then compile each chapter's tools and techniques at the end of the chapter for easy reference. I want you to engage with the book, take notes, write in the margins, and make it your own.

I also call out stealth leadership techniques to adapt certain ideas to the worker who isn't currently leading their own company or team. If you're not leading a team but are a member of one, I share subtle ways to create change around you without your having to possess a formal title.

STORIES

During the process of writing this book, I gathered stories from some of the most incredible minds today. I'm eternally grateful that my company, Mindvalley, has allowed me to become an intersection point for incredible leaders, and my interviews and work with hundreds from the fields of business, science, technology, spirituality, education, and relationships form the basis of my success and the ideas I share in this book.

In writing this book, I spent two weeks masterminding with Richard Branson and other business leaders on Necker Island. I spoke on stage at events alongside Michael Beckwith, Jay Shetty, and Gary Vaynerchuk. I sat down next to Marianne Williamson, Dave Asprey, Ken Wilber, Keith Ferrazzi, Chip Conley, and Shefali Tsabary for candid interviews. There are too many incredible names to mention that have contributed to this book. I don't say this to brag. I attribute my success to their mentorship and I am grateful to call many of them friends. These relationships have allowed me to connect the dots, see patterns, and build new codes for how to achieve unorthodox levels of success. I don't believe in guruship. I believe no one has all the answers, including me, so all my books integrate theories and ideas from multiple minds.

So, I'll be sharing personal stories from the intimate conversations I've had with many of the greatest visionaries of our time. This book is an homage to the knowledge they've shared with me, as well as the lessons I've learned from my own team, many of whom have influenced me in ways they'll never know.

MY VOICE AND STORY

The way I write is candid. I don't hold back. I've shared stories here that I'm nervous to tell. But I don't mind telling on myself to drive home the point that anyone can do what I've done.

I quit Silicon Valley in 2003 to become a meditation teacher. I then started Mindvalley with $700 with no VC funding or investors. And as I'm writing this book we're preparing to go for an IPO. And it didn't happen without serious hurdles. My success started in a backroom of a warehouse in a ghetto neighborhood in Kuala Lumpur, Malaysia. If you're wondering where that is, I'm not surprised.

Expect personal stories and a writing style that is raw and vulnerable, as if you and I are seated across the table from one another.

ONLINE EXPERIENCE

For people who want a deeper dive into the concepts in this book, I will share links to additional resources along the way. As a computer engineer at heart, I created several online tools to help you with the transformational journey this book might lead you on. You'll find hours of additional videos and trainings for specific sections of this book to make it easier to bring some of the ideas here back to your life.

DEFINITION OF *ENTREPRENEUR*

An important note about the use of the word *entrepreneur.* To me, the word *entrepreneur* does not mean you're running a company. You can be working for a company or part of a group like NASA and still have the entrepreneur mindset. It means you're innovating, creating, honing your skills, and contributing to the world —and not merely spinning a hamster wheel to earn a paycheck. When I refer to the term *entrepreneur* in this book, it applies to everyone who is choosing to make a difference in the world by doing their best work, whether you're self-employed, a contractor, running a billion-dollar company, or working for a company.

CONNECT WITH ME

I love connecting with my readers. I primarily use Instagram and share new experiments, stories, and ideas there regularly. I would love to connect with you on that platform. But, just in case, I'm occasionally on Facebook and Twitter, too.

Instragram.com/vishen

Facebook.com/vishenlakhiani

Twitter.com/vishen

MY WEBSITES

To learn more about me and my work:

Mindvalley.com

Vishen.com

INTRODUCTION

Nature loves courage. You make the commitment and nature will respond to that commitment by removing impossible obstacles. Dream the impossible dream and the world will not grind you under, it will lift you up. This is the trick. This is what all these teachers and philosophers who really counted, who really touched the alchemical gold, this is what they understood. This is the shamanic dance in the waterfall. This is how magic is done. By hurling yourself into the abyss and discovering it's a feather bed.

—Terence McKenna

I n 2019, I found myself in the Caribbean attending a four-day mastermind for entrepreneurs. It was on a gorgeous island with white sand beaches and sunsets to die for. One morning following an early session, I went outside to get some fresh air. I sat down at a wooden bench overlooking a rocky cliff. The ocean was calm, a mirror with tiny imperfections. Strips of light from the morning sun burned through a thin cloud layer and reflected across the expanse of glassy water.

I took a moment to take it all in, then turned to my iPhone. I pulled my

AirPods from my pocket, stuck them in my ears, and started going through the hundreds of messages from my team on the other side of the world. I was completely consumed with my phone when a woman approached me.

"I've seen you all day today and yesterday on your phone. You must be really working hard. What would make your day better today?" she asked. She was in the same business mastermind.

"Oh, thank you," I said. "But my day is already perfect. Nothing could make it better."

She seemed stunned.

"Were you asking me that because you saw me on a phone here on this beautiful beach?" I asked.

"Yes," she said.

In that moment, I understood where the woman was coming from. She saw me on a beach glued to my cellphone. I could understand why she thought I needed saving from my "work." And, truth be told, there was a time once when I did need "saving." My job and personal life were once separate. Work was what I *had* to do to pay the bills to survive. But that's not the case anymore. Let me explain . . .

"I totally understand you," I said. "But I'm not working. I'm communicating with my team. And my work is so inspiring that it never feels like work. I love my team. Communicating with them is like talking to my friends," I explained.

I held up my iPhone.

"And this isn't a phone. To me, it's a 'portal of love.' I'm doing what I love right now. Communicating with the people I love. Writing about what I love. Sharing on social media with more people around the world who I love. Sending cheesy videos to friends and family I love. I'm not disconnected—I'm deeply connected.

"When you do what you love, you never have to work a day in your life. So thank you, and I get your concern, and you're wonderful to check in on me, but I choose to experience this moment here on this cliff doing exactly what I'm doing now. It's what I love."

"Wow," she said. "I think I just learned something there."

I smiled and went back to my phone.

Work wasn't always like this for me. But today, my life has become the experience captured most eloquently in this L.P. Jacks quote:

> *The master in the art of living makes little distinction between his work and his play, his labor and his leisure, his mind and his body, his education and his recreation, his love and his religion. He hardly knows which is which. He simply pursues his vision of excellence at whatever he does, leaving others to decide whether he is working or playing. To him he is always doing both.*

Anyone can have this. Although for many it requires a total mindset shift. And that's what this book will do for you.

But first, you must stand in the belief that you *can* create a life where work doesn't feel like work. And you don't have to truly believe that yet. But you must be open to it. You have to at least believe that's possible for other people even if you don't yet believe you can have it yourself at this point. This book will get you there. It's designed to have you see yourself in an entirely new paradigm.

Second, you must understand the big fat brule (bullshit rule) about success: the false belief that you have to work harder than anyone else. To put more hours in. In other words, to *hustle.* Anyone who believes this buys into a lie that's simply not true.

This book shows you how to go beyond the myth of hard work. You'll tap into a higher level of work where you'll access heightened states of consciousness that allow you to effortlessly glide through the world while creating impact. When you operate from these states, you will notice that you merge two beautiful states of being human. I call this the merger of the Buddha and the badass.

The Buddha is the archetype of the spiritual master. The person who can live in this world but also move with an ease, grace, and flow that come from inner awareness and alignment. I'm not necessarily talking about the literal Buddha; i.e., someone who has achieved enlightenment, but instead someone who recognizes and uses the power of the world "within us."

I grew up in Southeast Asia in a family that practices Hindu and Buddhist traditions. I speak of the Buddha with reverence and sought the advice of Buddhist spiritual teachers before choosing the title. This book, however, does not bring in any of the cultural or religious aspects of Buddhism, but deep scholars of the field will notice some similar worldviews within this book.

The badass is the archetype of the changemaker. This is the person who is out there creating change, building, coding, writing, inventing, leading. Pushing humanity forward to bring life to new structures in the physical plane. The badass represents the benevolent disruptor—the person challenging the norms so we can be better as a species.

To truly be a master of life you need to integrate the skillsets of both. When you do, you live life at a different level from most people:

1. **Bliss:** You find great joy in what you do. Work and play become one.
2. **Immunity to Overwhelm:** You're no longer burdened by thoughts of overwhelm. Multitasking becomes easy.
3. **Relationships:** You're able to create a positive vibe and generate energy with the people you're working with. This means all relationships are win-win and all interactions are imbued with positivity and care.

4. **Inspiration On Demand:** You're able to tap into ideas, inspiration, and creativity on demand so that you become a source of innovation and creative output.

5. **Abundance:** Whether it's financial or health, love, and life experiences, you start to see abundance emerging in all areas of your life.

6. **Flow and Ease:** Life flows almost as if it's blessed by luck and synchronicity. It almost feels as if you are held by a benevolent Universe.

7. **Bend Reality:** What you want comes to you with ease; you feel as if you are supported by the Universe.

These heightened states of awareness may sound mystical or spiritual, but they are real. All human beings can access them. Don't get me wrong, hustle has its place, but only for people operating at ordinary levels.

Of the seven traits I mentioned above, please take a pen and highlight the top three that you want to learn from this book. This simple action will help you gain even more out of this book. Pause for a moment and do this. It will make you read this book with a deliberate *intention*.

Regardless of where you're at now, I want you to know this: You can experience life at an expanded level. And no matter where you might be in the stages of your business or career, the book is designed to give you new ways of discovering yourself and looking at the world that will cause a massive upleveling in how you function.

I know this from experience. It wasn't long ago that I was thirty-two years old, living in a bedroom in my parents' home, driving a Nissan March, and barely making $3,000 a month. That was in 2008. But today, as this book goes to press, I am blessed to run a multimillion-dollar empire that's transforming global education. And my life today would seem to be an unrealistic fantasy to my 2008 self.

You can do that too. You can achieve whatever it is your soul was sent here to do. And in this book I will share all the tools I've learned so I can support you to get there easier and faster than I did.

Ten Years of Experiments

In 2008, my company, Mindvalley, was an eighteen-person operation. We built websites and online courses for personal growth authors. I had no major hot product. To be honest, I was burning through $15,000 a month and running low on cash. My small team operated out of a small three-bedroom house in a residential area.

I had big dreams but no idea how to get there. We were bringing in $250,000 a month in ecommerce sales from little shopping sites, but we were still *losing money*. If I kept burning money, my venture would soon be dead.

As a result of this dilemma, I sank into a period of depression. I had a one-year-old baby boy. I couldn't fail at this business. But goddamn it. It was hard.

Yet what I did have in my favor was an obsession with personal growth. I was committed to constantly growing so that I could become the best version of myself. I picked up every book I could read. Studied every author and attended every personal growth seminar I could. My daily routine was:

Grow Myself.
Grow My Business.
Repeat.

We often don't pay attention to personal growth when it comes to business or work. Instead we focus on business strategy, product innovation, and culture. Well, I'd tried that. I'd even given a huge chunk of my little business to a Stanford MBA so I could bring in the latest innovations in modern management. It did not help.

But that wasn't all. I started Mindvalley in the United States. As an immigrant I couldn't get a work visa. I had to relocate the entire business to Malaysia, my country of birth. (I'll share the full story in Chapter 2.) I envisioned Mindvalley as a globally recognized brand. Here I was, stuck in Kuala Lumpur, Malaysia. This situation wasn't helping.

And so I had no product. No money. And I was in a highly disadvantaged location.

So I turned my focus on one singular objective: Create the No. 1 Place in the World to Work (the exact story of WHY I chose that goal and how it emerged will be shared in Chapter 2). I figured if I could nail this, everything else would come. The people. The talent. The product innovation. And the money. If I focused on creating such a great workplace, I would also enjoy my job more. And have more time to thrive, grow, and love life.

This obsession became the Mindvalley experiment. And through it all I discovered the principles that make work a playground of innovation, productivity, creation, and joy. But more than that, these principles create a new type of employee or entrepreneur: the person who has merged the badass and the Buddha of their nature and is able to create massive results with magical ease.

In the ensuing ten years, a lot has changed:

- Mindvalley's office is on *Inc.* magazine's 2019 list of Top 10 Most Beautiful Offices in the World. As you'll learn soon, it started in the backroom of a warehouse in Kuala Lumpur, Malaysia. We've reinvented the office and today it's a case study for workplace interior designers.
- Our work culture at Mindvalley is so attractive that people from around the world relocate to Malaysia to work from our headquarters. Mindvalley employs brilliant minds from sixty

different countries. Walking into our office is like walking into the United Nations with all its diversity.

- Our team dynamic is vibrant and thriving. Our team scores significantly above average for multiple metrics of well-being and health. People join Mindvalley and get younger, fitter, happier, and healthier. I myself beat my health metrics every year as I get older. Recently we were awarded "Healthiest Employer" in our city based on insurance data. Our people get sick less and score well above average in multiple areas of health data.

- But the biggest result is this: As this book goes to print we will have also pulled off something rather unusual. We will have approached $100 million in revenue as an EdTech company with NO venture funding. This is a rarity in the industry. Our competition at the same level of revenue have raised between $75 and $300 million in funding. We did it with no venture capital.

- Best of all is that I live my life in balance and happiness. I feel blessed and grateful waking up every morning. I have close connections and love surrounding me. I get to work on things that light me up. I also get to travel, see the world with my two kids, meet the most amazing people, and experience tremendous fulfillment in what I do to serve the world.

This is what makes this book unique. I created my own test lab, and despite being in a disadvantaged location and not having access to capital, I'm building this company into $100 million in revenue using the ideas in this book. And I documented every painful lesson and brilliant "aha!" so that you can replicate this success.

The Magic and Power Within You

I'm an engineer. I have a degree in electrical engineering and computer science. I've been a science nerd all my life. My mind is attuned to processes, numbers, code, and spreadsheets.

But I've always been intrigued by people who seem to operate from a space beyond the hard data. They generate ideas on the fly. They magnetically attract the right people. They seem to be unusually "lucky." Others crave joining their missions, their companies, their teams. If these types of workers are in an organization, they move with fluidity and ease, nailing projects with a smile on their face. Getting the coveted raises and promotions. Many of them are able to handle multiple projects at once. Juggling dual roles and responsibilities while making each project thrive, much like Steve Jobs juggled the roles of being a leader at both Pixar and Apple. Yet the forces of overwhelm dare not touch them.

These superstar workers are often able to get in the zone at ease, displaying remarkable focus and creativity. And producing great work at dizzying speeds, like how Elton John released four albums in a single year and became responsible for 5 percent of all the music sold globally that year.

They are often also masters of relationships, forging close ties with their teams, their vendors, and everyone around them. They are intensely likable. When they do business, it's about win-win and not win-lose. I've witnessed this in charismatic leaders I've come to know, like Richard Branson of Virgin and Oprah Winfrey.

One of the most unique qualities they seem to have is remarkable luck. Things just go easily for them. They are the ones who get the raises. The recognition. Easy business success. It seems like the Universe bends in their favor.

Their personal lives thrive too. Many of them are in great health, and they just don't seem to age as fast. They have wonderful families, friendships, and connections with everyone around them.

These men and women are not blessed by a particular genetic edge like intelligence. Rather, they run their lives by a distinct set of rules. These superstars are embodying the qualities of both **the Buddha** and **the badass.** All human beings have access to these two qualities—and that's the journey this book takes you on.

The Myth of Hard Work

So why the obsession with hard work, hustle, and toil at the expense of everything else? Simply put, we don't understand what is normal. Our broken education systems teach us to survive at a job but not to thrive as a human. Success is often defined as the amount of money in your bank account or the title on your business card. But people are far more complex than a title or position. To understand this you must understand the two worlds we all live in.

There is our outer world, which is shared with other humans. This is the world of jobs, careers, culture, rituals, and shared meaning with others. We place so much emphasis on regimenting and ordering this outside world. We have laws, rules, structures, and processes to govern our lives.

But we also have an inner world. This is the world inside our own heads. It's our hopes, fears, aspirations, dreams, daily cascade of emotions. It consists of every doubt, every hope, every brazen thought, every secret desire or aspiration. And this world for most people is completely unstructured, messy, and disorganized.

To attain balance a person must bring order to this inner world. This requires knowing what this world consists of and having clear intentions for what you want to experience in this inner world before you go after getting them in your outer world.

And this means refusing to buy into the lie of hard work. Replace it with this:

The Soul's Experience on Earth Is Not Meant for Hard Work
and Toil. It's Meant for Freedom, Ease, and Expansion.

I've traveled the world meeting everyone from billionaires to spiritual teachers from the mountains of China. And I discovered that truly extraordinary people are not working "hard" but rather are focused on nurturing certain inner states of being and identities that allow life to unfold for them effortlessly.

Changing Our Mental Models of Work

The first step on this journey is changing your mental models, the operating system for your entire experience of life and work. A mental model is made up of your beliefs. And your beliefs are the master switch for your life. That's because reality is subjective.

In 1977, the famous physicist David Bohm lectured at Berkeley. An excerpt of his speech was later published in the book *The Quantum and the Lotus* by Matthieu Ricard and Trinh Thuan, where he offers a beautiful formulation of the interplay between our beliefs and what we experience as reality:

> *Reality is what we take to be true.*
> *What we take to be true is what we believe.*
> *What we believe is based upon our perceptions.*
> *What we perceive depends upon what we look for.*
> *What we look for depends upon what we think.*
> *What we think depends upon what we perceive.*
> *What we perceive determines what we believe.*
> *What we believe determines what we take to be true.*
> *What we take to be true is our reality.*

In short, reality doesn't really exist. We make it all up. All the time. And you can bend reality. You can shift it and mold it and play with it. It's quite fun. When you get it right, work and life all become one. A masterful act of living perpetually in play as you seem to have superhuman abilities to juggle it all.

The Multidimensional Human Being

As I built up Mindvalley I was blessed to have access to many of the most brilliant minds in the world. For my very first book, *The Code of the Extraordinary Mind,* I conducted some two hundred hours of interviews with leading thinkers about the human mind. I then integrated what I learned into several transformational models.

I coin specific names for these models to make them easier to understand and apply in your life. Here are some of the transformational models I will use in this book.

1. CONSCIOUSNESS ENGINEERING

Consciousness engineering is a framework for expanding your level of awareness on any subject. It suggests that if we want to grow in a field we pay attention to two things:

1. **Our Models of Reality.** A *model of reality (MOR)* is a belief. And your beliefs become your reality. If you believe that hard work is necessary for success, it will be. *For you.* Someone else could have a totally different belief.

2. **Our Systems for Living.** A *system for living (SFL)* is a process. It's your optimized set of procedures for getting something done. For example, a particular routine for the gym. Applied to work, a system

might be a way for aligning your goals with your team. Or for multi-tasking. Or for bringing on superhuman levels of focus and flow.

Every chapter of the book will end by collecting the chapter's models and systems so that you can easily reference those processes as you implement the ideas in the book.

If you think of the human being as a computer, then your beliefs are like your hardware. And your systems like your software. If you want to get a faster computer you can either *upgrade your hardware* or *download a software update*. Likewise, you upgrade your beliefs by dumping ideas that hold you back and taking on new empowering beliefs. And you upgrade your systems by taking on better, more optimized systems for working.

You can apply this to understanding how any genius or superhuman performer works. My friend Jim Kwik, the world-famous brain trainer, once said in a video he posted to Instagram:

> *I want to make the invisible visible. I want to expose the method behind the magic. Whenever you see someone doing something incredible in health, in sports, in business, there is a method to their magic. Because genius leaves clues.*

When you apply this approach to life, you get very very good. Very fast. Every chapter in this book will unwrap new models of reality that you are free to adopt, as well as new systems of living that you can apply in your life.

2. BRULES: BULLSHIT RULES

We all live by a set of conditioned-into-us rules. I call these beliefs: *B*RULES*. It stands for "bullshit rules."

They are all around us. And when we don't question them they trap us. They can rob us of a fuller version of life that we could be tapping into. Now it's time to disrupt your long-held brules around work.

3. BENDING REALITY

This is a concept that is going to reappear throughout the book because it's fundamental to achieving the Buddha/badass mindset. Many of the most creative and powerful people at the art of work seem to be able to access this state at will. *Bending reality* is a particular state of mind where it seems like life unfolds magically. Luck, synchronicity, moments of extreme flow—all seem to line up. You've probably experienced this at some point in your life. The trick is to be able to access this state on demand.

Interestingly, the phrase "bend reality" was used three times in Walter Isaacson's biography of Steve Jobs. Isaacson wrote of Steve:

> At the root of his reality distortion was his belief that the rules did not apply to him. He had evidence for this, in his childhood, he had often been able to bend reality to his desires. . . . He had a sense that he was . . . a chosen one. "He thinks that there are a few people who are special like Einstein and Gandhi and the gurus he met in India—and he's one of them."

In *The Code of the Extraordinary Mind*, I offer what I notice is a curious layering of mental states that seems to allow people to bend reality. I suggest that it has to do with having access to blissful emotions and passion almost as if work is play (you will learn this in Part II of this book), combined with powerful visions that pull you forward (you will learn this in

Part III of this book). This dual pillar of *bliss* and *visionary thinking* leads to enhanced states of functioning in the world.

Steve Jobs wasn't the first business legend to talk about this state. One hundred years ago when he was in his eighties, the titan John D. Rockefeller penned this poem. It was later published in the book *Titan* by Ron Chernow.

> I was early taught to work as well as play,
> My life has been one long, happy holiday;
> Full of work and full of play—
> I dropped the worry on the way—
> And God was good to me every day.

Rockefeller was the wealthiest person of his time. And you'll notice the same duality in his writing: bliss and visionary thinking.

In addition to mental models like consciousness engineering and bending reality, this book will look at elegant systems to run a business. But we're not going to go into MBA-speak.

The only systems I will cover here are systems for managing a business and growing your career that take into account the human being as a multidimensional being.

4. STEALTH LEADERSHIP

You might be the CEO of a Fortune 500 company or bootstrappy entrepreneur in start-up mode working from a Starbucks. Or you might be an employee in a much larger organization. No matter what, you can choose to be a leader. You have the power to transform your work and influence the people and teams you work within. If you don't have an official title you can still apply strategies from this book to shine at your career and influence your peers. It's a practice I call *stealth leadership*.

The reality is that every human is a leader—but most people fail to claim their power over their own lives and their experiences. You don't need the title of CEO to influence the people around you. Being a stealth leader means you exert your influence even when you don't have those three letters after your name (and, in fact, I'll tell you why I stripped myself of the CEO title and how that made me even more effective at leading my team).

You Are Not Just a Meat Body Controlled by Neurons

As long as we see humans as nothing more than meat bodies controlled by an exquisite set of neurons we'll think of work in a particular way. A highly limited way.

I prefer to think that we are much more than that. We are multidimensional beings.

Meat bodies—yes. Neurons—yes. But we are also a spirit and a soul. We are energy. We are complex creatures filled with deep longings, soul cravings, and unique superpowers ready to be unlocked.

If you thought you were buying a traditional business book, I'm sorry. I hope your bookstore has a good refund policy.

The Three Sections of This Book

There are three parts to this book. And each chapter goes extremely deep. This book is heavy on ideas and tactics. So if you find something useful you might need to read it twice to really let it sink in.

But this book does not have to be read in a linear way. You can jump chapters or go straight to whatever chapter pulls you best. Below I've explained what each chapter covers. If you're in a rush and can't read this cover to cover, go straight to the chapter that attracts you most.

PART I: BECOMING MAGNETIC: GO INWARD TO ATTRACT OUTWARD

What were you born to do? Once you are aligned with your true purpose and your *soulprint*, everything else becomes a lot easier.

Imagine your business as a powerful magnet that draws everything in the world toward it. The talent you need comes running to you.

The people you envision, with the skills, beliefs, and attitudes that fit with yours like the missing pieces of a puzzle, suddenly appear. The whole experience happens without effort and feels strangely supernatural.

In Part I, I'll train you to become a powerful magnet. That comes from aligning your work—whether it's your organization, initiative, project, or mission in life—with your innermost values and soul identity.

Chapter 1: Uncover Your Soulprint

Every person's life unfolds in a way that is unique to them. Each significant event you experience leaves a trace: every high, every low, every elation, every suffering. These experiences shape you into who you are meant to be. And when you decode them, you'll discover that the Universe has a plan for who you are meant to be. You are here to fill your unique role, career, and mission. Your greatest job is to uncover these unique values, stay true to them, and act from them.

Chapter 2: Attract Your Allies

Greatness is best achieved with others. The world is too complex to strike it alone. People are drawn to you not because of your business plan, but because your dream gives them hope. Humans are moved by emotion more than logic. The greatest gift you can give someone is to invite them to share in a dream. This is how you become magnetic and align yourself with the people you need to make any vision a reality.

PART II: FINDING YOUR POWER: THE FOUR ELEMENTS THAT TRANSFORM WORK AND AMPLIFY RESULTS

After interviewing thousands of people for jobs at my companies, I uncovered an astonishing truth about human behavior.

There are four dominant human needs people crave from any work they engage in. When you understand and apply this knowledge, people fall in love with their work and the culture they are a part of. And you need this too. When you mix these human needs into your work, your work becomes a place of healing and amplification of your power.

None of this is mystical. It's all backed by remarkable theories developed by the world's leading psychologists, philosophers, and spiritual leaders.

Chapter 3: Spark Deep Connections

Humans desire to come together. The need to belong is in our DNA. While we may see ourselves as separate from one another, the truth is, we are connected by invisible bonds. When you understand how to influence this space, you create communities where everyone is greater together than apart.

Chapter 4: Becoming an Unfuckwithable Masterpiece

In a world of many options we seek to follow others rather than follow our own inner guidance. The key is to learn to love yourself deeply and learn to trust your inner yearnings. As you do, you can channel these dreams, visions, and desires into a masterpiece of a life. As a leader, you can bring this out in others too. When you do this, the shared visions you create become reality with elegance and ease.

Chapter 5: Make Growth The Ultimate Goal

Your soul isn't here to achieve. Your soul is here to grow. Most people get this wrong. They become seduced by success and broken by failure. They add great meaning to what is essentially meaningless. The true reality is that success and failure are illusions. The only thing that matters is how fast you're evolving. Your journey is about removing all the barriers that hold you back from Self-Actualization.

Chapter 6: Choose Your Mission Wisely

As you self-actualize you gain an edge in life. The next step is to use this edge to lift others up and enhance the world—this is Self-Transcendence. When you live from this plane you will tap into a level of fulfillment beyond anything you can imagine. The goal is no longer to just refine yourself or sit in endless introspection. Rather, it's to use your newfound abilities to make the world better for others, multiple generations down.

PART III: BECOMING A VISIONARY: MERGING THE BUDDHA AND THE BADASS TO CHANGE THE WORLD

In Part III, you'll learn how to become a visionary. How to create visions and goals that truly inspire and excite the world. You'll then learn how to move rapidly toward these huge goals with ease. And as a bonus how to do so without sacrificing your health, your love life, or your family. We will bust the insidious idea that hard work is necessary for remarkable results.

Chapter 7: Activating the Visionary in You

There is no greater experience than to live your life working to achieve a vision so bold that it scares you. Any vision you commit to should be so inspiring that you stay up at night as it pulls you and flirts with you. Now, here is a big secret: The bigger your vision, the easier it gets. When you live this way, you may find that the vision is not coming from you. Instead the Universe is choosing to go through you to realize what the world needs.

Chapter 8: The Unified Brain

To tackle a truly grand vision you need to have many brains; you need a team of people to act as one unified superbrain. For the first time, we have incredible tools for this. Yet most teams work inside of age-old collaboration systems. When you learn to create a unified brain you move with amazing speed and prowess.

Chapter 9: Identity Upgrading and the Beautiful Destruction

The Universe acts as a mirror. It reflects back to you what you are. The miracle of this is that you can shift your identity and the world will obey. But you must shift it so deeply you believe the new identity and live life in accordance with it.

A Few Final Words . . .

Now more than ever, it's time to make work matter. It's time for you to find that inner power and magic to transform the way you function at work and, as a result, inspire everyone around you.

If you're looking around at whom to transfer the responsibility to, it's time you start relating to yourself as much bigger and much more powerful. Who is the trailblazer you admire? You're no different. Bezos. Branson. Musk. Huffington. Winfrey. Pick one. Or if it empowers you, forge your own identity.

It's time to ask yourself: What type of leader do you want to be? What do you want to experience in this lifetime? What legacy do you want your kids to remember you for? It's time we band together to set work straight.

Now let's get on with it.

PART I

BECOMING MAGNETIC

GO INWARD TO ATTRACT OUTWARD

Too many people end up hiding their own unique gifts to fit into the world around them. Entrepreneurs are no different. We imitate more often than we radiate.

By radiate I mean to discover the unique foundational values within your own soul. Values, I suggest, that the Universe placed within you for a reason. And to infuse everything you touch with these unique values. You seek to leave your "soulprint" on everything you create, whether it's a new app or a book or a company. And when you do this, you become magnetic.

In **Chapter 1: Uncover Your Soulprint,** you'll do a critical exercise to understand what you were born to do. This also allows you to consistently make the right decisions on whom to invite into your ecosystem. You'll learn why you need to mark your creations with the unique stamp of your soul. The process you learn, which I call the The Origin Story Exercise, is designed to extract your deeply ingrained values. You'll come to understand that core values can't be made up. Instead, they have to come *from* you.

In **Chapter 2: Attract Your Allies,** you'll learn how to turn your idea—whether it be for a business, organization, nonprofit, community group, or project—into a magnet that draws the people you need toward it. You will learn a process for effectively sharing your ideas by communicating with emotion first, then logic. You'll learn the first steps to formulating any idea and bringing it to the world so that the people you envision, with the exact skills, beliefs, and attitudes, and who are on the same mission as you, suddenly appear.

When you do the work presented in these two chapters, you'll be effortlessly aligned with your values, and others who share your values will be drawn to you. You will be surrounded with the exact people you need to make your vision a reality. You will shift from reacting to life to shaping it.

CHAPTER 1

UNCOVER YOUR SOULPRINT

Never forget what you are, for surely the world will not. Make it your strength. Then it can never be your weakness. Armour yourself in it, and it will never be used to hurt you.

—George R. R. Martin, *A Game of Thrones*
(*A Song of Ice and Fire*, Book 1)

Every person's life unfolds in a way that is unique to them. Each significant event you experience leaves a trace: every high, every low, every elation, every suffering. These experiences shape you into who you are meant to be. And when you decode them, you'll discover that the Universe has a plan for who you are meant to be. You are here to fill your unique role, career, and mission. Your greatest job is to uncover your story, stay true to it, and act from it.

FROM 2013 TO 2016, my company, Mindvalley, was burning through cash. A series of disastrous events nearly wiped out the business. This three-year period was a battle for survival.

One evening after another horrid day in survival mode, I flopped onto a chair at my kitchen table in distress. I was in crisis. It was 11 p.m. I wanted to smash my head in my pillow, turn the lights off, and go to sleep. But I had an appointment. I had a call booked with a potential Mindvalley teacher to discuss his appearance on one of our popular content shows. *And thankfully I kept it.*

I dialed the number of Srikumar Rao. And that night, I experienced his sage wisdom for the first time.

Rao is a famous business professor who has lectured at places like Columbia and London Business School. His classes have waitlists because his teachings are so revolutionary. Rao mixes the wisdom of long-dead philosophers and spiritual teachers with modern American business school ideas. It's not your classic MBA curriculum. It's more like the love child of Rumi and Jack Welch.

Rao lives in New York, but he is not the classically brash New York type. He's a humble, down-to-earth Indian man. He's the kind of person that only occasionally opens his mouth in a group, and he speaks slowly. But whenever he speaks, every person in the room shuts up because they know he's going to blow their mind.

That night we were strangers. But he's good at reading people. The tone of my voice clued him in to the fact that I was stressed.

"Vishen. Enough business talk. Are you okay?" he asked.

"Yes, I am," I said.

This was a lie, of course. Rao knew it too. So he probed further. He struck me as so loving, so sincere, I felt safe with him. I'd been struggling to hold in my anguish, and now I let it all out in a big messy stream of confessions.

"I'm burning out, Rao. I am so stressed. My health has gone to shit. I'm questioning my ability to lead and be a CEO. I am fighting to keep this company above water. And I can't share this with anyone. I've been keeping it all in. And I just don't know what to do," I shared.

Rao listened. Then he said, "Vishen. I want to read you a poem. Just listen. It's by a thirteenth-century poet named Rumi."

"Okay," I said.

But in the back of my mind I was thinking, *Poetry? Is he serious. I'm pouring my heart out and he wants to give me a damn poetry lesson?!*

But he did.

Here is that poem Rao read to me:

> When I run after *what I think I want,*
> my days are a furnace of distress and anxiety;
> If I sit in my own place of patience,
> what I need flows to me, and without any pain.
> From this I understand that what I want also wants me,
> is looking for me and attracting me.
> There is a great secret in this for anyone who can grasp it.

I didn't get it then. I only came to *truly* understand what this poem truly meant two years later. But at the time, Rao asked me what the poem meant, and that started me on the journey of understanding. So now I turn this question to you.

What do you think this poem means?

Pause for a moment. Consider your answer before you read further. Better yet, write your answer down. *What do you think this poem means?*

At the end of this book, I will remind you of it. I'll ask you to again consider what you think it means. You might surprise yourself with a new interpretation.

Rumi expresses that there are times where you feel a need to run after what you want. But is this a want that is emerging from your innermost self? Or is this an artificial want; a desire programmed into you by cultural conditioning?

That is different from *true wanting.* No one can explain those moments. There are people, places, ideas that we may feel drawn to for no particular reason. I'm sure you've had experiences like this. It may be an idea that pulls you or a vision that keeps you up at night. Sometimes it makes no sense at all. It may seem eerie to you. Yet you feel pulled by this vision despite common sense.

Just as each of us has a unique fingerprint, what if we also have a unique *soulprint*? A unique marker for our soul based on the experiences that soul seeks to have in this lifetime?

Discovering Your Soulprint

I've learned to listen to my soul. You may call it your inner knowing or gut instinct. I'm sure there are times you've listened to it too. And when you do, the Universe sends you what you need. This is when magic happens.

Your soulprint is an underlying set of instructions that you are operating in sync without realizing it. In business-speak, your soulprint is created by uncovering your foundational values.

What you'll learn in this chapter is that these values can't be made up. They come from you. They are the unique markers of your soul. And I'll walk you through a process for how to do this.

This is what it means to think like a Buddha. Instead of getting tied to the illusions of the world, which train you to want things that don't truly matter, you must strip away the brainwashing. When you learn to listen to the voice that's authentically yours, you will understand what your soul is actually driven to do in this world. And this is *the reason you were truly born.*

Your soulprint is represented by a unique set of values built into you. Values make every decision simple. When you uncover yours, you obtain a newfound resonance in your life that attracts more of what's in harmony with your real desires and repels what is not.

Too many of us are running after *what we think* we want because we've been brainwashed to believe these are our needs. We take jobs that crush our soul. Or build businesses that have no resonance with our deepest longings. I know because I've been there.

In 2010, I started a venture-backed start-up in the then-hot Silicon Valley digital coupon space. I had no interest in digital coupons. I only co-founded this company because I knew the space was booming. We closed a $2 million round of funding and the business took off. But six months in, I realized how miserable my life had become. I dreaded going to work. And I saw no value in our product. So I gave up most of my shares to my cofounders and quit feeling like a failure.

I was making false starts because I was woefully unaware of my foundational values, my *soulprint*. If I had only known to ask myself this philosophical question that I learned years later, I wouldn't have endured the turmoil:

If I am a soul choosing a human experience, why *am I here?*

If you run a successful business, are building one, or lead a team, what you learn next in this chapter is vital. Perhaps even a complete game-changer.

So often we're told to build products based on product market fit. We're told to ask, "What product do you want to sell?" or "What's the market asking for?" These questions should be asked inside a context of values. The question most people fail to ask is: "Given my values, given what fulfills me and how I want to grow, what can I uniquely offer the world?"

Before you take a job or start a company, begin first by knowing your values. Your book, your blog, your clothing line, your app, your career should be infused with your unique set of values. If you're not in a leadership position, identifying your values is the easiest way to align yourself with the right people and the right career where your gifts will shine.

Your values are what give you and whatever you create that special edge. More than that, they make your work meaningful to you so you know you've truly made a dent in the world. Market research, data, customer surveys are *subservient* to your values.

And make no mistake, your values are already shaping the choices you make. When you clearly uncover them they help you steer clear of putting yourself in positions that go against your deeply ingrained beliefs. Life becomes easier. Unlike so many other people, you know who you really are and what you truly want.

In this chapter, you'll get a glimpse of your unique soulprint by uncovering your values. But before we do that work, since there are so many misconceptions around core values, let me clear up the muck.

Your Values Point to New Visions for the World

Most entrepreneurs get core values wrong. In Mindvalley's early days, I certainly did. In 2008 when I assembled my team to do a values exercise, I was imitating Silicon Valley start-ups. We went through a democratic voting process to choose the company values.

Every member of my team has an equal vote, and our forty-person team identified some three hundred different attributes of Mindvalley. We clustered them and came up with a ten-point list of our supposed "values." The list included lines like:

> We Turn Customers into Raving Fans
> We Dare to Dream Big
> We Evolve Through Learning

It was democratic. It was fair. It was also very, very wrong.

Eight years later, I realized the folly of this method. I had confused my personal values (*foundational values*) with my company's values (*organizational values*). Almost all founders or start-up entrepreneurs make this mistake.

I needed to learn the difference and importance of the personal founding "why" and the company's "why." This happened in 2016 when an ex-employee, who was known as Amir Ahmad Nasr at the time, took me to lunch.

One of the best decisions I've made was hiring Amir. He was twenty-one when he came to Mindvalley in October 2007. Five years later, he published a well-regarded memoir, *My Isl@m: How Fundamentalism Stole My Mind—and Doubt Freed My Soul,* which led to his sharing the stage with Nobel laureates, former heads of state, and world-changing entrepreneurs.

This courageous book caused such a stir, it forced him to relocate to Canada, where he now resides. Today he is more widely known as the Toronto-based musician, singer-songwriter, and creative entrepreneur Drima Starlight. As an artist who loves to teach, he is a trusted strategic adviser to accomplished founders and CEOs, Forbes 30 Under 30 entrepreneurs, Grammy- and Emmy-recognized storytellers, *New York Times* bestselling authors, and TEDx speakers. I'm proud that Drima got his professional start at Mindvalley.

During his explosive career growth, Drima became obsessed with origin stories and core values. He invited me for lunch one day to gently point out that I was thinking of values in the wrong way. He spent five years at Mindvalley and knew the company intimately. As he became a world authority on designing company values we remained friends, and now he was in a position to expand my mind.

Drima explained the two types of core values and why so many people get values wrong.

Foundational values define the soul of a company. They bring the right people into the ecosystem. They give a product a unique edge. Great brands, great books, great restaurants are often unique because of the unique "flavor" given to them by their founders' values. Think Nike, Apple, or Starbucks. These values are also the key principles, guiding beliefs, and foundational ideas that shape the culture. Foundational values come from the founding team of a company. They are used to decide who gets IN the door. If you're a solopreneur or freelance, they are your values for how you operate.

Organizational values are developed once people are in the door. They are the rules that govern the expected behaviors required for day-to-day collaborations to run smoothly. They are agreed upon by the company as a whole. As you grow your team and company, organizational values become increasingly important.

Mindvalley had a clear set of organizational values that came from the team. This was the list I shared earlier. But I, as the founder, had never properly articulated the foundational values, the reason my soul drove me to start this company in the first place.

Drima set me straight. But what he was about to tell me would cause me to make such a dramatic shift, I would lose 30 percent of my team members in a single year. (More on this to come.)

"Vishen, think of your personal foundational values like America's founding document. The US Constitution is sacrosanct, and throughout history, it was only amended after significant measures for major important reasons unforeseen or blatantly ignored by America's founding fathers," Drima explained. Organizational values, in his analogy, are like the laws passed by Congress.

"Your personal foundational values are similar," he continued. "They take shape in the crucible of your life's earlier formative experiences, especially during childhood and your adolescent years. They rarely change in adulthood unless you experience massive turmoil, trauma, or major changes in your life's circumstances. But other than that, they stay relatively the same and quite unchanged for long periods.

Organizational values are formed when you bring people together. They emerge by consensus. They evolve more frequently as new team members come and go, and as circumstances in your marketplace and the world shift and change. They play a crucial role similar to the laws introduced, updated, and passed periodically by Congress.

The laws are like a living blueprint that guides and organizes societal behavior as appropriate, representing the will of the people. They must be in harmony and alignment with the US Constitution, because otherwise they would be deemed unconstitutional and therefore rejected.

This is why organizational values are not enough. For organizational values to truly matter, they need to be rooted in the underlying *why* of foundational values, which come straight from the founder or founding team.

Yet most businesses forget this. And most founders forget the importance of their own values. They bury them out of modesty or a desire to appeal to the status quo. But remember this:

> *In most cases anyone can imitate your business.*
> *But nobody can imitate your business if it's built based*
> *on YOUR STORY. When your values infuse your business,*
> *you've given a special life to your creation.*

Steve Jobs infused Apple with values of aesthetics in an era when personal computers were ugly. Oprah infused her talk shows with the values of love and healing in an era when talk shows were using scandal and family gossip to gain viewers.

If you're a founder or leader, you of all people can't ignore that you have deeply held personal foundational values that are driving you. You've got to become aware of them and how they're animating you, or else, as Carl Jung said, "Until you make the unconscious conscious, it will direct your life and you will call it fate."

So how do you discover these value systems? Well, you start with foundational values. You can't BS your way into them. They come straight from your core. The trick is to uncover them.

What's Your Seed?

I was one of the first guinea pigs to try the core values process called the Origin Story Exercise, which allowed me to discover my four foundational values and transform the way I work. When I asked Drima how he developed it, he told me a story that I'll never forget. He called it "Wisdom in the Shade of a Lime Tree," and it came from a profound lesson he learned from his grandfather.

WISDOM IN THE SHADE
OF A LIME TREE

When I was a young boy, I spent most holidays in Khartoum, the capital of northern Sudan, the place where the White and Blue Niles converge, the city I was born in and where most of my extended family members live. I visited my grandfather's home there. In their front yard and garden, he had a lime tree that by then was beginning to produce fewer and fewer lime fruits.

He and I would sit underneath the tree in the shade and we'd play chess almost every day. My grandfather always used this time to teach me life lessons and to bond with me. He was very much a mentor figure in my life.

One day, we were playing chess under the lime tree, and he picked up a fallen lime from the grass. He opened it. Pinched it, plucked out a seed, and said:

"Grandson, look at this. This is a lime seed. It gives you a lime tree. It can't give you a mango tree or an apple tree. A lime seed only gives you a lime tree. Obviously you have to put it in the right type of soil, give it some water, and make sure it has sunshine.

But at the end of the day, no matter what, the lime seed will only produce a lime tree."

Then he went on to say:

"This lime tree is getting old and it's dying. Just like me. I am getting old, and one day I will die too, and so you have to understand something. As you grow old, before your time is up, it's your duty to answer this important question: 'What's my seed?'

"Your seed will produce only what it's meant to produce. That's it. Don't get caught up with distractions. Don't get caught up in manipulation. Don't get caught up in the noise of society. Tune in within.

"Ask yourself: 'What's my seed?' Once you know it, pursue the answer.

"Pursue the answer with humility, and you too can fulfill your life's purpose."

Drima's story so poignantly articulates the inner truth of the billions of people in this world. None of us is a clone. Every person is unique with a blueprint of deeply ingrained core values that shape our behavior. Values are simply the beliefs we operate from that are as much a part of us as our DNA.

And like DNA, when you bring awareness to the beliefs that drive everything you do, it becomes much easier to make choices, which allows you to then speed up your rate of achieving the business outcomes you want.

The Origin Story Exercise

This is the exercise Drima led me through in the summer of 2016. It was a defining moment in my life because for the first time, I realized how my past was shaping my present.

STEP 1: CHART YOUR PEAKS

Drima began by getting me to think about the highs and lows in my life. "Close your eyes and remember some of the most painful experiences you had as a child."

During each of these times, values emerged. The low points—experiencing racism, being bullied—caused me to gain values such as an appreciation for diversity and compassion for others. The high points like seeing a product take, or seeing the faces of people light up at the events I created, ingrained me with values for innovation.

STEP 2: EXTRACT WHAT MATTERS

Drima then asked me to write down the values on a list. "What matters to you in life?" he asked. In around twenty minutes I came up with this list:

Transformation

Connectedness

Compassion

Growth

Humanism

Aesthetics

Vision

Happiness

Transcendence

Love

Change

Self-Directed Learning

Questioning

Innovation

Futurism

STEP 3: DISTILLATION

The next step was to look at this list and cluster the related values. Four clusters immediately became apparent.

VALUES RELATED TO UNITY

Connectedness

Compassion

Humanism

VALUES RELATED TO SELF-GROWTH

Transformation

Growth

Transcendence

Self-Directed Learning

VALUES RELATED TO INNOVATION

Aesthetics

Vision

Change

Innovation

Questioning

Futurism

VALUES RELATED TO LOVE

Happiness

Love

STEP 4: NAMING THE VALUES

The next step was to name these clusters. It became apparent to me that these four values had become like a part of my DNA. As you do the exercise at the end of this chapter, try to cluster your values too. Each cluster should get a name. Example: For cluster 3, which involves values related to innovation, I decided to use the title "Envisioning."

Here are the four foundational values that emerged from me as I did this exercise.

- Unity
- Transformation
- Envisioning
- Love

This is where the magic happens. So many founders, consultants, or experts become replicators. They create companies, work, and products that imitate the status quo. In today's world this is no longer enough. It's yet another reason why you must infuse your work with your values.

If you're working for a company and are not a founder, then your foundational values are the assets you bring to work every morning. They apply to the job you do no matter how small you might think it is. I know a customer support agent whose value is joy. Every single email she sends to a customer is infused with this value.

My four values went on to infuse Mindvalley with a unique edge. This is how we described it internally.

1. **Unity:** We fiercely believe in diversity, humanism, and environmentalism. We as the human race are in the evolution toward a better future together. Unity is the idea of seeing similarities over differences and embracing the human race as a whole.

2. **Transformation:** We believe in supporting individuals to transform

into the best versions of themselves—this holds true for our customers, partners, and employees. We believe that your personal growth should be the most important thing in your life.

3. **Envisioning:** We are not afraid to question the status quo and will never settle in our pursuit to push boundaries and create a better future. Our default approach is innovation, creation, and invention.

4. **Love:** We care deeply about our team, our partners and customers. We treat each other with care and love.

Each of the four values made our company stand out in our industry.

- Unity as a value is why we employ people from sixty countries in one office.
- Transformation is why everyone in Mindvalley takes their own personal growth so seriously.
- Envisioning is why we constantly reinvent our products and services to stay on the cutting edge in our industry.
- Love is why we have a culture of close friendship among our team members.

I used each of these values as an edge to craft our brand. With the exercise at the end of this chapter, you can do the same. Turn your values into your brand story. But your values will do more than that. Uncovering them will also make you understand your own behaviors.

The Hidden Forces Guiding Your Decisions

Now, before I uncovered the foundational four you read above, I did not realize the underlying forces guiding so many of my decisions. I would find myself in deals with partners I didn't work well with, or feeling conflicted about important decisions. Before I knew that *transformation* was one of my foundational values, I tried starting companies in other fields only to fail and fail again. But when I started companies or projects in the field of human transformation, they were always a raging success. When you know your soulprint, you know your unique edge.

Envisioning, or the act of dreaming up new creations, was another one of my values I discovered from this exercise. As a kid who grew up on LEGOs and a former engineer, I always feel that I'm at my best when I'm building, creating, and inventing. Nothing stays constant for me. Innovation is a way of life. But before 2016, I didn't know how deep this value ran. Before I established envisioning as a value, one of the biggest negative reviews of Mindvalley from former employees was that "things change too fast."

To me, however, change was a necessity in our industry. By establishing and clearly defining envisioning as a value and thus making change our way of life, we now attract people who thrive in fast-paced environments. The complaint that the business changes too quickly virtually disappeared from the company. Instead the people we bring aboard relate to innovation as a necessity. The result: happier people and a healthier business.

These four values—unity, transformation, envisioning, and love—now radiate in everything we do at Mindvalley and in everyone who works for us. They are featured on our career pages in a section that says: "Do you align with our values?"

The vetting for core values starts right there. We challenge our prospective employees from the moment they find us, and this continues through the hiring process until we invite them to join us. It's why the people we attract embody these same qualities.

Most individuals are living their lives blindly, without knowing the deep guiding beliefs that shape their behavior. It's just not something we are taught to pay attention to, which makes no sense. Especially when Drima said it this way:

> *Vishen, your values have to come from your soul. You created*
> *this company. There's a reason you were born and a reason*
> *for the events you experience in your life. Listen within*
> *and decide what values matter to you. Don't look outside*
> *or bring in some bullshit voting process.*

Remember this: If you are the founder of your company, you must discover and infuse your values into the budding organization. Don't diminish them. Your values were deliberately placed within your soul. They are the seeds of what the Universe is seeking to create through you. Listen carefully to what's emerging.

As Steve Jobs said in his famous 2005 commencement speech at Stanford:

> *You can't connect the dots looking forward; you can only*
> *connect them looking backwards. So you have to trust*
> *that the dots will somehow connect in your future.*
> *You have to trust in something—your gut, destiny, life,*
> *karma, whatever. This approach has never let me down,*
> *and it has made all the difference in my life.*

Look back at the events of your life. The failures. The sufferings. The highs and the lows. They shaped your values. And these values must guide your decisions about the type of company you create and the work you do.

Values have to come from you. They get ingrained in you during significant events that shape your life. What I've come to understand is that usually those moments are painful. But in those moments we grow the most. There is tremendous value to the toughest experience. It's the silver lining to life.

The Hidden Gifts of Your Pain

Now, this is the great secret of foundational values. They sometimes emerge from the pain and suffering that you may have experienced in life. Your values are often your unconscious desire to ensure that other people don't experience the same pain you do.

Your values become the healing you want to give to the world because of the pain you've experienced. Or, to drop another Rumi quote:

The wound is the place where the light enters you.

Being put on a security watch list (a story I'll tell in the next chapter) and having to leave the United States was painful. But I don't regret it. It helped me recognize my key value: unity.

And when you see how your suffering may contain within it a hidden gift, something special happens. This is perhaps what Viktor Frankl, author of the famed book *Man's Search for Meaning*, meant when he said:

Suffering ceases to be suffering at the
moment it finds a meaning.

Now, it's typically not just one value that defines you. There will be many. The idea is to start with a large list and consolidate and number the top ones.

The Origin Story Exercise might radically alter the way you run your life and business for the better. It did for me. My guess is, you will have a similar experience when you go through the process at the end of this chapter. And when you do, remember:

Your past pain is often the breadcrumbs that will lead you to the meaning, values, and purpose of your life.

Bringing This to Your Team

Now, there is one caveat to introducing foundational values to a team. There can be a temporarily inconvenient, even slightly painful aspect to the process. In the year 2016 when I implemented foundational values into Mindvalley, we saw 30 percent of our team resign. This shouldn't be surprising. When you bring in new values, you change a company. It's why it's better to build a business from them and do this process before you build a team.

But if your business is already running, do the exercise and bring in your foundational values. Not everyone is going to be happy with this change. It doesn't make them wrong. It just means that the working relationship might no longer be a match.

The upside? Within twelve months we launched into a three-year period of accelerated growth. The organization aligned around these new values. The people who joined the "new" Mindvalley in 2016 stayed almost 50 percent longer, produced twice as much revenue per employee, and were overall happier, because our values aligned.

The benefits significantly outweigh any short-term downfalls. Foundational values lead to higher-performing teams that are more connected. So stick to this rule: Foundational values come first.

Jump ahead to get started on the Origin Story Exercise now. Or keep reading to learn about what you'll focus on once you've set your foundational values—organizational values.

Here is how foundational and organizational values look together.

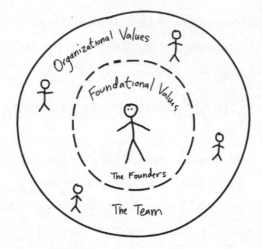

Foundational values come from the founder and emanate throughout the company. Organizational values come from the team. In the closing exercises for this chapter, I explain a process of creating organizational values. This is optional, and you can skip it and move on to Chapter 2 if this does not resonate with you. Organizational values are done with your team members.

But first, stop now and do the Origin Story Exercise below. It's time you discovered your unique soulprint.

Chapter Summary

MODELS OF REALITY

You Must Know Your Foundational Values.
Whether you're aware of them yet or not, your values are what are shaping all your decisions. Once you clearly define them you'll understand what you need to do next and whom you need to connect with, to build a life and business that inspires.

When you understand the values you operate from, everything in life gets easier. You understand why you do what you do, whom you need to have on your team, what projects you need to take on, how your business will change the world. You'll feel like a Buddha, serene and sure of your actions. Your good attitude will ripple outward. You'll lead with your attitude and behavior.

Once you know what you want, your next job is to magnetically attract the right people, which is what you'll learn in Chapter 2.

Systems for Living

EXERCISE 1: THE ORIGIN STORY EXERCISE

Follow the instructions below to define your foundational values. Remember that these values can't be made up. They must be extracted.

When you go through this process you will come up with a list that will help you figure out what businesses, movements, or projects to start, and how to position your organization so that you align with the best partners.

Step 1: Reconnect to peak moments in the past. Values tend to emerge from painful moments, because it's at these times we make powerful decisions on how we will choose to behave in the future. But they also emerge from peak moments, moments of awe or joy so grand you never want to forget them. Think about the peak moments in your life, highs or lows. NOTE: If you've experienced significant trauma it may help to have the support of a loved one or counselor while engaging in this process.

Ask yourself: *What is the most painful experience you went through as a young child?*

Step 2: Write out the story in detail. Bring yourself back to that moment in your mind. Describe it vividly. Who was there? What happened? How did you feel?

Example: "I fell off the swing and into the mud and all my friends laughed at me."

Step 3: Repeat the process for ages five to twenty-five. Scan through your past and repeat Steps 1 and 2 for each memory. If it helps, you can draw a timeline and mark in the major moments where you experienced significant pain.

Step 4: Write the values that emerged from those moments. Consider what you learned from all your painful experiences and your major achievements. What beliefs did you take on? Beside each memory write one word to describe the belief or core value that you think came from that moment.

Example: "Truth," "Courage," "Connection."

Step 5: Define your values. Review all the values and beliefs you wrote down. Define what they mean to you.

For an extended version of this exercise I've created a bonus video with Drima guiding you through this process. You can get this at www.mind valley.com/badass.

Today, Drima Starlight leads executive workshops and privately coaches top leaders from major North American and global brands with his training partner David Anthony Childs. For more information on the services they provide, visit: www.DrimaStarlight.com.

Optional Bonus: Understanding Organizational Values

Organizational values are the attitudes and behaviors team members should exhibit. That's why coming up with them is a democratic process.

Also, when the team changes and the culture shifts, you need to review organizational values at each stage of your business. Developing organizational values never stops. It's an evolutionary process. The teams I had in 2008, 2015, and 2019 all had slightly different versions. It's important to constantly go back to organizational values and review and iterate. (By comparison, foundational values rarely change.)

Here is how we came up with our organizational values in 2019. I assembled a group of colleagues that quite frankly I'd love to pop in a machine and clone. They are all team players and high-performers, experts of their craft, with attitudes we as a team wanted to codify.

We'd prepped before that day. It had taken a few months of collaborative work, which started with me. I began with my foundational values. Taking them into consideration, but then also reflecting on what the business and team needed, I came up with a list of ten values I wanted this new evolution of the culture at Mindvalley to embody. Then we had all the high-performers add to, and question, the initial list.

One Friday afternoon the group came together offsite, at a nearby hotel. We wrote each value on a whiteboard. There were about fifty of us. We split up into teams where each member had a say in the behaviors we'd like our coworkers to exhibit. Then we regrouped the teams and continued to consolidate.

We eventually solidified a list of organizational values to replace what we had created in 2015. Here is a partial list:

1. **Transparent Communication**
   - I create a safe space so people feel free of judgment and ego.
   - I would rather overcommunicate than undercommunicate.
   - I seek to understand before being understood.

2. **Visionary Leadership**
   - I take bold actions. Win or fail—try the idea, even if I'm not sure about the outcome.
   - I lead through not only words, but action. I demonstrate the behaviors and attitudes I expect.
   - I hold others to the highest version of themselves.

3. **Teamwork**
   - I constantly brain-sync ideas to co-create as a group.
   - I listen to the ideas of others and I am open to feedback.
   - I collaborate rather than compete.

It's fine to pull ideas from other companies, but keep in mind that every team has a unique culture code that is unlike any other. And also, as the business evolves you must always revisit your organizational values.

Remember that organizational values should come AFTER foundational values. If you want to implement this in your team, here's a rough guide.

EXERCISE FOR ORGANIZATIONAL VALUES (OPTIONAL)

Organizational values are the rules that govern the expected attitudes and behaviors required of team members for day-to-day collaborations to run smoothly. Follow this democratic process to create a list that defines the code of conduct for any team.

Step 1: Refer to your foundational values list. Consider the desired attitudes and behaviors of existing team members, and attitudes and behaviors you want your future team to operate from.

Also consider the day-to-day experience of workflow. *How do you want the team to work together? What is the business working toward now? What attitudes and behaviors are needed to get there?*

Create a list of six to ten core values you believe that represent the desired conditions you want to see in your team culture.

Step 2: Review your list of six to ten core values with the executive team first. Have them review, pick apart, ask questions, add to the list. Decide on the final six to ten core values.

Step 3: Assemble your team. Select all the high-performing individuals who have been with the company for a long time, who understand the current team dynamics and what the business needs. Or work with the entire team on the following process.

1. Share the six to ten core values with the entire team. Have each individual write down behavioral statements that they believe showcase the desired core value. *Example: Visionary Leadership—"I question the status quo."*
2. Divide the entire team into smaller groups of three. Have these teams review and consolidate the behavior statements each team

member wrote down that are the same, so they create one single list for their team.

3. Have teams of three pair up to become teams of six. Have them continue to consolidate and review the behavior statements each team member wrote down.

The groups of six then must write down their final list of behavior statements to an official list without replicating statements provided by other teams.

4. Bring the entire group back together and review each core value list to solidify the final statements.

Step 4: Share the list with the entire company. Taken a step further, you can get creative and come up with a team chant, code, or saying, which makes it easier for team members to learn and memorize the final list.

CHAPTER 2

ATTRACT YOUR ALLIES

*Find a group of people who challenge and inspire you,
spend a lot of time with them, and it will change your life.*

—Amy Poehler

Greatness is best achieved with others. The world is too complex to strike it alone. People are drawn to you not because of your business plan, but because your dream gives them hope. Humans are moved by emotion more than logic. The greatest gift you can give someone is to invite them to share in a dream. This is how you become magnetic and align yourself with the people you need to make any vision a reality.

ON A DAY LIKE any other, in 2003, I showed up at JFK Airport. I was returning home to New York after visiting my parents in Malaysia. But when I arrived at Immigration, instead of getting my usual passport stamp, I was ushered into a security room.

I sat anxiously watching every slow-motion tick of the clock on the wall, waiting for the immigration officer in the cubicle to pull the yellow file with my name on it. My leg bobbed up and down with an uncontrollable nervous tic, like a busy telegraph machine.

I was tense for two reasons. I was nervous about my bags lying uncollected at luggage claim. And I had no clue why the hell I was there.

Three hours later, an officer called, "Mr. Vishen Mohammad."

No one got up. I wondered if he was calling me.

Again he said, "Mr. Vishen Mohammad."

I stood, arranged my bags, and scrambled toward his glass encasement. He slid the window open and looked at me, stone-faced.

"Did you mean Mohammad or Mohandas?" I asked.

The officer looked down at the passport in his hand, then replied: "Oh, yes, Mohammad, Mohandas, whatever . . ."

Perhaps the difference in names was subtle, but it's easy to see how callous this entire situation was. Back then, I carried the middle name of my father, which was Mohandas. A fairly common Indian name. Gandhi's first name was Mohandas. But the proximity of its syllables to those of the Arabic name Mohammad was apparently enough to arouse suspicion.

"I'm sorry to inform you, your name is on the special registration list," said the officer.

Immediately, I felt guilty, even though I had absolutely no reason to be. Have you ever been accused of some infraction, yet despite knowing your innocence you still scanned your memory to see if there was something you actually did to warrant the claims against you? That's how I felt.

"What does that mean?" I asked.

"You've been added to a watch list," he said. "Probably because you were born in Malaysia."

"But my name is not Mohammad. I've lived here for nine years," I replied.

"Doesn't matter. The State Department refuses to take chances anymore," said the officer.

The "special registration" was a database of approximately seventy thousand men, mostly born in Muslim countries. More commonly, it is known as the Muslim watch list. It was initiated by the government to monitor security threats and mitigate terrorist attacks. The special registration program required all male foreign visitors already in the United States, aged sixteen and older, from specified countries, to register at designated immigration offices within a given time period. I wasn't a Muslim. Nor should that matter. Regardless, I had been added to the list.

At the time, it had only been eighteen months since the 9/11 terrorist attacks. America was in a state of hypervigilance. And for good reason. But I had done nothing to get pegged as a potential security threat. For the record, I was removed from the list in 2008, and in 2013 the entire program was axed after it was found to be practically useless. (That didn't stop Trump from trying and failing to revive it in 2018.)

But on that day in 2003 when I was added to the list, the United States had been my home for nine years. Abruptly, I was denied my right to board a plane or even get off a plane without a special interview that could take up to three excruciating hours. Flying became an agonizing ordeal.

This was nothing compared to my mandated monthly check-in duties. Those were the worst. Even if I chose not to fly, every four weeks, I had to stand in a line of foreigners that wrapped around a government office in downtown New York City to report myself. Some days it was bitterly cold. I showed up once in February and joined the tail end of a line that ran four blocks. I shivered for three hours. Finally, I was let into a warm building—though the service I received was still quite icy.

When it was my turn, they took my fingerprints. Then my mugshot. And they'd rifle through my credit card statements, inspecting them for suspicious activity.

The United States was my home. It was a country I loved. I wanted my children to be born and raised there. But it quickly became a difficult place for me to live.

By month three of obediently repeating the government-sanctioned rituals, I came home one night, looked at my then-wife Kristina in the eyes, and said, "I just can't do this anymore." I loved America. But we couldn't live there. So we left our home.

Let me be clear. I don't bring this up to blame anyone. The country I loved had gone through a devastating attack. I had lived in New York not far from the towers and had spent many summer days Rollerblading around the area. The World Trade Center was in my neighborhood. The attacks were painful for me. Like any American-born citizen, I wanted the country to be safe.

We left the country I loved not because I didn't want to be there, but because living there became too painful. Due to the newly imposed security structures, I no longer felt welcome.

Landing in Kuala Lumpur, Malaysia, was nightmarishly surreal. I walked down the aircraft stairs onto the tarmac, and looked across the airport at the lush green palms lining the airport's runway. I breathed in the humid jasmine-scented air. I thought, "Shit, what now?" Malaysia was almost alien to me. I had spent my adult life in the United States. Mindvalley was founded in America. My clients and partners were all in the USA. I felt I had been kicked out of my home.

But I was determined to continue building my business. I had no idea how, but I knew I would find a way.

The Inner Voice

It was June 2004 when I found myself back in Malaysia. Back then, the country was suffering from a serious brain drain issue. At the time we arrived, Malaysia was losing around three hundred thousand of their best and smartest people each year. The country's most talented professionals were moving to countries like Singapore, Hong Kong, the UK, or Canada.

There were simply far better opportunities. Malaysia was seen as a career dead end. Friends asked: "Why the hell are you back? There are no good jobs here." At least in Malaysia we had the comfort and support of my immediate family. My mom and dad still lived in Kuala Lumpur.

The question was: *Could I achieve my dreams of building a Silicon Valley–style start-up catering to the US market in a country on the other side of the planet with a severe shortage of talent?*

I had four suitcases and the love of my wife and parents. And I was now moving back into my parents' home at the age of twenty-eight. They also believed in me and gave me the space to be foolishly stubborn.

That's when an inner voice spoke to me.

Have you ever noticed an inner voice nudging you? Even though you're really not sure if there is such a thing? Is it your soul? Intuition? Gut instinct? Or was it that salad you ate that was past the expiry date?

One of my favorite quotes of all time comes from the movie *Babe*. It's a movie about a talking pig who wants to be a sheepdog. There's a moment in the movie when the pig's farmer has a feeling that his pig is special. He believes his pig is so unique that it might be able to win a sheepdog competition. As he realizes this, the narrator of the movie says:

> *Little ideas that tickled, and nagged, and refused to go away should never be ignored, for in them lie the seeds of destiny.*

Remember this. It's one of those quotes to live by.

Now, I'm sure you've experienced moments like that. Call it the inner voice, or intuition, creativity, the soul, gut instinct, a hunch, the Universe, or God. Choose whatever words empower you to describe it. But make no mistake, all humans have inklings like this.

And this is what happened to me when I returned to Malaysia. I couldn't get my inner voice to shut up. It was telling me:

Inner voice: *You're here for a reason. Quit feeling bad for yourself and start building up this company you call Mindvalley.*

Me: *Piss off. I'm not in the mood.*

Inner voice: *Be honest, you don't have much of a choice. The work culture here is horrendous. It's decades behind New York and Silicon Valley. You can't find a job here that will keep you happy. So create your own world.*

Me: *You make a good point.*

Inner voice: *What makes you think you can't attract talent in Malaysia? Sure, the country suffers from brain drain and there might not be much talent around, but think outside the box. What if you drained brains from other countries and convinced people to move here?*

Me: *Well, that would be pretty amazing! But HOW?*

My inner voice was quite jazzed about this idea, but my logical mind was not. So I went through this idea loop for many weeks. It seemed like an eternity. But my inner voice wouldn't shut the heck up.

My greatest challenge was that I still didn't have a successful product. I didn't *know* what I was going to do. I was kind of at a point of just stumbling through business and life. I had brilliant ideas, but my circumstances didn't lend themselves to an easy path to achieve any of them.

This same scenario I now see playing out for many of my colleagues, friends, partners, and students. They have brilliant ideas. Their intuition keeps nudging them. But they stop there. They are paralyzed by the fear of not having all the answers. The ideas die because they know the *what*, but they don't know the *how*.

When that happens they also lose faith in themselves and life. It becomes a secret failure only they know about. Once again, they feel they have settled for their circumstances. And they condition in beliefs that "life is hard" or "I can't do that" or "that's too much work." But then, they never learn the true power all humans are born with.

There is one lesson I learned at this time in my life and repeatedly since then. It's now become a knowing that frees me when I am stuck. It's this:

You don't need to know how to achieve an outcome. Forget knowing
HOW.
All you need to know is your WHY and WHAT for doing it.
Then, you share this with passion.
The people you need will come to you.
And they will bring the answers you need.
And usually much faster than you expect.

That's what this chapter is about. It's about unlocking your dream and sharing it with such potency that the world is drawn to you. The people you need come. And together you bend reality with more force than one person ever could alone.

"I'll Drain Brains from Other Countries"

One sleepless night it hit me. What if I could create a workplace so attractive that talent from around the world would willingly relocate to Malaysia and help me build my dream company?

In my head, a Buckminster Fuller quote was on replay. Bucky once said:

You never change things by fighting the existing reality.
To change something, build a new model that makes
the existing model obsolete.

This vision of building a new type of business, the World's Greatest Workplace, fueled me. And it wasn't going to be in New York, or Silicon Valley, or London or Berlin, or in any of the world's most popular cities. It was going to be in Kuala Lumpur.

I gave myself until 2020 to pull it off. My personal mantra became: "Screw brain drain. Our company will drain brains from other countries and bring them into Malaysia."

Now, I admit, the level of delusion required to say something like this is pretty high. Especially when you're broke and working from a backroom office of your father's factory in a ghetto part of town. (Thanks, Dad, for the free office space.) But oddly, this wild dream started coming true.

Magnetically Attracting People

Whether you run a company, work for one, or you are starting your own business, nonprofit, or movement, the first step to massive success is to turn yourself into a magnet for the people you need to achieve your mission. For you, this might be colleagues, partners, or customers.

The good news is, there's a formula. For most people, it starts with a total mindset shift. Let me tell you, you don't need to have it all figured out. You need to have a vision and then start with the *who*. Don't try to figure out every step in making the vision a reality. Give up needing to know all the answers and instead focus on attracting the people who will make the vision a reality. Once you have the right people on board, they will help you figure out the *how*.

At this very moment, there are talented people around the world yearning to join forces with you. They believe in the same (perhaps misfit) ideas. They envision the same future. They are desperate for the same change you ache for.

This is the genius of the Buddha mindset. It's not about knowing every answer. It's about believing in your idea and in the fact that other people have similar dreams and are willing to collaborate with you. It's about submitting to the mystery of your gut instinct, and trusting that others share your inner knowing.

What's most brilliant about this is, many of these people have skills you don't have. Skills you need. And they need you. Team up with them, and together you become an unstoppable band of mission-driven rebels that can change the world.

To make this happen, you must do the work of this chapter and build your business, movement, or self into a magnet. Then it's easy. You draw the people you need right to you. And the best part is, you don't need to have a fancy office or any perks or (in my case) a viable company to bring them to you.

Be the Bus Driver

In the book *Good to Great* Jim Collins writes: "You are a bus driver. The bus, your company [or your project, idea, or movement] is at a standstill, and it's your job to get it going . . ."

He goes on to explain, "Start not with 'where' but with 'who.' . . . start by getting the right people on the bus, the wrong people off the bus, and the right people in the right seats."

I took this advice to heart. And to be honest, this wasn't just good business sense. I was lonely. I missed my friends in America. I longed for social connection with like-minded people just as much as I wanted a successful company.

I did everything I could to get the talent pool even partially filled. But sadly, I couldn't afford a real office. So I worked from Starbucks, until they canceled their free Wi-Fi service to keep guys like me from buying one venti cappuccino and hogging a table for seven hours.

Now, this was 2004, the era before start-up funds were easily available. I was twenty-eight and broke. I was forced to do what many start-up entrepreneurs do. I went to the Bank of Dad and asked for help. That was when my father willingly offered me the makeshift office at the back of his warehouse.

Mindvalley was me plus a Labradoodle named Ozzy in a run-down warehouse. Ozzy was great company. But Ozzy couldn't use a keyboard and never delivered much in results.

But then my college buddy Mike from Michigan joined me. He became a cofounder. Together we placed an ad for two interns. Adelle and Hannu were my first hires. We had little to offer them, just a meager salary and a dream. Our first tech product was still years from launching. But they both saw our venture as a training opportunity.

Mike and I now had two interns on board, and the four of us built the business to a place where we were desperate for talent. Our focus was primarily building innovative Web applications for the then-emerging space known as Web 2.0. We were competing with start-ups in Silicon Valley. But our growth was stalled by our desperate need for talented engineers, marketing minds, and branding experts. We needed smart workers fast. And I was spread thin—it was an obvious sign that we needed to hire.

Then quite by accident we stumbled upon the solution. One day, just for fun, I wrote a manifesto to describe the new type of business I wanted to create.

TACTIC #1: THE MANIFESTO

Office 1.0 was in a bad area. The morning walk to get there took me over broken sidewalks where street vendors ran their roadside food stalls, and the air always smelled like curry and fried chicken. In the alley behind the warehouse, transport trucks loaded up with cheap woven baskets, pallets of wholesale T-shirts, or crates of exotic fruit—items destined for much trendier places.

Naturally, the first computer programmer I interviewed turned down the job. Honestly, I didn't blame him. At least he was nice enough to say, "I'll think about it."

This was code for "Hell no! I'm never working in this place."

To come to our office, he had to walk past ten-foot crates laden with Chinese and Indian garments ready to be loaded onto trucks.

So the question was how to get brilliant people to move to Malaysia, to work for a no-name start-up with no money. After months of frustration, I realized regular job ads would not work. We needed a new approach. One night, I got resourceful. I grabbed a scrap piece of paper and scribbled out a manifesto, which stated not *what Mindvalley was* (which honestly wasn't much) or what skills I was looking for, but instead, *what Mindvalley stood for* and what the company would be. The idea that came to me would open the floodgates, and it's still an idea we use today. I call it the Manifesto Technique.

A manifesto won't simply get you more applications. It'll get you people who jell with your values and beliefs. It will get you the *right* kind of people.

Here was the first manifesto I wrote, in all its imperfect glory. As you read this, remember it was written in 2005, when the world was a different place.

TOP 10 REASONS TO WORK
FOR MINDVALLEY (2005)

1. Freedom: We understand that brilliant people hate rules and shackles and desire the freedom to do their work, in their way.
2. Thinking BIG! We're not aiming to create email software, we're aiming to create the biggest revolution in email since Gmail. We're not content with creating blogging tools, we aim to create the world's first "intelligent" blog. When we build an ecommerce site, we aim to put it in the top 1 percent of sites for performance rates. We aim to be as influential in improving people's lives through technology as Yahoo!, Google, or Apple. We love Big, Scary, Audacious Goals.

3. Profitability: We're fully profitable, and continue to see our profits grow by at least 10 percent each month.

4. Great People: We hire only the best. For a typical position we sift through one hundred résumés and interview at least ten people. Make it in, and you'll be working with some of the best minds in the business. We understand that "A" people attract "A" people.

5. Treats: We treat our employees well. This includes rent subsidization, occasional concert tickets, Starbucks coffee, dinners and drinks. Our founders have worked at Microsoft and eBay and believe in the Silicon Valley model of spoiling employees.

6. Creativity: Your typical workweek is 45 hours. Of this time, we allow you to spend 5 hours a week working on your own projects or inventions. If your project is successful, we'll help you launch it. We've modeled this after Google's and 3M's styles of nurturing creativity within the organization.

7. Stability: We've never taken a drop of investment and so have no investors to pull the plug on us. Our business also spans multiple industries such as Internet marketing, product development, publishing, and coding. This protects us from short-term market trends in any one industry.

8. Fun: We put the "FUN" in "Business Fundamentals." Don't get us wrong—we're a disciplined, well-oiled engine of growth. But we believe that business should be fun and people should look forward to going to work each day.

9. Idealism: 100 percent of our employees have spent significant time volunteering or working for nonprofits. We started this business to change the world. Profits come second. As a result, we will devote our time and attention to causes that may not bring in short-term profits, but might result in positive social change.

10. Entrepreneurship. We understand that great people dream of start-

ing their own companies. We help you attain this dream. We provide training and mentorship to help you grow. We do not require any employees to sign a binding contract. Simply put, you're free to learn from us and then move on when you're ready and start your own business. We respect entrepreneurship.

The ideas in this manifesto resonated deeply with people. This ten-point manifesto resulted in a horde of applicants. Within a month, our gloomy backroom operation was packed with interviewees. We weren't simply drawing in local talent. We were getting résumés from highly skilled workers across the world. It was astonishing. But more important, we were getting the *right* talent. People driven by values with rockstar skills—in short, people who were both Buddhas and badasses.

One of the applicants we hired was Khailee Ng. Today he's the managing director of the hot seed investing company 500 Startups. He is one of Asia's most famous investors and start-up founders. He was one of our early brilliant hires (Employee #11). And he joined us despite having a pick of pretty much any job.

What I didn't fully understand at the time was why our manifesto approach was so effective. Our company certainly hadn't changed. It was still only the four of us and Ozzy. We still worked from a crummy warehouse. Applicants who came to see us still had to walk down the same broken streets and past the same food vendors.

Instead of using a bulleted list of regular job skills to lure high-level talent, and believing that would work, we had crafted an inspirational vision. Our manifesto was a promise. It was an attitude. It defined who we were and how we planned to play our business game to win. Smart, talented people care about that. They did back then. And they do today. Now more than ever.

This was my first major lesson. People don't care *what* you do. They care *why* you do it. And when you share your big *why*, you want to get raw, real, and authentic. This means publicly sharing your innermost beliefs about the world and your personal vision.

Now, here is an important rule: Your manifesto is not meant to appeal to everyone. You want to generate feelings of extreme attraction or extreme repulsion. Hopefully most people will love some of the aspects of your manifesto. It's okay if others hate some of the aspects of your manifesto. But whatever you do, stay away from the zone of apathy.

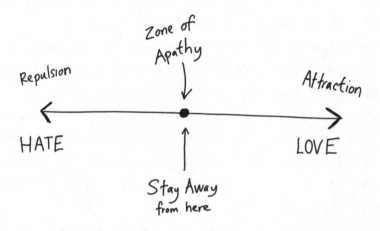

In my new manifesto for my company (you can read it on mindvalley .com/careers), I talk about how I view Mindvalley as an Earth company and not an American or Malaysian or Estonian company. This repulses some people who might say we're unpatriotic. That's okay. But it attracts more people than it repulses. We attract people with world-centric views, and that's exactly what I want. If you're too afraid to offend the *few*, you won't attract the *many*. So stay away from the zone of apathy. Don't be vanilla.

At the end of this chapter, there's an exercise to support you in creating the process of building your manifesto. You don't need a business to do this. This applies to the stealth leader just as much as it does to anyone in a leadership position. However, before we get there, I'll share some ideas to help you really dive deep into your beliefs and reason for existing.

TACTIC #2: FIND YOUR BIG WHY

In his famous TED Talk, Simon Sinek, author of *Start with Why*, says, "People don't buy what you do; they buy why you do it. And what you do simply proves what you believe."

Sinek also said, "There are only two ways to influence human behavior: You can manipulate it or you can inspire it."

This is where most people go wrong when they share their ideas about a business. They fail to explain their *why*. And thus, they fail to inspire. It doesn't matter if you're the CEO of a business, you lead a team inside one, or you're a junior at a company wishing to bring ideas forth or shift a team dynamic. To inspire people, you must unlock your company's *why* and communicate it effectively.

Sinek uses Apple to illustrate his point. Apple never says, "Buy our computers because they're beautifully designed and user-friendly." Instead it communicates a deeper purpose. Apple challenges the status quo. It thinks differently. And it just so happens it does so with beautifully designed, user-friendly products.

Starbucks is another global brand that's done this. While Howard Schultz certainly cared about quality coffee when he took the helm of Starbucks, it was the community-centric experience that was the differentiator for the business. The Starbucks *why* is "Inspire and nurture the human spirit." And they do it "one person, one cup, and one neighborhood at a time."

This is why if you're traveling somewhere you've never been, and you see the green, crowned mermaid on a café front, you might recognize it as a place where you can go to immediately feel connected to people and the community around you. It's also why the company's coffee buyers support fair trade. And why baristas label cups with a person's name. In this ritual, the customer feels acknowledged and appreciated.

How about Nike. Its brand promise is "to bring inspiration and innovation to every athlete in the world." It's not simply to make great athletic gear or sell some nice-looking shoes with slick checkmarks.

Human beings are biologically hardwired to make decisions from their emotions. This is why we gravitate to companies and people that arouse emotion in us. In fact, a study by neuroscientist Antonio Damasio proved just how deep the connection runs. Damasio studied individuals with damaged amygdalas, which is a region of the brain responsible for processing emotions. He found that these brain-injured participants could conceptually discuss decisions but could not make them. Even simple decisions like what to eat were impossible for them to make. The field of neuroscience now has empirical data on how emotions are intrinsically tied to the decision-making process.

Yet, when people make decisions, they think they are basing them on facts and data. In other words, using their neocortex, which is the brain region that deals in practicality, reasoning, and conscious thought. But really they are using their limbic system, the neural network that processes emotions.

So, to attract workers, clients, and partners who are the right fit, you need to connect in a way that's authentic and arouses emotion. In other words, in a way that's human.

Throw out the dispassionate corporate-speak. For many business leaders, this requires a wholesale mindset shift. This is why talking about your beliefs, your values, your vision for the world all matter. It's why my 2005 manifesto worked so well.

Now, let's say you're a stealth leader who wants to transform an unhealthy team environment at your workplace. Your job is to consider your vision for that team. Then you share your vision and your *why* with the people on the team and start to create alliances with the people who will work with you on your mission. You can even craft a manifesto outlining the changes you want to create and WHY you want these shifts. You can use that outside the workplace too, to build incredible social connections and align yourself with the right companies, brands, and organizations.

What if you're in a traditional industry? Or what if you're manufacturing a commodity good? There's still a way to share your "Big Why."

FINDING THE *WHY* IF YOU'RE IN A TRADITIONAL INDUSTRY

I learned this lesson from Srikumar Rao, the MBA professor and my personal mentor whom I mentioned in Chapter 1.

One night, Rao gave a speech on the importance of sharing a company's values publicly. Following the speech he opened the floor for a Q&A session. The first hand up was from the owner of a glass-manufacturing company.

He stood up and said, "Okay, okay, I get you, Rao, but tell me: My company makes glass for window panes. How am I ever going to inspire people?"

Rao ran through a line of questioning with the man. He asked him to describe the company, what made him excited to go to work, how he cared about his employees. The *why* they uncovered was pretty remarkable.

This glass manufacturer provided jobs for some 170 people in his city. The founder was deeply passionate about giving back to the community. Once a year, every employee would get a chance to volunteer for a week in a soup kitchen or a charity and still get paid their full salary. The founder believed in providing steady jobs for families in his small town and turning his employees into caring fellow citizens. This is what made him encourage his employees to volunteer for a week every year.

"Imagine telling that story," said Rao.

Instead of a dry marketing statement about "making the best windows ever," the company's manifesto should focus on its volunteerism and community-focused mission. It might look like this:

> *Giving Back to Our Community: This company is run by caring, community-oriented people who believe in giving back. Not only do we build and install the clearest, toughest, most storm-resistant windows in our state, but we care that our people always feel safe, warm, and protected in more ways than what a humble window provides. Therefore, our entire team spends one week every year outside our factory and volunteering in soup kitchens and other places where we get to serve our community from our hearts.*

Doing this requires that you step away from logic and connect to your heart instead. Go within and try to understand your own inner motivation for what you do. Consider the business or initiative or project you're truly committed to bringing to the world and the difference it makes in the world. When you start there, you'll be surprised how it comes naturally.

If you are currently hiring, look at your job website, your job ad, or any piece of content that talks about whom you're hiring. Are you speaking in dry terms and talking about skills, day-to-day tasks, and the nature of the work? Or are you speaking from the heart about your beliefs, your world vision, and *why* you do what you do?

Always start with your beliefs, your values, and your *why*. Writing your manifesto is a great starting place. And that's how you get the right people in the right seats of the bus, to echo Jim Collins's sage advice.

Jim was super clear. You don't have to always know *where* your business or mission or project is going. But if you know *why* you're doing it and attract the right people on the bus, this motley crew will help you figure out *where* to go.

When Mindvalley was in its first two years, my small little team worked on several totally unrelated products. We worked on a meditation website that sold CDs. A social bookmarking engine called Blinklist.com that we ultimately sold. And a new type of blog software that we hoped would change the nature of email and blogging (it ultimately failed). Like many aspiring entrepreneurs, I had to try many things. Eventually, as we experimented and attracted good people, we began to rally around the ideas that worked best. This is why the manifesto comes first. Then, once you start getting good people on the bus, you zero in on the vision.

TACTIC #3: CRAFT YOUR VIVID VISION

Shared beliefs may be the first thing that will draw the right people to you, but the second is a future that inspires. That's what this tactic is about. People's actions line up with the future they want to create for themselves. Give them the future they want and they'll join you.

Cameron Herold is famously known in business circles as the CEO Whisperer. He has worked with hundreds of organizations, including a Big 4 wireless carrier and a monarchy. He teaches a process called Vivid Vision™ that's helped business leaders like me bring their ideas to life and connect authentically with their audience.

In an interview I did with Cameron in 2019 for the Mindvalley podcast, he told me that the biggest problem he sees with business leaders is lack of vision, which then reverberates through all levels of the company. The lack of vision infects the entire team, not to mention its consumers.

If you don't run a team or company at this point, apply this same idea to your life. Lack of vision for your life will have you taking unintentional actions that don't align with what you want. This is why crafting a Vivid Vision is critical work. Intentionality makes decisions easy and speeds up your rate of achieving what you want. The Vivid Vision exercise at the end of this chapter will support you in figuring out what you really want, at work and in life.

While a Vivid Vision is something everyone should learn in school, it's primarily business schools that teach the importance of vision statements. But they do it backward. The classic way is to gather top employees in a boardroom, think up a sexy-sounding paragraph to tell the story of the company, and then post it everywhere.

Cameron says this is wrong. Firstly, the Vivid Vision must come from the founder of the company. Or the leader of the team. And if you're a solopreneur or leading a division in your company, congratulations, you're it. It's your responsibility to create that Vivid Vision for your division.

Cameron provided me a useful piece of advice: "Forget mission and vision. These words are too confusing," he said. "Instead you need to think of it as one; your core purpose."

Your Vivid Vision holds everything together. Herold then showed me this diagram:

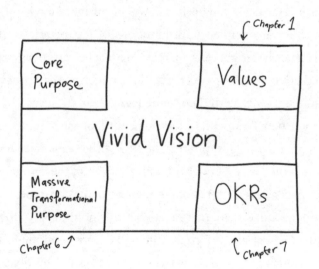

Think of the Vivid Vision as holder of the other elements of your work. We've simplified and covered Core Purpose in this chapter.

Values are what you learned in Chapter 1. Don't worry about Massive

Transformational Purpose (you'll learn that in Chapter 6) or OKRs (Chapter 7). For now just pay attention to Vivid Vision.

A Vivid Vision brings the future to life. The process entails crafting an experiential walk-through for how the world will be transformed in the near term because of your business. It encapsulates why you exist but also how you plan to achieve it. Then you reverse-engineer how the company will get there.

A Vivid Vision gives clarity to team members, clients, customers, partners, and media. It creates alignment. It helps them see what's possible. It also becomes a motivating draw that gets people excited for the future that's being built now. And most important, it extracts ideas from the leader's head, and allows them to be shared so the ideas can multiply quickly through the power of the team.

Cameron says the best way to craft a Vivid Vision is to think three years out. Amplify your business into the future and ask yourself: What does the future look like because my business exists? The three-year timeframe is important. It gives you ample time to achieve desired results, but it's not so far away that you can't get excited. In this way, Vivid Vision becomes the ultimate motivator that propels you and your team forward. And remember, as I wrote in *The Code of the Extraordinary Mind*:

> *As human beings we tend to overestimate what we can do in one year. But we tend to underestimate what we're capable of in three years. So always visualize your life three years ahead. And push that limit and dream bigger.*

Cameron suggests you map out your Vivid Vision in no more than four pages. Share it on a Google Doc and get input. Publish it on job websites and career pages. Cameron does a great job outlining the Vivid Vision concept in his book *Vivid Vision* and his book with Hal Elrod, *The Miracle Morning for Entrepreneurs.*

When you get clear on the Vivid Vision and you do the work to write it out and present it, you'll be amazed at how the right people come to you organically.

As an example, Mindvalley's Vivid Vision starts in the following way:

> *Imagine a school for humanity. A school with no borders, physical or imagined. A school that turns Earth into one global campus. It unites all genders, ages, countries, and cultures, all 7.5 billion of us. The practices taught there empower us to live extraordinary lives. Not only that, they teach us how to bend reality. How to craft lives we create regardless of what we're told. At this school, students are encouraged to think critically. They're allowed to question their beliefs and the collective systems they've adopted. This school reinvents the nature of work. People pursue their creative compulsions. In a world of exponential change, this school experiments with the latest tools. It's obsessed with innovation. And graduation never happens, because learning is lifelong. It's so fun, you never want to stop. This school rallies the world's best teachers and spreads its knowledge to every corner of the earth. It's not afraid to ask the big questions.*

And remember: Any department (or any person) can have its own Vivid Vision. If you're an editor for the blog of your company, you can create a Vivid Vision for the quality of posts you want to produce, the style and vision for the blog, the quantity of readers it would attract, and the conversion rates you aim for. You would also mention what would make the blog stand out and how you'd make it world class. All this helps your team understand what's in your head. It helps the writers you hire know the type of work to deliver.

Now, the challenging part for some people is to make the Google Doc public and share it with the world. You might be worried about people's judgments, but don't let that stop you. The *right* people will be drawn by your vision. The wrong people may be repulsed. But this is exactly what you want.

Every idea in this world starts with a vision, and that comes from one person. To make it happen, that idea must be shared. If you're fearful about that, think about this: An unshared idea is selfish. Sharing is critical to making an idea viable because it needs to be heard or witnessed by another to take its form and be birthed into the world. The Buddha mindset isn't concerned with judgment. It's concerned with expressing your inner truth. Anyone you lose in the process was never going to serve your mission anyway.

So what's your Vivid Vision for your company or your next project? Use the questions at the end of this chapter to guide you.

And don't worry about getting it perfect. Let your vision flow. Allow your team members, spouse, customers you trust, to read it and give you feedback. Magic happens when a vision is co-created.

When you get these ingredients right, you'll find that the right people will flow to you with ease.

And when they come, it's time to lead. The next section of this book and Chapters 3 through 6 go deep in these ideas. You'll learn how to not just create a remarkable life for yourself and an extraordinary impact at your work, but how to take the people you work most closely with on this ride.

Chapter Summary

MODELS OF REALITY

Attracting the allies you need is not a logical process. Be aspirational when you communicate. Use emotion. Dry mission statements are ineffective. Speak from the heart.

1. **Create a manifesto** that summarizes what you're seeking to bring to the world, your beliefs and values, and how you operate. Add this to your website if you have one. Remember to share the *why* of what you do.

2. **Find your big *why*.** Throw out the dispassionate corporate-speak. Talking about your beliefs, your values, your vision for the world will engage people's emotions, which is how they make decisions.

3. **Craft a Vivid Vision and make it public.** Speak three years into the future. Don't worry if you're currently small or operating from a warehouse. *Talk about the future as if it's happening now.*

Systems for Living

EXERCISE 1: CRAFT YOUR MANIFESTO

Your manifesto does not have to be ten points. It can be anywhere from three to ten. Our new manifesto is seven points and it's evolved signifi-cantly from the one I shared from 2005. If you don't run a company, create a personal manifesto to help you attract the right people from friends to people in your community and colleagues.

Ask yourself the following questions:

- What makes us weird/unique or edgy as a company?
- What do we do differently from our competition?
- What makes our culture unique?
- What makes people call us crazy, odd, or unusual?
- What do we believe about life and the world that might be seen as unusual?
- What are the things we will definitely NOT do? (For example,

an ad company refusing to take on clients that promote unhealthy food.)

See an example of the Mindvalley Manifesto on https://careers.mind valley.com/manifesto.

EXERCISE 2: CRAFT YOUR VIVID VISION

Think about the business, nonprofit, project, or movement you want to create or have already created. Fast-forward three years out. What does the world look like? How have you made a difference? What milestones will you have achieved?

Set aside ample time for this exercise, at least thirty minutes to one hour. Go somewhere that stokes your creativity—a coffee shop, bar, garden, even a hike with a dictation app—if it helps. Write out a three-to-four-page experience that vividly tells the story of you or your business, project, or movement, in the future. Use the questions below to guide you.

Don't just do this for your team. If you're an individual you can create a vision like this for your own career path.

- Where do you see your company, movement, skill, project in the next three years?
- If you don't exist, what would be missing in the world?
- What problems are you here to solve?
- What milestones will you have accomplished three years out?
- How is the world different because of you?
- Who are your partners?
- How do you want people to feel when they engage with your brand/creation?
- What groups have you impacted?

PART II

FINDING YOUR POWER

THE FOUR ELEMENTS THAT TRANSFORM WORK AND AMPLIFY RESULTS

Think about that person at work who just Gets. It. Done. But not only are they highly efficient, they also don't suck anyone dry. It's more like they fuel their coworkers and inspire them to do their best too. They contribute to an atmosphere that makes everyone healthier, happier, more creative. Those rockstar high-performers? Those are the badasses of the workplace, and anyone can transform into one.

There's a secret to being a high-performer: At a basic level, every person lives to satisfy a universal set of human needs. Only when a person's basic needs are met can they truly do their best work.

After interviewing almost two thousand people from sixty countries over the years for Mindvalley jobs, I noticed a pattern. What people really wanted in their jobs wasn't security or a steady salary—even if that's what they thought they wanted. What they wanted boiled down to four clusters of personal needs.

These requests emerged over and over again from candidates across all religious, cultural, and national backgrounds.

The four clusters of needs are:

HAPPINESS, LOVE, AND BELONGING

Most people want to wake up every morning knowing they're heading to a job they enjoy, in an atmosphere they like to be in. They want to genuinely like their coworkers. They want to feel like they can express themselves.

After many years, I found that when people say they want to be happy at work, what it really means is, they want to love what they do and whom they do it with. They want to feel like they belong. This is why the structures you learn in Chapter 3 focus on love and connection.

SIGNIFICANCE

Most people want to know that the work they do matters. They want to be appreciated. They want to be able to afford a nice home, or clothes they need to look their best, or the food they need to eat healthy. They want to feel heard and like their opinion matters. They want to be able to express themselves.

You will learn structures for making people feel appreciated and like they matter in Chapter 4.

GROWTH

Most people want to grow. They want opportunities to gain new skills and knowledge and further their capabilities. People want to be provided access to education and training to help them grow both professionally and personally.

We will cover this in Chapter 5, where you'll learn how to create a team dynamic where people challenge and support each other to be their best.

MEANING

Most people want to know that the work they do is positively contributing to society. That they aren't doing work that's actually moving humanity backward, or poisoning a population with some marketing-induced need for an unhealthy product. They care that their work is part of making sure our planet and species are better off several generations down.

This is what you'll learn in Chapter 6. You'll learn structures for propelling a mission forward and keeping people on task.

The four needs were so common I started drawing a diagram like this on my iPad as I interviewed people and asked them to talk about how they felt about these four. I referred to it as the Job Quadrant and it helped me understand the minds of the people I was interviewing to truly see if they were a fit for our culture.

friendship | abundance

mission | growth

Of course, people still need to get paid enough to cover their needs. Ideally, their work won't make them sick, age them prematurely, or threaten their livelihood in any way. Their work environment should at least make them feel safe. But beyond that, people care about a lot more than just the salary or title.

There's a compounding growth effect that happens in teams where each member's basic needs are satisfied. People put in 150 percent on everything they do, and not because it gets them anything but the result. They become intrinsically motivated versus extrinsically motivated people. In other words, they don't need to be incentivized with any perks.

When you learn to cater to these four fundamental needs you build teams of super-performers. And beyond that, you see your power and potential at your work rise too. Work becomes something more than just a means to earn a paycheck. It becomes an essential aspect of living a truly wondrous life.

CHAPTER 3

SPARK DEEP CONNECTIONS

> We all are so deeply interconnected; we have no option but to love all. Be kind and do good for any one and that will be reflected. The ripples of the kind heart are the highest blessings of the Universe.
>
> —Amit Ray, *Yoga and Vipassana: An Integrated Lifestyle*

Humans desire to come together. The need to belong is in our DNA. While we may see ourselves as separate from one another, the truth is, we are connected by invisible bonds. When you understand how to influence this space, you create communities where everyone is greater together than apart.

I LOVE HUMANS. BUT, let's be honest, we can be kind of absurd. This crossed my mind for a brief moment as I stood in a ring of a hundred of my teammates. We were on a company retreat held at a beachfront hotel on a stunning island called Penang, in northwest Malaysia. Our facilitator walked into the center of the circle and said, "This next game will have us get even more vulnerable with one another. But I know you guys are ready for it."

Now, before I tell you what happened next, I have to say this: Why is it that we need to play games to be *real* with each other? It's quite bizarre.

And that's not a comment on other people. I am certainly not exempt from that statement.

But let's face it, the workplace is usually not the place for deep conversations and profound human connection. We sometimes need some nudging to form deeper relationships.

And so, this exercise was part of our 2019 team retreat, which focused solely on the theme of connection. While our team retreats were once about company strategy and objectives and key results (OKRs), I've learned my lesson. Today our team retreats focus on connection and bonding first. We don't talk about the business or vision much. Rather we focus on becoming truly raw, open, and transparent with each other.

When you focus on *connection first* everything else falls into place. This is as true for leaders as it is for anyone else in the group. And if you're not officially a leader, keep in mind that the skill of building connections is perhaps the most powerful tool in the stealth leader toolkit. First of all, it enables you to covertly rise up the ranks in any organization. The second benefit is the social edge you gain when you have the ability to transform any disempowered team. For you this means never having to work in a toxic environment. And since it's been scientifically proven that your quality of life is determined by the people you spend the most time with, relationships matter far more than you might think.

That day at our team retreat, as I stood in that circle, I felt a sense of safety and peace. But it didn't stop the feeling of monster butterflies cavorting in my stomach. Later I learned that I wasn't the only one.

This particular game was called Anybody Else? One person stands in the center of the circle. They share something personal. Something vulnerable. Then they say, "Anybody else?" If the statement is true for anyone else, that person immediately joins the person in the middle.

Once the game got rolling it became a parade of courageous people stepping forward, one by one.

"Sometimes I feel weird in social situations, so I pretend I want to be alone and pull myself away or busy myself on my phone, but I really just feel insecure," said one person.

"I was bullied in my elementary school years and it's taken me more than a decade to get over it," said another.

Each time people joined them in the center. And there were more:

"It doesn't matter how many accomplishments I have, I never feel good enough."

"I'm afraid I'll never find a romantic partner and I'll be alone forever."

I then said my statement: "I've had moments in the past where I felt depression so deep and dark that I wondered if being alive was really worth it."

Ten people stepped in. It was an enlightening moment. The tremendous fear I felt just before I spoke those words dissipated. The eleven of us stood there taking each other in. The nonverbal message we sent to one another was, "I've been there too. I understand what that's like. And I've got you. You are not alone."

There were no tears, just smiles of compassion and relief in many of the faces as the exercise went on. I felt connected. So did many others. It was an uncommon exchange between workmates. In the beginning, it was perhaps a touch unnerving, but it led to an extraordinary level of closeness between us all.

As you'll learn in this chapter, deep connection is a key component of an engaged culture and a high-performing team. When colleagues move beyond "professional" surface relationships and relate to one another as human-to-human, they thrive.

This is not simply an opinion I have. There is ample science to back up the value of social bonds. Connection is a deeply seated desire for all humans. We *crave* it. And when we get it in the workplace, life and work fuse together seamlessly.

As the founder of a company in personal growth, I witness over and over how people struggle alone with thoughts and experiences that are universal. I've experienced hundreds of transformational events where people connect more deeply than they usually do in public—from Burning Man to A-Fest to Mindvalley University. It's magical when groups are given permission to share authentically. That's when our insecurities, challenges, weirdnesses even, dissolve. This allows people to shift from feeling alone, confused, and fearful to feeling supported, understood, and fearless.

Social bonds are the number one variable that raises a person's physical health, mental state, and day-to-day performance. In other words, pretty much any quality connected to a person's overall satisfaction with life is directly correlated to the strength of their social bonds. Today there is ample science to back that up.

The Science of Connection

Human beings are social creatures. Prehistoric man relied on his tribe to survive. To be cast out meant death. The need to belong is not a character trait. It's a basic survival requirement that is hardwired into our DNA.

This is why when a person's sense of belonging is filled, they might feel invincible. Conversely, when it's not, they wither. Numerous neuroscientific studies show that social connection causes reward centers of the brain to light up. On the other hand, experiences of social pain (like loneliness) cause activity in the same regions of the brain that process actual physical pain. A broken heart quite literally aches.

One of Harvard's longest, most qualitative studies was the "Very Happy People" study by Ed Diener and Martin Seligman. It spanned 80 years and followed the lives of 222 people who were screened on life fulfillment using multiple assessment filters. The scientists did an invasive analysis. They went through the participants' vast medical records and conducted hundreds of in-person interviews and questionnaires. The revolutionary findings were that social bonds have a 0.7 correlation (which is massive in the world of science) to life fulfillment.

Think about it. Of everything that the Harvard study looked at, only one factor truly correlated with happiness. It wasn't wealth or good looks or fame or living in a place with warm weather. It was the *strength of a person's social connections* that mattered most.

I wrote about my survey of job candidates in the introduction to Part II in this book and how it led me to identify four clusters of basic human needs that underlie top performance. There's more to the story than that. Later, I was getting into the work of Abraham Maslow and noticed a fascinating similarity: The four quadrants on my diagram almost perfectly matched the four upper levels of Maslow's pyramid.

Maslow's hierarchy of needs shows the universal stages of motivation that all humans go through. Maslow says that in order for any person to move from one level to the next, the underlying needs must be satisfied. For instance, when a person's physiological and safety needs are met, they are motivated to seek connection with other people. Then, once they have social support, their focus turns to proving they matter to themselves and the world in more impactful ways.

After someone has their physiological and safety needs met, according to Maslow, the things that actually matter are:

> *Love and Belonging:* To feel part of a tribe
>
> *Self-Esteem:* To know you matter
>
> *Self-Actualization:* To discover your true potential
>
> *Self-Transcendence:* To transcend your own personal concerns and see from a higher perspective

The similarity between the needs I stumbled upon in my interview process (what I called the Job Quadrant) and Maslow affirmed I was on the right track in building a new kind of workplace. This is how they line up:

MY INTERVIEW QUESTIONS (JOB QUADRANT)	MASLOW
Friendship	Connection and Belonging
Abundance	Self-Esteem
Growth	Self-Actualization
Meaning	Self-Transcendence

It's obvious to see how friendship aligns with connection and belonging and how growth and meaning connect to self-actualization and self-transcendence, but what trips people up is: How is abundance related to self-esteem?

Turns out that abundance was never about money. Rather it was about the respect that people felt money gave them. The money was a means goal. (More on this in coming chapters.) In Maslow the level of Self-Esteem includes confidence, strength, self-belief, personal and social acceptance, and respect from others. All of these were what people were really chasing when they thought they needed money.

When you look at Maslow's pyramid you realize something interesting. Governments are supposed to take care of us. But governments mostly stop at levels 1 and 2 (Physiological Needs and Safety). Who then provides the rest?

I believe the human structures best able to provide the next four levels are the structures of the workplace. Work should not just be about producing a product or service. It can be about so much more.

The next three chapters are based on Maslow and my own research with people I interviewed. For now, we'll discuss happiness through connection and belonging, and how bringing this into work changes the game and makes your life so much more fulfilling.

Work Is Today's Tribe

In the last half century, most people's need for belonging was met by institutions. Militaries, churches, and the flags of nations were structures for connection. Not anymore. The role they've played is weakening at a faster rate than ever before.

Something has to fill the void, and many people today are trying to get that need met at work. It may surprise you to know that the 2019 Edelman Trust Barometer reports that, globally, "my employer" (75 percent) is significantly more trusted than NGOs (57 percent), businesses (56 percent), governments (48 percent), and the media (47 percent). If you're running a company, congrats. You've got the monopoly on trust. And this trust gives you immense power to shift someone's life.

Companies today are blessed with an incredible opportunity, but most of them squander it by putting business needs before their people. In most workplaces there is little place for feelings, vulnerability, or emotional "nonsense." The instruction and expectation from management is to be *professional*. What a stupid concept.

That model is obsolete (if it ever was effective). It's a holdover from the mid-twentieth century. In the modern era, spanning back to the end of the Industrial Revolution, work was a bastion of masculinity. Sadly, many workplaces, organizations, and schools still run in a top-down authoritarian manner where subordinates follow leaders who have been elected by a handful of men in suits. A corporate *Lord of the Flies*.

Postwar leaders returned from serving in World War II and brought their militarized mindset into the boardrooms of corporations everywhere. A young soldier in the 1940s was forty in the 1960s and fifty in the 1970s. On the battlefield, there is certainly no place for feelings. A soldier is there to follow orders. To do a job.

That's how a pseudo-military culture was ingrained in the halls of industry, with no room for emotional outbursts, or talk of loving families, or much in the way of healthy social support. That was for home.

Today, many companies have allowed for a more relaxed environment (think Casual Fridays), but the authoritarian management style is not yet fully extinct. Allowing hoodies in the workplace or giving out free food at the company cafeteria is not sufficient for human connection to flourish.

Since most people spend eight hours of their day at work, colleagues may very well be the new tribe. Most people spend more time with their coworkers than with their families. Now, this is good news if the team dynamic you're a part of is a connected one. But there are horrendous implications if it's not. So let's bend the rules on how companies are *supposed* to run.

And why bother? Well, consider this:

We know today that social connection is the number one thing that correlates with happiness. And as it turns out science now says happiness is perhaps the biggest single contributor to the performance of your team. They go together in one straight line.

Social Connection ⟶ Happiness ⟶ Performance

The Truth About Happiness

Books on company culture sometimes lead to an illusion that workers should be in a constant state of bliss. That workers must be joyful at work all the time. And that leaders should implement structures for this. Frankly, that's rubbish.

It's simply not possible for anyone to be happy all the time. And it's certainly not any leader's job to prance down the company corridors tossing glitter and cupcakes into the air to make everyone smile.

Great companies have structures that encourage the growth of a quality I call positive optimism. Let me clarify.

A positive state is any feel-good mood, like happiness, which is easily achieved when a person experiences any number of stimuli. Watch some kitten videos on YouTube, or eat a piece of chocolate, or binge some Netflix, and you're sure to tap into a positive, albeit fleeting, state. Emotional states fluctuate from moment to moment.

You can be happily working at your computer in one moment, and then receive an email from a coworker about an error that's jeopardized your team's project. You move from happiness to upset very rapidly. That's how emotional states work.

No one can be positive all the time. It's not healthy or useful. And the truth is, "always-on" positivity takes away from experiencing true fulfillment. All emotions are useful. Feeling them fully is healthy. Acceptance is critical.

In an interview Big Think did with Harvard psychologist Dr. Susan David, she said that "society's preoccupation with happiness inadvertently has resulted in greater levels of unhappiness."

Ironic, don't you think?

The desire to feel happy or think positively all the time hinders many people's authentic existence. It lowers resilience.

Instead, Aim for Positive Optimism

So instead of happiness, aim for positive optimism. During negative emotional states, a positively optimistic person will remain committed to the outcome. They will see a bright future ahead even when they experience a setback, rejection, or loss. They accept negative emotions like sadness in the moment and view it as what it is: a temporary state.

Look, we all get sad. And sadness has its own gifts of learning and self-discovery. Let's not avoid sadness. Positive optimism accepts sadness while knowing that it's temporary and more blissful states will come.

My friend, the great spiritual teacher Reverend Michael Beckwith, refers to sadness as a "companion." I was filming with Michael just two weeks after he lost his father. I asked him how he was doing. He replied:

I am bliss. I am joy. I know these are my true nature. But right now I feel a sadness. I'm not pushing it away or denying it. I see this sadness as a companion. An energy within my field. I don't know how long it will be with me. Maybe a month. Maybe years. But I honor it's there. And I understand why it's there.

Michael was not trying to fight his sadness. Nor did he let it overwhelm him. He embraced it and understood its nature. But he knew that life in the long run would be okay. This is the nature of positive optimism.

Happiness is a *state* change. Positive optimism, on the other hand, is a *stage* evolution.

You can be happy in an instant on the right drug, but crash and be depressed the very next day as your brain chemistry changes. This is a state change.

Stage changes, on the other hand, are permanent and irreversible. They are the essence of wisdom and taking on higher worldviews.

Positive optimism is a *stage* change—this means it is a wiser, more developed worldview that governs your relationship with the world around you. Once you awaken to the idea that the Universe is benevolent and life is ultimately good, you never again revert back to your older worldview. You are permanently transformed. That doesn't mean endless bliss. Rather, as Michael Beckwith suggests, it implies a healthier, wiser way to deal with the occasional companions of sadness, grief, and loss.

The Benefits of Positive Optimism

A positively optimistic person is less reactive to their emotions. They have trained themselves to be more aware. They are a witness to what they feel and they proactively *choose* how to react.

> *Positive optimism is not the rejection of sadness, but the thought, even during sadness, that the future will be okay.*

This way of thinking can be trained. It's like building any skill. It simply requires learning how to think more objectively and see situations from other perspectives.

The best athletes in the world see challenge, danger, and uncomfortable moments ahead but still see themselves winning. When they fail, they get back up and go again. This is because they have been trained to deal with emotions, and most critically, they have a solid support system of caring people behind them. In the context of business, positive optimism is what you want your team to possess.

How do you measure happiness and positive optimism? There is a new field emerging called PQ that does just that. And the data that's emerging is something everyone with a job or career needs to pay attention to.

The Power of PQ

Positive optimism can equate to what Shirzad Chamine, author of the book *Positive Intelligence: Why Only 20% of Teams and Individuals Achieve Their True Potential*, would call a high Positive Intelligence Quotient (PQ). A person with a high PQ means they have a higher ratio of positive feelings to overall feelings. In a simple sense: a person who is feeling a little stressed or insecure or down 10 percent of the time would have a PQ of 90. The book is a meta-analysis of hundreds of studies on happiness and work, concluding that "higher PQ leads to higher salary and greater success in the arenas of work, marriage, health, sociability, friendship, and creativity."

Chamine writes: "Your mind is your best friend, but it is also your worst enemy. Positive intelligence is the relative strength of these two modes of your mind. Positive intelligence is therefore an indication of the control you have over your own mind, and how well your mind acts in your best interest."

So to develop a high-performing culture, leaders must focus on nurturing stage development. This does not mean solely providing opportunities for state happiness (let's call this the glitter and cupcakes approach).

Instead they have to provide opportunities for growth of positive optimism (personal growth and social support in the workplace).

And you don't need to be leading a team. It's obvious that developing positive optimism would benefit you no matter your work situation or your current goals. Simple tools like the Two-Minute Appreciation Technique (Chapter 4) can yield amazing results for anyone. (The company in the example I will share saw a revenue increase of over $300 million.)

And if you are leading a team or starting from scratch and hiring one, you must support your people to develop mastery over their own minds, so they can elevate their PQ.

In fact, in one stunning study, a comparison of sixty teams, Chamine suggests that the PQ of a team is the SINGLE BEST indicator of a team's success. Consider this:

- Higher-PQ CEOs are more likely to lead happy teams who report their work climate to be conducive to high performance.
- Project teams with higher-PQ managers perform 31 percent better.
- Higher-PQ workers take fewer sick days and are less likely to become burned out or quit.
- Managers with higher PQ are more accurate and careful in making decisions, and they reduce the effort needed to get their work done.

So how do you raise PQ? It's all about people. These are five tactics I brought into our culture.

Five Tactics for a Connected Culture

Whatever your role and future goals, master these next five tactics and you'll gain a superpower that will give you the ability to turn any group into a socially bonded high-performance team. The astonishing by-product is: Work becomes more like play, since you're with some of your closest friends.

If you're in a leadership role, allow me to stop you before you go tossing a fun company party, or doling out bigger Christmas bonuses. While these are useful ideas, and they'll raise positivity, these surface-level strategies produce only fleeting results.

If you're waiting for an authority figure to step up and fix the team dynamic at your workplace, more waiting won't help. Designate yourself. Anyone can shift an entire group dynamic through their own deliberate actions. You can also use these tactics for establishing a team or to deepen bonds with people in any other groups you're a part of.

Here are the five tactics for creating a connected workplace that I've found to be most effective:

1. Friendships at Work
2. Create an Environment of Safety and Support
3. Practice Vulnerability
4. Positive Contagions
5. Compete at Kindness

TACTIC #1: FRIENDSHIPS AT WORK

Time to challenge a mindset. What if friendship at work were as impor-tant to a company as productivity? What if companies didn't simply obsess about the latest time-optimization platform but also about encouraging people to connect deeply with one another? What if you worked with your best friends?

If you think these ideas are fluff, this data will change your mind. Gallup's Q12 Employee Engagement Survey completely shatters the idea that friendships at work are unproductive. The study concludes that one of the key determinants to engagement at work is having a workplace bestie. Co-workers who report a best friend at work are *seven times* more engaged at work than their disconnected counterparts. They score higher on all performance metrics. They are better with customers, bring more innovation to projects and have superior mental acuity and reduced rates of error and injury.

This is because having social bonds at work makes people feel good. It makes them happy. In 2014, I interviewed Shawn Achor, Harvard researcher and bestselling author of *The Happiness Advantage, Beyond Happiness* and *Big Potential.* Get a load of this data:

- When the brain is in a positive state, productivity rises by 31 percent
- Sales success increases by 37 percent
- Intelligence, creativity, and memory all improve dramatically
- Doctors primed to be happy are 19 percent better at making the right diagnosis

Social bonds raise positivity, and that's important. Yet when it comes to happiness and work, most people operate with an attitude of "Work hard now, be happy later." Or, "If I work hard, it will make me happy later." Achor encourages us to flip the formula. His equation might look like:

Feel good = Work better = Exponentially better results

The greatest way to do this is with social connections. That is how you create a team dynamic where people feel a sense of love and belonging.

These findings mirror one of the key arguments from Jim Collins in his book *Good to Great,* who writes, "The people we interviewed from good-to-great companies loved what they did largely because they loved who they did it with."

HOW TO SPARK FRIENDSHIPS

In Amy Cuddy's book *Presence,* the Harvard researcher explains that when two people first meet they both make a quick calculation to decide whether they like each other. People unconsciously seek to answer these two questions:

1. Do I trust this person?
2. Do I respect this person?

These are the initial building blocks of all relationships. If a person answers "yes" to both questions on the first encounter, this could be the start of a budding friendship. Adversely, in any relationship that doesn't work, one or both of these two elements is missing. A hint to anyone who has a personal or business relationship that feels hostile: Restore these two elements.

In an interview with the *New York Times,* the CEO of Shopify talked about establishing a metric for this, which he calls the "trust battery." He said, "It's charged at 50 percent when a person is hired and then every time you work with someone at the company, the trust battery between the two of you is either charged or discharged, based on scenarios like whether you deliver a project on time or not."

Perhaps the same type of metric could be created to measure respect? Thinking of relationships as having a trust battery or respect battery is one way to simplify their complexity, because the challenge with relationships is that they are subjective. The variables that turn two strangers into great friends is too complex to attempt to explain in this book. It can't be forced. That said, there are beliefs and practices that can be initiated by anyone to engineer for better odds.

First, people who have common values are more apt to seek friendships with one another. So if you're in a position to hire, nail that process first. Then periodically evaluate the team dynamic. Ask yourself an honest question: Are there people in the company that are preventing friendships from forming?

I once let go of a highly religious man who refused to shake hands with women. It was against his culture. He was a brilliant engineer but his presence on the team severely diminished the level of overall group cohesion and made women feel uncomfortable. This was not healthy, given our management at that time was 60 percent women. He had to go or change his beliefs. While we can respect religious beliefs, we can't let in someone who makes others feel uncomfortable.

Next create a cadence of social activities. Friendships are built over time. People need multiple opportunities to connect in different environments. I've discovered that two of the best methods to create solid social connections and bring love and belonging into the workplace are:

1. Social events
2. Rituals

One simple way anyone can support the growth of friendships at work is to initiate more social events. This might seem basic and pretty obvious. Yet most companies simply don't organize enough of these. Anyone can easily initiate very simple events that bring people together.

Below I've laid out a simple cadence to run your social events. There are five types: daily, weekly, monthly, quarterly, annually.

At Mindvalley, we have a weekly social hour, which is often extended late into the evening. We also do a monthly social night outside the office where the team gathers at a swanky restaurant for food and drinks.

If you're in a leadership position, show up. I always do. I've found that people open up to their managers differently outside the office. We are social machines but we are conditioned to operate in the cultural contexts we find ourselves in. No matter how open a workplace, most people abide by a code of rules that regulate how we speak, dress, and listen to each other.

After a beer or two, a programmer might gripe openly about a work-place struggle. Or, I'll learn about hidden talents of my coworkers, or their recent travel experiences, or personal triumphs and struggles. And I can be myself at these moments too.

When I worked for Microsoft in 1998 I admired how Bill Gates invited all the new hires to his home. I remember feeling such respect for Bill watching him in his backyard flipping burger patties for us employees. I admired how he brought us into his circle right away and gave us a space to share with one another. If Bill Gates can make time to fire up the grill for his employees, surely anyone can.

Here's some guiding advice for the five different types of events you can run.

Daily Rituals

Daily team connection rituals are vital. Many of my most effective team leaders insist on starting the day with a gratitude ritual. For a ten-person team this can take five minutes per person, but it helps everyone connect deeply and get to know each other.

The rule is that each person shares one thing that they are grateful for. It could be a cup of coffee their spouse made them that morning. Or the smile of a child waking them up with a hug. Or a work victory. For remote teams I've seen this done very effectively via Skype or even Slack, where everyone posts emoticon-filled messages.

Weekly Rituals

When my executive team meets every Wednesday, we open with Ezekiel, our CHRO, asking, "So what's going on in everyone's life and how are you all feeling today?"

The rule is that we then share our week, but we're not allowed to discuss work. We openly share what we're facing, our ups and downs and the latest events in our life. We often rate how we're feeling from a scale of 1 to 10. For example, during our last meeting, I shared that I was a 7 because I had gotten hooked on *Stranger Things,* season 3, and just after finishing episode 5 my Internet conked out and it took four days to get it fixed. Ohhh, the agony of waiting to see what happens in episode 6.

The sharing doesn't have to be serious or intense. It does have to be how real friends talk to each other.

Monthly Rituals

Every month Mindvalley runs a social night. Usually it happens in a bar. There is always great food, and nonalcoholic drinks for nondrinkers. We never make this compulsory. It's strictly optional. (If you don't have a budget for this, keep it more casual. Make it a potluck, for instance, and do it at someone's house.)

Personally, I often find that during these evenings I get to hear things people may not bring up in the office. I particularly enjoy hearing the programmers, who usually quietly work behind their computer screens, open up after a glass of whiskey. Engineering frustrations and problems that some introverts won't bring up in the office suddenly pop up on my radar at 11 p.m. over pizza and wine.

Quarterly Rituals

Once every quarter the company organizes a large party. We might rent out an entire bar or restaurant. In the early days, before we had a budget, we hosted it in my apartment. The parties sometimes have a theme or might be more classy and formal.

In the invitation, I often ask my people to bring with them the most brilliant person they know. These brilliant guests often then end up quitting their regular jobs and joining Mindvalley when they meet the team. Recruiting in this way is a powerful strategy.

Annual Rituals

At Mindvalley, one way we deepen social bonds and encourage vulnerability is by hosting an annual team retreat, as mentioned earlier. Mindvalley flies the entire company to an exotic locale for four days of getting to know each other. This is where we spend three nights and two days connecting and bonding. Each night we host an elaborate costume party. I've found that costume parties are a great equalizer. When you can be anyone you want to be, it somehow gives people more social fluidity.

TACTIC #2: CREATE AN ENVIRONMENT OF SAFETY AND SUPPORT

I've had direct experience on the wrong side of this at Mindvalley. One day in 2017, I ended up in the hospital after working myself into a state of exhaustion. I lay in bed thinking, *How the hell did I get here?* It was a stupid thought, because I knew very well how I'd gotten there.

If you've ever overworked yourself, you know it can be tough to stop when you're in the middle of a project. Even if you're tired, you keep going. You don't ask for help. And you do it all yourself. Which is what I did. I took on too much and inevitably, I collapsed.

We had just launched Mindvalley University, a pop-up-style university that lasts for an entire month. The first time we launched it, it was an experiment. We wondered if it was possible to reinvent the traditional university. Could we get people, families even, to travel to a new country, live there for two to four weeks, and connect with a pop-up community of brilliant minds and world-renowned teachers?

As you can imagine, an event that spans one full month and happens in a different foreign country every year is a massive undertaking. In the end, the experience was an amazing success. But it just about killed me.

The first time we did it, we asked students and teachers to travel to Barcelona, Spain. We had three hundred attendees. The next year, in Tallinn, Estonia, we had eleven hundred. And it continues to grow year after year.

But that first time around in Barcelona, I physically broke down during the event. I was hospitalized with severe bronchitis. I had no voice. I was depleted. I had managed to get enough of my work done to see the project to its end, but when it was over, I was swallowed up by a black cloud of depression. This happened thanks to an amplified workload and the stress that came with so many unknowns. It was one of the most stressful periods of my life.

And so, when we discussed Version 2.0 of Mindvalley U, in 2018, I appointed my friend and teammate Kadi Oja to take it on. But I had major concerns.

Given my previous year's experience, I feared for her mental and physical health. I internally wrestled with letting her or anyone take it on. But she is one of my best people. She often texts me late in the evening with ideas and suggestions for departments that aren't even hers. And she usually ends her texts with "Sorry, but you just know how much I love this company." She treats the company like it's her own. Which made it impossible for me to say no when the idea of her taking over Mindvalley University came up. I appointed her director of Mindvalley University. But there were conditions.

I promised myself that she would not go through the agony I did. So together with a small team on the project, we created a WhatsApp group called Angels. It was a structure to support everyone involved so that no one was going through undue stress alone. The group was a way for us to check in with each other every day. We used it to share grateful moments, work through challenges, and make each other laugh with silly videos and gifs that made us smile throughout the arduous planning process of our second go-around.

Beyond our Angels WhatsApp group we also connected in person over lunch every week. During one lunch, I was struggling with a personal dilemma. Because of the stress of the project, I broke down and sobbed in front of my team.

As a man, and the CEO of the company, crying in front of your team can feel horrible, and to some it may seem like a sign of weakness.

I don't remember what my teammates said that day, but I do remember how they made me feel safe and loved. I left lunch at peace. I knew everything was going to be okay. That day they were more than WhatsApp Angels for me. They were living ones. And it was one of the most beautiful experiences I've ever had bonding with my colleagues that I've had at work.

The experience reminds me of a quote from the movie *Almost Famous*. Philip Seymour Hoffman's character Lester Bangs says, "The only true currency in this bankrupt world is what you share with someone else when you are uncool."

Of course, this takes the willingness to be uncool yourself. But when you are, you'll find that people appreciate you even more. (More on this shortly.)

This is the dynamic you want to create in a team. A safe space where people can celebrate the good times and lean on each other during tough moments. In other words, where people can feel safe enough to ask for support and help and know they will receive it.

There is nothing that will truly get you through the hard times in work and life like a solid support system. It's a very special experience.

In teams it takes effort to have people feel okay being themselves. But once again, anyone can create structures for this. First, trash the grand myth about work, which is that personal life needs to be separate. When people feel safe with their teammates, it's true magic.

How do you build a group where people feel supported? There are two simple practices you can start to help move this forward:

1. **Group Sharing Spaces:** Create a WhatsApp where any team you're a part of can share personal matters. In Asia, it's common for families to connect over a WhatsApp group. My entire family is connected. It's what we use to keep each other informed. Why not do the same for your team?

Rule: Make the group about sharing personal aspects of the participants' lives. And make it clear that this group is for people to ask for support. When facing an intense project with the potential of high levels of stress, these groups are particularly useful. Like me, you can name this group Angels to make a statement that the purpose of the group is to provide a loving support network.

Also, please note, I'm suggesting WhatsApp because it's the most widely used tool, but feel free to use any tool common in your country.

2. **Intimate Dinner Gatherings:** Our monthly bar nights became so enjoyable that I now often invite teams over for dinners and evening gatherings.

As I write this book, I am designing a new apartment space. I told the designer to make sure I have room for twenty to thirty people at my home.

Every week, I plan to schedule dinner meetups with all my teams. When we meet it will be in a space where people feel able to open up and be more authentic.

Anyone can do this (and it's especially important if you lead a team), though it may require operating outside the conventional rules of business.

When you create these moments, you'll find that remarkable ideas emerge. When people are at work, they communicate with a syntax of professionalism, which can lower their self-expression. Where do friends and family gather? Over a dinner table. To create a feeling of deeper trust, it can pay to skip dinner at a restaurant. Instead, open the doors to your home.

TACTIC #3: PRACTICE VULNERABILITY

Virginia Woolf wrote, "What I value is the naked contact of a mind." When we know we are safe, we can be ourselves. When we know we have friends who care, we know we can share our inner demons and insecurities.

For a sense of love and belonging to develop in the workplace, for actual bonding to take place, there's an emotional ingredient that's required. And that is vulnerability.

The truth is, people want to be vulnerable (even if they think they don't). It's the ingredient for the biologically hardwired love and belonging they crave. And this is perhaps the greatest challenge for all of us. But let me tell you a secret that I've learned about leadership: Vulnerability is the mark of the truly great ones.

Vulnerability is uncomfortable. That's why it's hard. If you think you're doing it right but you don't feel scared, you're not doing it at all. Fear is a prerequisite.

WHY HIDING THE BAD ISN'T GOOD

I learned an important lesson about vulnerability one day in 2012.

My then-wife Kristina and I were trying to have a second child. We'd been trying to conceive for five years. In January of 2012, we discovered Kristina was pregnant. We were ecstatic.

Then, one day during the sixth week of the pregnancy while doing a routine checkup at the hospital, we received the devastating news. We learned that we had lost the baby.

I walked Kristina back to the car. She could hardly stand. Tears trailed down my cheeks. I had no idea how to deal with this heartache. It was a horrid paralyzing moment. I felt like all the joy or love I'd ever experienced in life had suddenly been sucked straight out of me.

I dropped Kristina off at home and went to the office. That particular day some filmmakers from Singapore had traveled down to interview me for a documentary on Mindvalley culture.

When I got to the film studio I crumpled to the floor. I told the production manager that I would not be able to complete the shoot. She understood and canceled it.

I told her what had just transpired, but I didn't tell anyone else. I didn't want my pain to infect the office. So I hid it. For several weeks. On the twelfth day, my colleague Grace walked into my office. Grace is a manager at Mindvalley. She's a very sweet and gentle-mannered woman.

"Vishen, are you upset with me?" she inquired.

"No," I replied. "Why would you even think that?"

"Well, for this entire past week you've been *different*. You seem angry and distant. I don't feel you've been yourself around me. So I felt I did something wrong."

In that moment, I realized that by trying to hide my pain from others I had inadvertently created more pain. Grace thought she'd failed me.

I changed my approach that day. Now, whenever I'm going through a particularly bad period in my life, I make a point to tell my team. It might be a child that's sick. Or a death in the family. But when I have a sudden dilemma that jolts my feelings and creates a sense of sadness, I share it.

I encourage everyone on my team to do the same. If it's something that can't be shared, then the rule is to simply state: "I'm going through some shit right now. So I'm in a bit of a bad mood. If I seem upset, please know that it's not you."

This statement removes people's assumptions. And can facilitate a deeper level of bonding. Being vulnerable in this way allows your coworkers to support you in their own way.

When I have shared these moments someone always gives me a hug. Or when I return from a meeting, I'll find a note of appreciation on my desk. This is what good friends and good coworkers do. They may not be able to feel your pain, but they allow you to go through it and let you know that they are there for you.

TACTIC #4: POSITIVE CONTAGIONS

Moods go viral, in a similar way as the flu. The phenomenon is called emotional contagion. It's what happens when what one person feels and behaves triggers the same emotions and actions in the people in their immediate environment.

This is perhaps why Shawn Achor wrote in his book *The Happiness Advantage*, "Studies have found that when leaders are in a positive mood, their employees are more likely to be in a positive mood themselves, to exhibit prosocial helping behaviors toward one another and to coordinate tasks more efficiently and with less effort."

One of the best ways to initiate a positive emotional contagion in groups is to be optimistically positive yourself. Set the tone. To take this a step further, initiate strategically planned rituals that infuse the team with good vibes, and make them a regular occurrence. Rituals are an incredible way to create the experience of belonging.

Ritual #1: Culture Days and Celebrations. At Mindvalley we do this with a monthly Culture Day. Since we have sixty countries represented on our team, we make people feel like they belong by having them spread the customs, food, and rituals from their native land.

On a Culture Day in our office you might see a team of loud and proud Middle Easterners dancing with plates of hummus, or a giant colorful dragon parading through the halls to celebrate the Chinese New Year. There have been Germans dressed in lederhosen, pouring beer and serving bratwurst. And cheerful Canadians delivering handwritten thank-you notes, because, well, leave it to the Canucks to go over and above to be ridiculously nice.

Steal our Culture Day tradition if it inspires you. But for every team, these rituals should be unique. It's important to consider your values and the emotional contagions you want to create.

Ritual #2: The Weekly All Hands Gathering: The Awesomeness Report. Another simple ritual any company can initiate is a company-wide gathering for celebrating wins. The A-Report (the "A" in our case stands for "Awesomeness") is a community meeting at Mindvalley that takes place once a week. We use this group time to share updates, celebrate new records broken, ideas, team achievements, and goals met. We recognize the talents, accomplishments, and success of the team and this inspires even greater achievements company-wide.

The agenda of the A-Report is structured as follows:

1. Share customer stories and press articles on Mindvalley
2. Visit each Quarterly Goal (OKR) and report on any possible wins
3. Share new records broken
4. Recognize individuals who contributed to the past week's successes

5. Recognize new hires who joined the company

6. Share updates on HR and new initiatives for employees

7. Close with a message or insight. Any key leader can choose to deliver a five-minute insight.

This simple ritual takes place for sixty to ninety minutes every week. It brings the entire company together in a group positive contagion. Following the A-Report we serve drinks and snacks and people bond over food and music.

Positive contagions like A-Reports and Culture Days are important. They create ripples of positivity that lead to greater group performance across the entire company and allow people to connect deeply and get to know and recognize their teammates.

TACTIC #5: COMPETE AT KINDNESS

If there was ONE thing you could do in under five minutes every day to dramatically boost your odds of getting a raise over the next two years, would you do it?

Well, here it is.

In an interview with me, Shawn Achor shared his concept of Social Connection Score:

> Social connection is the breadth, the depth and meaning in your social relationships. It's actually the greatest predictor of your long-term happiness. But the way scientists normally measure it is that we ask you, "Do you have a lot of social support given to you? If you're stuck at work do you have someone who will help you out?"
>
> I flipped around the questions to ask WHO is providing it. WHO is the giver.
>
> What we found is that IF . . .

- you're the type of person people want to talk to when they are going through difficult times,
- you have high levels of compassion,
- you're initiating social engagements,
- you're a positive and optimistic person (which we found in previous research makes you magnetic),

Then you have a high Social Connection Score. And it turns out that if you're in the top quartile of social connection (meaning the top 25 percent in your company), you're 40 percent more likely to get a promotion in the next two-year period of time.

Think about that for a moment. We sometimes think that raises go to the most brilliant or competitive people. But Shawn Achor's research shows that it's social connectivity that seems to matter in a big way.

He went on: "Happiness may be a choice, but it requires effort. Both on an individual level and also those of us that own companies. We have a moral and business obligation to make sure people in our team are in a positive state," Achor emphasized to me.

Feeling bonded, appreciated, or loved at work makes people feel good. And when people feel good they work better. Their life improves. This is why it's critical to encourage acts of kindness.

But how do we grow social connection for an entire company en masse? At Mindvalley we created a massive culture hack called Love Week. It's become so popular that Love Week is now practiced in more than five thousand companies worldwide.

Love Week happens every year during the week of Valentine's Day and it's not about romantic love at all. For five days straight, coworkers spread love and appreciation for each other.

HERE'S HOW IT WORKS

Each person becomes a "Secret Angel" to a "Human." The Secret Angel's duty of the week is to show affection to their Human in creative, mysterious, and secretive ways. These displays don't need to be lavish. It's as simple as leaving a favorite caffeinated morning brew on a desk, or delivering a bouquet of flowers or handwritten note. However, at Mindvalley, there have been French dinners, massage vouchers, and singing telegrams.

At the end of Love Week the Secret Angels reveal their identities. It's always a beautiful sight to see the surprise, love, and genuine gratitude that follow. To start a kindness competition in any team, follow the guidelines of the Love Week exercise at the end of this chapter.

Over five thousand companies now take part in Love Week, and it's amazing to see the sharing and stories on Instagram. I created an official Love Week implementation guide you can find on the resource website for this book at www.mindvalley.com/badass.

Now, if you're still not convinced, or you think that a few connection exercises don't have lasting results, I'll leave you with one last story. This was my personal highlight of our last team retreat in 2019. And it was completely unexpected.

Love in a Public Restroom

I knew our last team retreat was successful when I interrupted some colleagues in the men's bathroom at two a.m. on Rock Legend party night.

I walked in on a group of my male colleagues huddled around one of their coworkers, consoling him. When they heard the creak of the door, they all turned in unison to see who it was.

"Hey, guys," I said nonchalantly but feeling slightly awkward and knowing full well I'd walked in on something.

The guy in the center of the circle—let's call him Dan—looked up, and seeing it was me, offered an explanation of what was going on. "I am so fed up with being rejected by women. Like, is there something wrong with me? What do I need to do to get them to like me?"

All the guys gathered around Dan. They came together to help him. They were all offering ideas and support.

"Next week, let's do coffee. I want to help you with this," said one of the crew. Another teammate offered, "You need to read this book I read on dating."

A third chimed in, "I'd be happy to help you hit the gym if you want some support there."

It was amazing to see all of the guys connecting in this way. Dan was comforted by it. He was simply trying to figure out the barriers in his way and asking for support from his coworkers—actually, his friends.

Dan felt comfortable sharing about his struggle bravely in a public toilet in front of his peers and the founder of the company. He knew he wasn't going to be judged. In that moment I thought, *Wow, this is remarkable. That's what connection can look like.*

When you bring connection to your workplace you give people and yourself one of the greatest gifts in the world—and the gift with the highest correlation to human happiness. The gift of belonging.

In the next chapter we'll go one step higher on Maslow's pyramid. We'll go from Connection to Self-Esteem. And as you'll see, it's very possible to design your business in such a way that the people who join feel extremely significant.

I'll also share a simple exercise that Shawn Achor revealed to me. It caused one company to go from $650 million to $950 million in eighteen months—and all it involved was a daily two-minute exercise.

Chapter Summary

MODELS OF REALITY

Love and belonging are basic human needs. They are biologically hardwired into all people. Everyone wants to feel connected. This includes with their colleagues. Most people spend one-third of their life at work, which means workmates are the new tribe.

Social connections greatly influence a person's quality of life in and outside of the workplace. When people get their need for belonging met their productivity, intelligence, creativity, and health improve dramatically. This is because social bonds are the most important factor for individual happiness (a 0.7 correlation).

So to grow social bonds in any group the five tactics are:

1. Friendships at Work. Workers with best friends at the office are *seven times* more engaged at work than their disconnected counterparts. To deepen social bonds in any group, initiate social events and rituals. Anyone can do this.

2. Create an Environment of Safety and Support. For belonging to happen, people must feel safe with their peers. To put this in action, anyone can create personal sharing spaces both online and offline.

3. Vulnerability is one of the top qualities linked to unstoppability. Be a demonstration and anyone can create an environment where others can be authentic too.

4. Positive Contagions. An emotional contagion is when a mood spreads from one person to another in the same environment. Positive emotional contagions can be instigated by anyone. Use rituals to infuse teams with positive emotions and create community.

5. Compete at Kindness. Celebrate Love Week. To join the movement,

follow the steps below. For more information, visit the resource website for this book on www.mindvalley.com/badass.

In the next chapter, you will learn how to be someone who is unfuckwithable and how to spread that quality to everyone you touch. Honing this quality will make you invincible. And when you learn how to unlock the unfuckwithability of others, they are too.

SYSTEMS FOR LIVING

LOVE WEEK: A GUIDE TO INJECTING LOVE INTO YOUR WORKPLACE

Join Mindvalley in our annual Love Week tradition. Every year we share about the weeklong campaign. Follow and share by connecting with us on Mindvalley's Facebook page and Instagram and Twitter feed (@mind valley) using the official hashtag #SpreadLoveWeek.

Step 1: Preparing for Love Week: Before Love Week starts, everyone adds their name to a hat and then each person draws out a name (at random), regardless of gender or rank. The name each person draws becomes their Human, which makes them a Secret Angel.

Their duty as a Secret Angel is to show love and appreciation for their Human all week in creative, mysterious, and secretive ways.

Step 2: Find out about your "Human": No one needs to spend lavish amounts to show their "Human" love and appreciation. It's always the thought and effort that count. If they already know their Human, they will have a good idea about what they love, enjoy, and favor. If they don't know, it's a great opportunity to get to know someone better.

Step 3: Be creative! Team members are encouraged to collaborate with other Secret Angels to brainstorm and execute on gifts. Here are some ideas: Compile love notes from their friends, create a Spotify playlist, send them empowering quotes, set up a temporary Tumblr account dedicated to them, or create a customized (anonymous) Pinterest board of their goals and interests. The ideas are infinite.

Get the full Love Week Implementation Guide and see a behind-the-scenes video at www.mindvalley.com/badass.

CHAPTER 4

MASTER UNFUCKWITHABILITY

To be yourself in a world that is constantly trying to make
you something else is the greatest accomplishment.

—Ralph Waldo Emerson

I n a world of many options we seek to follow others rather than follow our own inner guidance. The key is to learn to love yourself
deeply and learn to trust your inner yearnings. As you do, you
can channel these dreams, visions, and desires into a masterpiece of
a life. As a leader, you can bring this out in others too. When you do
this, the shared visions you create become reality with elegance and
ease.

I HAVE A MEMORY of my grandfather driving me to school when I was a
teen and sharing a profound bit of advice. He told me, "Be like Bill Gates.
He's the richest man in the world. Be like him. You must study computers."

My grandfather was of Indian origin. And that year Gates had made
a much-publicized trip to India. My grandfather had been watching the
news and was fascinated by Gates.

His advice stuck in my head.

"Be like Bill."

"Study computers."

And because of the reverence I had for my granddad, I started to move in the direction he implanted in my mind.

I worked hard in school and got the grades. I applied to every major university with a computer science program. And in 1995 I was accepted into the University of Michigan School of Electrical Engineering and Computer Science. And so I began my life as a student engineer. I found university challenging. I hardly enjoyed my engineering classes, but I pressed on.

Then one day in 1998 Microsoft came to campus. Their recruiters were there to encourage the students of our prestigious school to apply to join the company. I was delighted to be selected for the interview.

A few months later I was accepted. I had become one of the select few engineers to be chosen to spend the summer of 1998 in Redmond, Washington, as an intern at Microsoft. And unless you absolutely screwed up, this was a path to a full-time job at one of the most amazing companies in the world back then.

And so I found myself one day in my own office at Microsoft. It was an amazing feeling. I had my own room. They provided me with a swanky apartment. I had triple monitors on my desk at work. And an invitation to visit Bill Gates's home for a barbecue.

My grandfather would have been proud.

But something was eating me up inside.

Frankly, I hated my job. I was a software test engineer. And I woke up every day dreading going to work.

One weekend I found myself on the shores of Lake Washington. Our class of new hires had been invited to visit the man himself, Bill Gates, in his gorgeous home overlooking a lake. I was awestruck and honored to be there.

At the center of the lawn was Bill himself. He was wonderfully kind and charming. I had the utmost respect for the man. And there he was, serving burgers to my fellow engineers, who circled him to hear his stories and shake his hand.

I walked toward Bill to say hi. In the back of my mind I wondered if my grandfather was watching from heaven. But then I stopped.

Something didn't feel right.

I hated my job.

I shouldn't be there.

Why was I pretending?

I admired Bill, but I knew I was lying to him. And lying to myself.

I quit Microsoft shortly thereafter. (Okay, I got myself fired.) I lasted eleven weeks in the company.

As I boarded my taxi to fly out of Sea-Tac Airport, a part of me felt like a failure. But there was another part of me that felt elated. I promised myself to never again try to mold my vision for my life around what someone else wanted for me.

Not for Bill.

Not for my grandfather.

Almost five years of my life had been spent chasing a degree and a vision for my future that I never truly cared about. Once I attained that dream of working for Microsoft, I realized within weeks that I wanted out.

And this taught me something curious about dreams. So often what we think we want isn't what we really want.

We confuse our dreams. We pursue visions that others implant within us while squelching the visions truly emerging from our soul.

And we do this . . . to feel significant.

All people are born with a need for significance. To feel whole and self-empowered and valued and loved. As kids, we relate to ourselves as if our opinion is the *only* one that matters. Then we learn that we're not alone on the planet. Inevitably we experience some pivotal event that shakes our self-esteem.

Parents or teachers might tell us: "Why can't you be like your sister or your brother or classmate?" Or we might be ridiculed in class for raising our hand and giving the wrong answer. Or teased by our peers because we look different in some way.

In these instances a person questions whether they are good enough, and the memory of the hurt gets etched into their being. There's a chink in the core belief "I am enough."

From that moment, life becomes a quest to prove they matter to the world. I don't know anyone who doesn't deal with this in some manner. And I am no exception.

The chasing of significance aligns with the fourth level of Abraham Maslow's pyramid, which he categorizes as Esteem. Maslow's theory suggests that when a person's Physical Safety and Love/Belonging needs are met, being appreciated and respected predominantly motivates behavior.

I studied something I didn't enjoy and took a job I didn't like because I wanted to feel significant and raise my self-esteem. I wanted to feel like I made my family proud. But in the process I crushed my own dreams.

We all go to extreme measures to remedy the feeling that we're not enough. Some try to validate themselves with their careers or their bank accounts. Some staunch the fear with a sporty car or a grand home. Some work themselves into misery to chase that elusive title and raise. Others seek fame. Some fail to validate themselves, and their inability to feel whole drives them to addiction or despair.

But when people are liberated of their need to feel significant, when they believe they are good enough, they start operating at a level of incredible power. It's the quality of being unfuckwithable.

Becoming "Unfuckwithable"

I don't know who coined the word *unfuckwithable,* but it was popularized via an Internet meme. It was an image with the following text:

> Unfuckwithable: When you're truly at peace and in touch with yourself. Nothing anyone says or does bothers you and no negativity can touch you.

Truly, being unfuckwithable is synonymous with being a badass. But most of us are far from it.

You go on a date with someone who doesn't text you back the next day and you can't stop wondering what you did wrong. You get a negative performance review at the job you're not passionate about and you can't stop feeling inadequate. You see your peers, your siblings, your colleagues all progressing at a faster pace than you seem to be progressing, and you start feeling afraid of getting left in the dust. These are all tiny blows individually, but they eat away at your confidence over time. And the reason they have such a big effect is that you are *fuckwithable.*

If your goal is to get a particular person to love you, you are fuckwith-able. Your failure or success lies in the hands of somebody else. However, if your goal is to bring as much energy, love, and enthusiasm as you can to the lives of the people around you, you are unfuckwithable. You are in control of that situation. Any love or acceptance you get back from it is simply a bonus.

Let me break that term down for you. People who are fuckwithable are people who do not feel whole. People who place their self-worth in the hands of others and only feel good enough when they are accepted, admired, or praised. We are all born as fuckwithable people. We exist in a social ecosystem and it's difficult to tear ourselves apart from our natural craving for approval. But if we're able to retrain that craving and transform ourselves into badasses who are unfuckwithable—that's when we truly move into our power.

Getting your worth and becoming unfuckwithable isn't a process that happens overnight. It's a process that happens through a series of delib-erate, conscious steps you take that move you away from self-doubt and toward self-confidence.

Because the end goal of being unfuckwithable is to move from having holes to being *whole*. When you know that you're enough just as you are, absolutely nothing can stand in your way.

And you can give this gift to people (more on this later in the chapter).

Anyone can build their unfuckwithability. The strategies in this chap-ter will train you how to override insecurities, and to support everyone you touch to do the same. Unfuckwithability has an expanded effect. When you cause others to unleash their greatness you raise the unfuck-withability in yourself. So there are two key components that go into being unfuckwithable:

1. Feeling You're Enough
2. Creating Your Life as a Unique Masterpiece

RULE #1: START FEELING THAT YOU'RE ENOUGH

The first component of being unfuckwithable is realizing that you are enough. Not that you will be enough in the future, once you complete a certain project or fall in love with a certain type of person. Being unfuck-withable means that you are enough, exactly as you are, right now. With no changes or upgrades or tweaks.

When people realize they are enough, tiny issues that used to preoc-cupy them throughout the day suddenly disappear.

Their self-esteem is no longer attached to the person who did not text them back or the job they aren't passionate about. They have the energy to devote themselves to greater causes. They have the resilience to persevere through failures. They have the confidence to dream without restraint be-cause their ego is not on the chopping block if something goes wrong.

Two of the most powerful ways to move toward unfuckwithability are self-love and self-gratitude.

Tell yourself *I love you*. It sounds ridiculous. But if you do this daily you'll experience a major difference. You should never miss a chance to tell the people you care about how much you love them, and the number one person you should care about if you want to be unfuckwithable is you. Stand in front of the mirror every morning, while you're brushing your teeth or combing your hair or whatever and tell yourself, "I love you." It will feel silly at first. Keep doing it until it stops feeling that way.

Practice self-gratitude. Every morning when you wake up, give thanks for all of the good things in your life and start the list with you. Thank yourself for the hard work you do, the passion you pour into your proj-ects, the love and patience you show toward your family. Begin to appreci-ate the best parts of your personality, because what you focus on grows. And people who are unfuckwithable are always growing the best parts of themselves.

While the two exercises above are powerful (I go into the exact nuances and protocols for them in my book *The Code of the Extraordinary Mind*), there is another technique that I want to introduce you to.

I believe the best way to raise your unfuckwithability is to elevate others. By appreciating others, you feel good about yourself. And you realize your own strengths. It comes from the concept of projection, which means we can better see in others what we already possess. When you appreciate someone for being creative, it's because you have that spark of creativity within you too.

I was introduced to this exercise by Shawn Achor. And it's a true game-changer: The Two-Minute Appreciation Technique.

Oddly, it seems that the most important way to start feeling enough is to spend a few minutes every day making someone else feel enough.

Shawn Achor wrote the book *The Happiness Advantage,* and his TEDx Talk on happiness is listed as one of TED's twenty-five most popular talks, with more than twenty million views online. You already learned about Achor's research on social connections in the previous chapter. But now here is one of the simple yet incredibly powerful tools he taught me when I interviewed him in 2014.

Achor's team had conducted a workplace experiment that grew a nationally recognized insurance company's revenues by $300 million in one year. The result was caused by a two-minute daily practice that is as simple as brushing your teeth.

"We had people do this at Facebook and at Nationwide Insurance in the U.S. Every morning when they got to work, the very first task they had to complete for twenty-one days in a row was to write a single two-minute email praising or thanking one person that they know," Achor explained.

"The email could be as simple as '*Thank you for helping me with my work yesterday*' or something more meaningful like '*You're the reason each day. You are my best friend here*' or '*Thank you so much for covering for me when I had so much work going on yesterday.*'

"What that person is doing is providing praise for someone else, and after three days they get addicted to it. And people started writing emails back about how grateful they are."

This shows how expressing appreciation with a small act like an email has a reverberating effect. Achor continued:

"If someone did it for twenty-one days in a row it turns out their social connection score is in the TOP quartile. A simple two-minute habit each day moved them exactly where they should be, not only for higher levels of happiness, but also for promotion, for productive energy, sales—every business outcome we know how to test for." (Remember that if you are in the top quarter in your company in terms of Social Connection Score, you're 40 percent more likely to get a raise or promotion in the next two years!)

Shawn continued, "When we did this at Nationwide Insurance, we were working with the president, Gary Baker, who said he was a numbers guy. He said, 'I thought happiness research was fluff.' Until we showed him the numbers. So he allowed us to do this intervention with his team. Over the next eighteen months, they had a 50 percent rise in their revenue and 237 percent in their application rates. They went from $650 million to $950 million in a single year with no new hires, which was phenomenal."

Similar experiments were conducted in other organizations. One school had a cute story with results that were more than quaint. Bus drivers wrote handwritten thank-you notes to the kids on their bus. The standardized test scores of the children rose by about 22 percent. The school went from a bottom 10 percent school in the United States to one of the top 150 schools to work for in the United States.

Anyone can introduce these types of simple daily rituals. Create your own practice to let the people in your life know that they matter, or replicate the Two-Minute Appreciation Technique in your own team or business. The results you create when you focus on making other people feel special might shock you.

If the first part of becoming unfuckwithable is about elevating others, this next section takes it further. It's about turning your life into a masterpiece and infecting everyone around you to do the same. Since I created the exercise called the Three Most Important Questions in 2012, an estimated one million people globally have done it. We'll cover this in detail in Rule #2.

RULE #2: CREATE YOUR LIFE AS A UNIQUE MASTERPIECE

The second component of being unfuckwithable is having your own dreams and goals versus imitating the world around you. Everyone has their own unique vision for their life. It requires a process of understanding why you're here on this planet and having your own original list of goals and visions for yourself outside what the world is telling you to do, be, or have. You'll learn the specific technique to identify your unique vision shortly.

But first, understand that most people are conformists. Even if they don't agree with conventions, they will often choose to do what everyone else does anyway. This is because most people have an innate desire to fit in and be liked. So when the rules of the group rub up against what a person *authentically wants,* an existential crisis presents itself. They are pulled between what their intuition tells them to do—what they personally believe is right—and what the majority are doing.

This is one reason why most people design lives that don't fulfill them. They are not leading their own lives but imitating what teachers, preachers, fathers, mothers, and mass media have drilled into them.

Don Miguel Ruiz, the author of *The Mastery of Love,* once drilled this into me. I asked the great spiritual writer what was the essence of the "Toltec Wisdom" he espoused. Ruiz said, "Toltec means 'artist.' It means having the wisdom to be the artist of your own life."

Too many people don't create lives that feel like original art. Rather they create lives that feel like photocopies of the world around them. They imitate. Their goals for themselves come from the outside world rather than the depth of their own unique soul. They have forgotten an important distinction—that there's a difference between the means to an end and the end itself.

Means Goals Versus End Goals

If you read my first book, *The Code of the Extraordinary Mind*, you'll remember that I defined the difference between mean goals and end goals. And if you know the expression "It was a means to an end," you already know the gist of it. People often invest years—even a lifetime—of toil and money into a goal that they think of as the end goal, but which is really just a means to an end. This is a major mistake. As I wrote in *The Code of the Extraordinary Mind*,

> End goals are the beautiful, exciting rewards of being human on planet Earth. End goals are about experiencing love, traveling around the world being truly happy, contributing to the planet because doing so gives you meaning, and learning a new skill for the pure joy of it.
>
> End goals speak to your soul. They bring you joy in and of themselves, not because they confer any outward label, standard, or value attached by society. Nor are end goals undertaken for the purpose of pay or for material reward. They are the experiences that create the best memories in our lives.
>
> Means goals are the things that society tells us we need to have in place to get to happiness. Almost everything I wrote down as a goal was actually a means to an end, not an end in itself, including:

- Graduating from high school with a good GPA.
- Qualifying for the right college.
- Securing a summer internship.

My chasing of a degree in computer engineering and the job at Microsoft was me pursuing means goals. They were a means to an end. But not the end in itself.

So how do you identify your true goals? The end goals that come from the soul? I created a useful exercise in 2012 that became popular with millions of people worldwide called the Three Most Important Questions (3MIQs). When you answer these three questions, you start to dive into yourself and bring out what truly makes you YOU.

The Three Most Important Questions (3MIQs)

Although means goals are useful, achieving them is not what life is about. Life, ultimately, is not about doing well on a test, achieving a job title, or driving a sports car. But instead of getting clear on our end goals, most of us are obsessed with the means.

This is where the 3MIQ comes in. When these specific three questions are asked in the correct order, this exercise can help you jump straight to the end goals that really matter in your life.

I've found that all end goals fall into three different buckets.

The first is experiences. No matter what you believe about humanity's origins, one thing is clear. We're here to experience all the world has to offer—not objects, not money, but experiences. Money and objects only generate experiences. Experiences also give us instant bliss, not some type of artificial bliss that happens when we jump through a society-defined hoop (like scoring well on a test). We need to feel that daily life holds wonder, love, and excitement to sustain our happiness. And happiness, as you already know, is a superpower.

The second is growth. Growth deepens our wisdom and awareness. It may be growth we choose or growth that chooses us. Growth makes life an endless journey of discovery.

The third is contribution. It is what we give back from the wealth of our experiences and growth. What we give is the special mark we can make on the world. Giving moves us toward true fulfillment by providing meaning in our lives, and it's a key component of the extraordinary life.

Think about these three essentials framed as questions. Notice how each question ties to the one before it.

1. What experiences do I want to have in this lifetime?
2. To be the person who lives life with these amazing experiences, how do I need to grow?
3. If I had a life with these amazing experiences and had grown to this level, how do I now give back to the world that has rewarded me so much?

Answering these questions gives people an original vision for their life. It becomes their expression of what they would like to achieve by the end of their life.

Take out a piece of paper and create three columns like this. Label each:

EXPERIENCES	GROWTH	CONTRIBUTION

In these columns you're going to make a list of your visions for yourself in these three areas. The paper should eventually look like this.

Give yourself five minutes each to write the answers to each question. You'll be surprised by what you discover. The full exercise only takes fifteen minutes. You can find videos of my guiding this exercise online by searching on Google for "Three Most Important Questions Vishen."

Now imagine everyone in a workplace being able to see each other's 3MIQ. That's when the real magic starts to happen.

When Work Fulfills Dreams

All Mindvalley employees are asked to design their 3MIQs as part of our onboarding process. Then they stick them to a public bulletin board. Copies of the response are also photographed and shared with their manager. I keep a picture of every single employee's 3MIQ on my phone and Dropbox for convenience.

It's an incredible way for teammates to get to know each other below the surface. And also to support each other to reach their goals. It gives leaders insights into how they can best support their colleagues to become the greatest possible version of themselves.

Miracles emerge from the 3MIQs. Luminita Saviuc was a classic example. She joined Mindvalley from Romania as a customer support agent. She had written on her 3MIQ that she wanted to be a published author and speak internationally.

During her time at Mindvalley, she wrote an article called "15 Things to Give Up to Be Happy" on her personal blog. Six months later, it went viral: 1.2 million people shared the article on Facebook. That's when she got a call asking her if she wanted to turn her article into a book. She left the company two years after her start date, when Penguin Random House cut her a check for her own book deal.

I was sad to see her go. But I was proud for her. And she appreciated Mindvalley and the work that we had done together. She asked me to write the foreword for her book, which of course I did.

The book opportunity gave Luminita the platform to speak at conferences around the world. This helped her attain her "speak internationally" goal.

So while it might be scary for some leaders to allow their people to dream and grow for fear of losing them, I urge you to think bigger. Luminita is an ally. And when she became a speaker we worked together in new, more exciting ways for both of us. Don't be afraid to let your team grow. They will expand and you will too.

Then there was Jason Campbell. He's the host of Mindvalley's podcast *Superhumans at Work*. When he joined Mindvalley in 2012, he wrote on his 3MIQs that he wanted to become an engaging speaker. Then, at one event, it happened.

One of our regular speakers canceled. I was frazzled. I was behind the curtain with my team, trying to figure out what to do. Jason stepped up. He begged me to put him on stage. I had no idea if he was capable or not. He'd never spoken before. But he had written a speech he wanted to share with the world. This made me nervous, but I turned to Jason and said, "Okay, go. Do it. Make us proud."

Jason received the award for best speaker that A-Fest. Today, he is an amazing host for our podcast dedicated to optimizing work (look for *Superhumans at Work* on Spotify or iTunes) and speaks around the world.

3MIQs is also a way for people to connect or take on shared goals together. When everyone's 3MIQ is laid out publicly on a wall for all to see, people can collaborate on goals. One year, four coworkers learned they shared the desire to hike the Himalayas. They teamed up and did it together.

There is beauty in offering people opportunities to explore and expand. Work should not limit people's personal lives. It's remarkable when the people around you grow, because they expand you too. Community has a miraculous compounding effect.

So care for your people and show them they matter. Even in small ways. Because then the work you're doing together will matter to them.

The Future of Work

Bill Jensen, author of *Hacking Work: Breaking Stupid Rules for Smart Results,* once visited Mindvalley HQ.

"What do you think will be one of the biggest trends in the future of work?" I asked.

"Work will no longer be just about getting employees engaged in the company vision," he told me. "Companies will need to be engaged with the employee's vision."

Bill is an oracle. I really believe that workers who are given the right to explore their passions are simply better workers. They don't resent their company for holding them back. And, in workplaces where people feel they matter, their output increases. As a by-product of how awesome their employer is, loyal bonds are strengthened.

Bill also said that the 3MIQ process was one of the best examples he had seen of how companies can engage in their employees' vision.

Today when I sit down with new hires for lunch I have their 3MIQs with me. It instantly gives me a glimpse of each individual. You see beyond the facade. And when we can all see each other's 3MIQs, we become a better team and can support each other in being our own unique badass self.

If you're running a large company and have a big budget, you can take this a step further. You can implement a Dream Manager program. Here's a story that blew my mind.

The Dream Manager Program

I met my friend John Ratliff, the founder of Appletree Answers, at an entrepreneurs event. John's stance on leadership is refreshing. He says, "Anyone that's a principal in a company should wake up every day with so much gratitude for all the people that have said, 'Hey, I believe in your vision. I believe in your mantras. I believe in your style and your strategy and where you're going.' And then they show up and get behind you. We need to honor that."

John's team was determined to set a new industry standard for the call center business, where the average annual turnover rate is 150 percent. That's devastating. It means that every year he loses essentially all his staff. And that is the average for his entire industry. So one day he met with his executives at a quarterly meeting to discuss employee engagement. What surfaced was that one of the company's core values—"We take care of each other"—was not being honored.

To fix it, one of the management team pitched the idea to create a program that mimicked the Make-A-Wish charity model. Make-A-Wish is a nonprofit organization founded in the United States that grants life-changing wishes for children with a critical illness. But the idea here was not to do it for customers, but internally for staff. They would call it Dream On.

To kick it off, the management team sent a heartfelt email to everyone in the company. They expressed how the company wanted to support employees to achieve their life goals. They asked workers to share their dreams, and the board would grant a series of wishes. No strings attached.

Well, no one seemed to care. Initially, no one responded to the email. That's how bad the trust level was at the company between workers and management. Nobody believed the offer was genuine. It sounded like another corporate gimmick.

But John's team pressed on. They sent a second email and received a reply that came out of desperation. It was from an incredibly courageous team member who had fallen on seriously difficult times. Her husband had left her. She was sleeping in her car with her two small children.

The management team immediately booked a hotel room on the corporate credit card. They helped her negotiate a lease for a new apartment. They gave her a paid leave of absence so she could focus on her personal affairs and children until she felt more stable. She was amazed. And she told others. Word quickly spread.

There were more dreams like this. One employee wrote about being tight on cash for diapers. These types of requests were immediately granted, though the management team would always reply with an email asking for a real dream. Basic necessities weren't considered dreams. Dreams are different. They are personal passion-driven requests that come out of the realm of the seemingly impossible.

Here is one dream with a remarkable story.

One October, a request came in from one of a pair of sisters who worked for the company. One sister submitted a request for her brother-in-law

Dan. He was twenty-eight years old and had Stage IV Hodgkin's disease with a 10 percent chance of survival. Dan's dream was to go to one more NFL game. He was from Philadelphia and was a big fan of the Eagles.

When the Philadelphia Eagles got wind of the dream, they sent Dan tickets. That wasn't all. They arranged for Dan to sit on the sidelines with the cheerleaders before the game. They put him up in a VIP suite with the girlfriends and wives of the players. After the game, they brought Dan down to meet the players one by one as they walked out the door of the locker room. The team signed a football for him. He spent quality one-on-one time with his favorite player.

This was all amazing, but it's not the end of the story.

One day John was in his office and he received a phone call from our mutual friend Verne Harnish, another incredible leader and founder of the Entrepreneurs' Organization and the Association of Collegiate Entrepreneurs. Verne was a fan of the Dream On program and he asked John how it was going. John shared Dan's amazing story.

"Hmm, that's curious," Verne said. "Is there any chance Dan has an estranged relationship with his father?"

Then he explained, "I'm on the board of a prestigious medical clinic and we do alternative medicine analysis and studies. I just read a study about Hodgkin's. It said that firstborn sons with an estranged paternal relationship have a wildly higher incidence of Hodgkin's."

"That's crazy. There is no way that's true," said John.

So Verne sent him the study and John got curious.

He called Dan's wife. "Is Dan estranged from his father?"

"How do you know that?" she replied.

"I don't."

John sent Dan's sister-in-law the study. It was true that Dan had had a falling-out with his father. The two hadn't spoken in seven months. Both men were torturing themselves over the breakup.

When Dan learned about the study, he was shocked. He had also been thinking about reaching out so they could both gain closure. Dan didn't have much time. So he called his dad and they went to therapy. A few weeks later, they had repaired the relationship.

A few weeks after, Dan went back to the doctor who had made the original diagnosis. This doctor had told Dan, "You're not going to be here at Christmastime. You have to start preparing your kids."

But Dan's scans came back clear. The doctor could not find any sign of Hodgkin's. Astonished and confused, the final conclusion was that it may have been a case of misdiagnosis. This was after testing for cancer and months of physical decline.

When John told me the story he said, "Now, we don't take credit for any of this. No one knows if there is some kind of psychosomatic connection at play," he said, adding, "It was kind of the punchline for me as an entrepreneur. Leaders don't realize how much influence, impact, authority, and ability they have to alter the lives of the people who show up every single day to make their vision a reality."

Dream On is now in hundreds of other companies across North America. What's remarkable about the program is the overflow of generosity it creates. Often, workers use their wishes for their coworkers' dreams. Beautiful bonds emerge. Dream On creates leaders at all levels. And when given the opportunity, people step up for one another. It's in our authentic nature as humans to want to contribute.

Whether you run a business or organization, coach a sports team or teach at a school, or you're a member of a team, practice seeing people wholly. Get invested. It's everyone's responsibility to treat people like the rounded individuals they are versus one-dimensional characters, which is a twentieth-century capitalist mentality.

When you relate to people human-to-human, they care about you too, and the company. When they leave the team they never forget the impact it had on their lives. Best of all, they eventually become dream managers too. They might go out and build their own empires.

You will form a band of forever allies with good people who care about humanity. Investing in the dreams of the people around you has a ripple effect. But you need to give them opportunities to explore. Most people have no clue what they really want. It's why 85 percent of people are in jobs they hate. It's not their fault. It's the way they've been conditioned to build their lives. And in most societies, the entire goal-setting model is flawed.

Start Co-Visioning

Co-visioning is when a company (or person) takes an active interest in an employee's (or their teammate's) vision. It means you're not just focused on the company's vision as a team. Team members support each other in attaining each other's private goals. The 3MIQ and programs like Dream Manager help make this a reality.

> *Companies should not just ask people to be engaged in the company vision. Companies should be engaged in an employee's vision for their own life.*

You may have a smaller team. You may not have the budget for a Dream On program. But with the 3MIQ process you can take an avid interest in employees' dreams.

And what I'm about to share here might be the SINGLE most powerful tool in this entire book. It will create a remarkable transformation in your culture and in the relationship you have with anyone in your team. And it doesn't matter if you're the founder, CEO, a team leader, or an entry-level employee.

The Unexpected Gifts

I frequently go through people's 3MIQs and look for opportunities to support them. And then I buy them a book.

One person dreamt of moving to Italy one day. I bought her a copy of the Lonely Planet guide to Italy and gave her the book with a note: "When your dream comes true, this should come in handy."

Another wanted to start a nonprofit someday. His name was Yusop.

Yusop had written a number of goals on his 3MIQ, and one of them really moved me. It was to start a nonprofit. I immediately thought of a book that I loved on the subject, *Start Something That Matters* by Blake Mycoskie.

I went to the bookstore, purchased the book, and wrote a note inside: "I thought this book might help you achieve your dream of changing the world."

Yusop was dumbstruck. He'd never had a boss relate to him like that before. He went on to become one of our best designers. He even remembered my birthday. He bought me a wonderful shirt as a gift, which is actually pretty rare for someone to do for his boss. And now, years later, he's someone who's made an incredible contribution to our culture.

You can genuinely care about people, and I bet you do. But the fact is, unless you make a demonstration of it, everyone's internal piddling doubts will overshadow their sense that you care.

It's not enough for you to assume *people know that you care. You need to show it.*

By taking the effort to get to know people via the 3MIQ and then taking action to support their dreams, you bring incredible magic and loyalty to the workplace. Unexpected gifts show people you appreciate them.

The way you and others perform when you believe you are enough is next-level. When you feel significant your motivations shift. Now your primary focus becomes growth.

Chapter Summary

MODELS OF REALITY

All people are born with a need for significance. To feel whole and self-empowered and valued and loved. When it's met people become unfuck-withable. This is when you're truly at peace and in touch with yourself. Nothing anyone says or does bothers you and no negativity can touch you. The first step in becoming unfuckwithable is to realize that you are enough. You were born enough. If you don't believe this about yourself yet, believe it about other people. You'll start to get the same message back about yourself.

To unlock the unfuckwithability of the badass, do this:

1. **Tell yourself "I love you"**
2. **Practice gratitude**
3. **Practice the Two-Minute Appreciation or bring it to your team**

Remember what Don Miguel Ruiz said about being the artist of your own life. To do this, set goals with a mindset that asks the questions:

1. What do I want to experience?
2. How do I want to grow?
3. How do I want to contribute?

This same process can be brought to groups. It's a powerful practice when people help their community members achieve dreams. And this can be done in simple ways, like the gift of a book or an email acknowledgment that takes two minutes to send.

Systems for Living

EXERCISE 1: THE TWO-MINUTE APPRECIATION TECHNIQUE

Step 1: Make an agreement with your team that they will start every day with the appreciation exercise. Make a commitment to do this for twenty-one days and see results.

Step 2: Before anyone opens their email for the first time in the morning, they have to set a timer on their phone for two minutes counting down. And in those two minutes write a simple, short email of appreciation to another member of the team or company as a whole. If you use tools like WhatsApp or Slack to communicate, this works too. Audio notes can be just as precious.

Step 3: Hold each other accountable. A good way might be to ensure that everyone is connected in a Slack or WhatsApp group and reports in when their appreciation is sent. The idea is to make this a habit.

Step 4: Run this for twenty-one days. Notice the difference in moral and emotional states of your team and the company as a whole. Most likely you will see immense benefits. If so, decide if you want to continue it. After twenty-one days it starts becoming a habit.

EXERCISE 2: THE THREE MOST IMPORTANT QUESTIONS

Discover what it takes for you to know you truly *lived* life.

Important note before doing this exercise: Take no more than ninety seconds to answer each of these questions. The point is not to overthink it, but let the answers flow through you. This is how you will hear the answers that instantly come to you, straight from your heart. Keep on writing for the full ninety seconds and do not stop. At some point, your critical mind shuts off and you start writing what matters.

There are no right or wrong answers here. This is about discovering what makes your soul shine and makes your life a wonderful experience. Dare to dream big.

1. What do you want to experience?

Think about any experience that you wish to have in this lifetime. Consider your love life, your relationships, your sexuality. Think about what experiences you'd like to have with your friends and family. What would you like your social life to look like?

Assume you have unlimited access to funds. What type of car would you want to drive? What type of home would you want to live in? Are there any other things you dream of having in your life? And what places do you want to travel to? What type of activities, hobbies, or sports would you love to explore?

Write down everything that you could possibly dream of doing or having that would make you feel happy and joyful.

2. How do you want to grow?

How would you like to develop yourself? Think about your intellectual life, for instance. What skills would you like to obtain? What languages would you want to master?

But also: What character traits do you admire in others and which would you like to master? For instance: How do you want to deal with stressful events in your life?

What are your health and fitness goals? How long would you like to live? How would you like to feel and what would you like to be able to do in your old age? Is there a particular aspect of your spiritual life that you'd like to dive deeper into?

Jot down anything you'd like to develop in your life.

3. How do you want to contribute?

Lastly, think about all the various ways in which you want to contribute to the world.

How could you contribute to your family, friends, society, city, or even the entire planet?

No matter how big or small your ideas, write down everything that comes to you.

What will be your legacy? How will you make the world a slightly better place? Which problem would you like to solve for the planet and humanity?

It could be volunteering or giving your time to specific people. It could be a certain work you'd like to create. Anything you can think of that would be of benefit to others and the world we live in.

Full guides and videos of all of these exercises are available on www.mindvalley.com/badass.

CHAPTER 5

MAKE GROWTH THE ULTIMATE GOAL

Grow so fast that your friends who haven't seen you in a
month have to get to know you all over again.

—Unknown

Your soul isn't here to achieve. Your soul is here to grow. Most
people get this wrong. They become seduced by success and
broken by failure. They add great meaning to what is essentially meaningless. The true reality is that success and failure are
illusions. The only thing that matters is how fast you're evolving.
Your journey is about removing all the barriers that hold you back
from self-actualization.

IN 2013, MY COMPANY turned ten years old. At this point in our growth,
you'd think that the business was running fairly smoothly. And that after
more than a decade as CEO, I knew what I was doing. That, however, was
not the case. Between 2013 and 2015, we suffered a series of ugly misfor-
tunes that almost wiped out the company. And it caused me to question my
own abilities as an entrepreneur and leader.

It started with a rude wake-up call. I discovered that my accountant,
whom I trusted, and who had been with the company for five years, had
been stealing from the company coffers for four and a half of those years.

Little by little, month by month, this person pocketed $250,000 using fake accounts. The betrayal shook me. She had been one of my most trusted team members. And she had been stealing from us the entire time. I had many sleepless nights. I questioned my ability to hire the right people, to lead, to run my business.

But it got worse. One month later, just after Christmas, my head of operations called and said, "Vishen, we're not going to be able to meet payroll this month."

This meant our employees would not get paid at the most crucial time of the year. This was a double whammy. It had been a weak December. Part of it was due to the emotional upheaval I had experienced from discovering the theft. I was off balance. To backfill the shortfall, I considered selling my car. It was better than lying to people who put their faith in me for years. In the end, my executive team jumped in. Collectively, they decided not to take their pay so everyone else could. It was a miracle. And it restored my faith in the greatness of people. Thankfully, January was a good month for us. We launched a major product that replenished the withering bank account.

We'd barely made it out of the company's first major near-death experience when we were broadsided by new problems. First, we lost our biggest client when that company changed CEOs. Immediately 15 percent of our revenue was wiped out. Next we had a huge technology platform failure when an email service provider we relied on for being in touch with customers was acquired by a larger company. In the acquisition, the tech went awry, causing us to lose access to 40 percent of our customer base. We started bleeding millions. It felt as if the Universe was against us.

I want you to pause as you're reading this for a moment and think back to your life and career. Have you been in situations like this where you felt you were failing due to turmoil outside your control? When I ask that question in rooms of CEOs or employees at any company, almost everyone raises their hand. We've all experienced pain and failure. Know that you're not alone. To be a badass, you're going to have to learn how to cause change in the world. And you will commonly encounter resistance. If it was easy, everyone would do it. Failure and pain are part of the game. But while failure is common, the pain you feel can be optional. This chapter is about a mental model shift that will help you and everyone on your team move through failure with the grace of the Buddha while becoming stronger and more powerful with each "failure."

Now, in my life, this repeated set of failures had caused my usual confident demeanor to erode. All of a sudden I was kicking back two glasses of red wine every single night to cope with the stress. And I was too stubborn to ask for help. I figured hard work would pull me out of this mess. Yup. Hard work, hustle, and grit. Those were my solutions.

But each month got scarier as I saw our burn rate and our bank balance shrink. Then, unexpectedly, a blessing occurred.

What Work Is *Really* About

I happened to meet up with Srikumar Rao, the business sage I mentioned in Chapter 1. Rao often spoke of the idea that we should adopt a mental model that we live in a benevolent Universe. Trust that the world has your back. And everything happening to you is for your own good.

But I pushed back and asked him, "If this was true, why did I feel that the world was against me and why was I going through so much failure and pain at work?"

Rao replied, "The common misconception, Vishen, is that people think their work is about their work. This is wrong."

The next piece of wisdom out of his mouth spun me around:

The most important thing that our business schools need to teach us is that your work is not about your work. Rather, your work is nothing more than the ultimate vehicle for your personal growth. If your business fails, it doesn't matter. The question is, how did

you GROW? If your business becomes a billion dollars, it doesn't
matter. The question is, how did you GROW?

That interaction was a pivotal moment. I started to see new actions I could take to free myself of the torment I was suffering. I certainly wasn't viewing the situation from the perspective that it was growing me in a new way as a CEO and business owner. This simple context shift immediately gave me relief. Oddly, I now saw the same situations that had been keeping me up at night for months through a lens of appreciation.

The entire model most societies have for success and happiness is flawed. Most people learn that to attain life fulfillment, you must acquire three things:

1. A certain role or title (which gives you prestige)
2. A certain balance in your bank account (which gives you wealth)
3. Acquisition of specific material positions like a car or a house with a white picket fence

The result: Success.

Right? Nope. Rao would call that an "if/then life." He says you have to stop hanging your happiness on your title and your money and your stuff. Stop thinking, "I need X to be successful or happy." (How many times have you gotten X and *still* not felt happy?) The Rao formula to reclaim your happiness is simply . . . Growth.

The only point of life is to grow. Pain can lead to growth. Success can lead to growth. Look at it this way and pain ceases to exist. Success ceases to be so intoxicating. Growth is the only thing that matters.

Real success is actually much simpler than most of us have been led to believe. There is nothing you have to *get to* or *be* in order to have finally made it. The secret formula is this:

Growth = Success

The Happiest Millionaires

My friend Ken Honda is the most prolific personal-growth writer in Japan with over fifty books published, and his focus lies in the mindset of millionaires. Honda once did a survey of some twelve thousand millionaires in Japan. He found that no matter how rich someone was they always wanted more. Ken explained to me: "I interviewed a guy who had a million in the bank and I asked, 'Do you feel rich?' He said no. Because he didn't yet have ten million dollars. But I also interviewed a guy who had ten million dollars in the bank and he didn't feel rich because, he said, 'I don't yet have a private jet.' And then I interviewed a man with a private jet and I asked him if he felt rich. He said, 'No.' 'Cause his jet was only a six-seater!"

These millionaires were effectively trying to catch the horizon. You can't catch the horizon. As you get closer it moves away. Such is the illusion of tying your goal to a specific wealth marker.

So what, then, made people feel rich? Turns out it was a different type of goal. In fact, it wasn't a goal at all. It was a state of being. More on this later in the chapter. But here is what is important to understand: As long as you are growing (by your own measure) you'll be fulfilled.

Maslow places growth near the top of his pyramid. He calls it Self-Actualization, which he describes as: the fulfillment of one's talents and potential, especially considered as a drive or need present in everyone.

Bottom line here is: **Growth is a goal in itself.** When you understand how you want to grow, you can take responsibility and be the driver of your own growth. You can turn every work opportunity into an experience for becoming a better version of you.

Growth by Learning Versus Transformation

Learning is what you get from school. When it comes to classes like history, geography. and algebra, schools teach you facts and ideas—most of which you're going to forget. This is LEARNING.

But true growth comes from something else. Something much more powerful than learning. It's called TRANSFORMATION.

When you learn a fact you can forget it the next day. But a transformation is when your entire worldview shifts. When a transformation occurs there is an opening for a new way of seeing the world. It's a complete shift in perspective. A transformation causes an exponential jump in who you are as a person. It may jolt you and rejig some of your long-held beliefs and values.

Edmund O'Sullivan is a transformative learning expert at the Transformative Learning Centre in Toronto, Canada. In academic terms he defines a transformational moment in this way: "Transformation involves experiencing a deep, structural shift in the basic premises of thought, feelings, and actions. It is a shift in consciousness that dramatically and irreversibly alters our way of being in the world."

In the case of the Japanese millionaires discussed above, Ken Honda told me that the difference between the millionaires who felt rich and those who didn't was a shift in worldview. They had gone through a transformation that shifted their view of money. They had taken on a belief that money is like air. It's everywhere. And it flows to them when they need it. There was no goal for money. No goal for a jet. They simply believed that the right amount of money they needed in their life would come to them as and when needed. And this was when they could answer YES to the question "Do you feel truly rich?" This is what transformation is. It's a radical shift in your worldview.

Now, there are strict conditions for this to happen. It usually requires a person to be introduced to a revolutionary idea or concept that starkly challenges their long-held beliefs. If the new idea presents stronger evidence that they can't dispute, the old information is replaced by the new information. Here's the greatest distinction to take note of:

When a person experiences a transformation, they can't go back to being the same as they were before.

It's a perspective shift that's irreversible. In short, a person whose mind is expanded and stretched by transformation cannot revert back to their old beliefs.

Here's a real-world example to illustrate how a transformation works, using an event most of us can relate to.

Remember when you first learned to ride a bike? Likely, you conceptually learned how to ride it first. You went through a traditional learning process. The directions would go something like this:

a. Put your helmet on.
b. Sit on the bike.
c. Put one foot on one pedal.
d. Put the second foot on the other pedal while thrusting forward to pick up speed.

But until you physically get on the bike and achieve balance, you haven't gone through the transformation required to go from nonrider to rider. Then, miraculously, as soon as you find your balance, you're transformed. You can't go back to having no balance. It's not possible. That's a transformational experience.

The Two Things That Cause Transformation

Now, here is the tricky thing with growth by transformation. It happens in life in two specific ways:

Cause #1: The Disorienting Dilemma. This means growth through some painful lesson or life circumstance. Example: Someone you deeply loved cruelly breaks your heart. It's awfully painful. But you grow by understanding what qualities to look for in a future partner.

Cause #2: Evolution of a New Meaning Schema. This means gradually gathering new ideas and layers over your life that lead you to ultimately see the world in a totally different way. This often happens in slower progression over time. For example, this is the growth that happens when you apprentice with a master or read biographies of legendary people and slowly come to understand some of their unique worldviews. This is the attainment of wisdom.

Reverend Michael Beckwith of Agape Spiritual Center has labels for these two experiences of transformation. He calls them *kensho* and *satori*.

Kensho is growth through pain, while growth by satori is gradual and slow. So slow, in fact, you might not even notice it as it happens. Satori can actually be pleasant. Put in a simple graph, kensho and satori look like this. Notice the dips? That's the painful kensho moments. And the sudden rises are the satori moments.

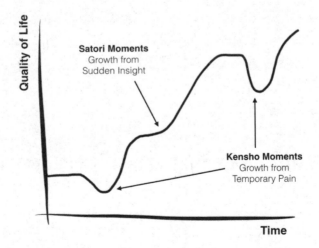

Let's look at kensho and satori more closely.

Kensho: The Disorienting Dilemma

Jack Mezirow, who is credited with being the father of Transformational Learning Theory, coined the term *disorienting dilemma* (oh, how academic he makes it sound). He defines it as a life crisis or a major life transition.

A disorienting dilemma in the real world can take the form of a business owner's company going bankrupt and learning what NOT to do for his next business.

Or going through divorce, and learning what to correct for their next relationship.

As the poet Rumi said: "Oh ye who can't take a good rub . . . how will you ever become a polished gem?"

What that means is, it often takes struggle or pain for new information to find its way into a person. But this often makes them a more resilient, compassionate, and open person than they were before.

In his book *Exponential Organizations*, the author Salim Ismail shares a fascinating discovery Google made about its best workers. He writes: "Google recently demonstrated that its best employees were not Ivy League students, but rather young people who had experienced a big loss in their lives and had been able to transform that experience into growth. According to Google, deep personal loss has resulted in employees who are more humble and open to listening and learning."

These individuals had been able to suffer through a negative experience, a "disorienting dilemma," and reframe it as a moment of strength, learning, and personal growth.

Satori: The Evolution of a New Meaning Schema

The transformation that happens when a meaning schema evolves over time happens after an accumulation of sporadic moments of awakening. A person experiences small revelations. These can happen in any environment. They can come from an exchange with another person, or from a walk outside, or from reading a book or listening to music. Enough of these moments and one day, there's a significant shift in a person's values.

For instance, a person with an unhealthy diet may receive numerous signals to eat better. Let's say they are watching TV and an advertisement scares them and makes them question their habits. Then maybe one day they start experiencing symptoms of diabetes. Perhaps the final cue to take action is that they step on the scale and see a number that shocks them. This causes a shift that knocks them harshly onto a better path.

The beauty of transformation is that no one can avoid it, in a similar way that a tree in the forest grows even though it doesn't move. The bears still rub on it. The bees still nest in it. The squirrels forage there. External factors transform the tree over time. And so, whether people actively seek out their own personal growth or not, challenges and situations naturally arise that they are forced to deal with.

But here's the problem. Because transformation comes from disorienting dilemmas or a gradual accumulation of meaning schema, it is unpredictable. And awfully slow. And usually painful.

Transformation: Unpredictable. Slow. And Painful.

But what if we can create deliberate transformation in people? So they grow before they have a painful wake-up call? And what if we can do this in a predictable and fast way? So people grow so rapidly that they seem to evolve into a different human being almost month to month?

I believe the soul craves transformation. Your soul is here to grow. But if you're not deliberately putting yourself through opportunities to transform yourself, your soul will have to smack you on the back of the head to wake you up. This is what painful kensho moments are like. True masters of the art of life create deliberate daily processes to transform and evolve themselves. They dedicate themselves to the continual expansion of their mind, body, and soul. These masters seek satori or awakening on a regular basis.

The more you transform through deliberate practices, the less you have to transform through painful kensho moments. And the workplace is the best place for it. Imagine that you design your work so that it becomes an accelerator of transformation, where you unlock the best in yourself and everyone around you.

The Transformational Organization

At a very young age most people's goals are implanted in them by whichever company has a bigger marketing budget. Or whichever religion dominated their culture. Or what their parents told them. Or their government drilled into them. Unfortunately schools don't do the best job with this, either. But this is where work comes in. Schools focus on traditional learning, while work is for continuous growth.

Author Neil Gaiman wrote in *The Sandman, Vol. 9: The Kindly Ones*:

> *I've been making a list of the things they don't teach you at school. They don't teach you how to love somebody. They don't teach you how to be famous. They don't teach you how to be rich or how to be poor. They don't teach you how to walk away from someone you don't love any longer. They don't teach you how to know what's going on in someone else's mind. They don't teach you what to say to someone who's dying. They don't teach you anything worth knowing.*

School teaches you to memorize facts quite well—something your smartphone can now easily replace.

Sugata Mitra is a professor of educational technology at the School of Education, Communication and Language Sciences at Newcastle University, England. When he won the TED Prize for education, he said:

> *Human beings are not smartphones. We own smartphones.*
> *We don't need heads filled with useless facts when we all have*
> *access to Google. What we need is a head filled with the right*
> *wisdom, beliefs, practices, and knowledge to help us deal with*
> *the messy, confusing, beautiful aspects of being human itself.*

There's a great opportunity for our work to fill the gap that other institutions currently don't. If you run a company today, I might argue that you have a moral obligation to do so. The best leaders care that their team members are constantly growing. Because people who are growing and transforming are the best kind of people to have around. And they will drive up every metric associated with a company's success.

If you don't run a business, remember your personal growth is up to you. It's your responsibility. It's always under your control. It's your job to put yourself in situations that stretch you. Work provides the best opportunities for this. It's the perfect self-growth feedback and reward system. And if you're growing as a person, you're going to do better at work. Work is the ultimate laboratory for personal transformation.

Remember the wise words of Srikumar Rao:

> *Your Work Is Not About Your Work. Rather Your Work*
> *Is the Greatest Vehicle for Your Personal Growth*

Now, any workplace can be turned into a growth-centric environment. Leader or stealth leader, in the remaining sections of this chapter, I'll teach you to construct your personal environment for accelerated growth and then how to bring a growth mindset to any team environment. The first step is to understand the true definition of the "leader."

TACTIC #1: REDEFINE LEADERSHIP TO BE ABOUT GROWTH

I used to believe in the Dwight Eisenhower mode of leadership. He said, "Leadership is getting other people to do things you want done because they want to do it."

Today that's outdated. Leaders do many things. They set a vision. They raise the energy and emotions of the team. They coordinate and set direction. But I'd argue that the number one job of a leader is to always evolve and to GROW other leaders.

Everyone is a leader. And great leaders create other great leaders. To stress this at Mindvalley, I created this definition and made sure all my managers understood its meaning.

> *Leadership is recognizing that we are all ONE. That every person you lead is as brilliant as you, as talented as you, and has the same capacity for growth and accomplishment. They simply need to be reminded of this fact.*

When I first created this leadership creed it was based on intuition, not on direct evidence. But years later a research study on managers conducted by Google revealed that the number one most important behavior of the highest-scoring managers was that they were effective coaches. This meant that they listened, guided, and helped their people grow.

But to do this best, you have to be the best damn version of yourself you can be. And this means embracing self-actualization as a principle for living. You should be viewing your life as a project to make yourself into the most extraordinary human possible. After all, the best leaders lead by example. So keep your focus on your rate of self-evolution and support others to grow theirs too.

TACTIC # 2: LIVE A PERSONAL GROWTH LIFESTYLE

I have a confession to make. I was going to tell this story but pass it off as some guy I know that had this Mars bar problem.

But, full disclosure, the Mars bar guy is me. You can't preach vulnerability if you don't practice it, right? Okay, here goes.

I used to have this daily Mars bar ritual.

Around 5 p.m., as my team started heading home each day, I would go to my desk, open the bottom drawer, and slip out a Mars bar. I'd scarf down the chocolate in a couple of bites. Chomp. Gulp. Gone.

This Mars bar nap routine was my afternoon reboot. I knew it was not healthy, but there was an addictive quality to it, and I became reliant on it. It was pretty awesome actually. I really enjoyed it.

Then one day I lingered a moment longer than usual in the mirror. There was me, but I had this "dad bod." I had become this chubby, pinch-an-inch kind of pudgy dude.

I looked in the mirror and I knew I was failing on my health. My hair was falling out. I had gained weight. And yes, there were those two glasses of red wine I needed to drink every night to fall asleep. So I made a commitment to embrace health. In February of my fortieth year I signed up for a program called WildFit. It was a program designed to transform your relationship with food.

By May my body fat percentage had dropped from 22 percent to 15 percent. I tossed most of my clothes because they all became too loose. My transformation had been so great, my face changed. People asked me if I had had surgery, because I started to look years younger. But it was not just my shape that changed. My energy went through the roof. My cravings for sugar almost disappeared. My skin cleared up. I was so blown away by my personal results, I decided to bring my team into the program. Over a hundred people at Mindvalley enrolled in the WildFit ninety-day program that August. And by December the very culture of our company had shifted. Gone were the soda cans. Liquor consumption at company socials dropped by almost half. People started cooking healthy meals and concocting veggie juices for each other. One engineer set the record for most pounds lost: fifty-one. He was a big man and, for the first time in his life, could finally shop in a regular store.

Around the same time as this shift we also started to notice health metrics across the company shift. Profits went up. Retention soared. Employee NPS hit new records. And more and more people started joining WildFit and achieving excellent health. As my team's relationship with food changed, their energy levels shot up.

By 2017 we had a new culture. That year I decided to take up strength training. We brought in fitness instructors and set up a lab to create a rapid strength and muscle gain protocol. We called it 10X and again a large number of our employees participated. Now they were not just eating healthy, they were operating like athletes.

By 2018 we were ready for the next evolution. We started actually becoming athletes. Dozens of our employees would train together and compete in the ultra-tough Spartan Race challenges. For the uninitiated, a Spartan race involves serious physical obstacles like rope climbing, running through pits of mud, and swinging on monkey bars. At the time this book was written, more than forty of our people had competed together at the same time as a team.

By 2019, the office was a different place. The conversations around the water cooler were unusual. To join Mindvalley meant to embrace total health. Today, if you join Mindvalley you will likely lose an average of ten to fifteen pounds in your first year. In our company we have pull-up bars and kettlebells and an indoor gym. And instead of eating chocolate bars to get through the afternoon lull, I now walk to a pull-up bar and knock out ten pull-ups.

We don't force any eating plans or lifestyle on anyone. But change happens by simply being part of a health-conscious ecosystem. It's contagious.

As for me, as I turn forty-four, I'm in the best shape of my life.

To live a personal growth lifestyle means to actively enroll in programs designed to transform you. And to bring these programs into your team. When people are focused on transformation, their performance at life and work goes up. This brings us to Tactic #3.

TACTIC # 3: MAKE TRANSFORMATION THE NUMBER ONE FOCUS

A person who embraces personal growth naturally takes others with them. Growth has an incredible compounding effect. Powerful people with healthy habits encourage the people in their team to follow suit. It's why a core philosophy of mine is that personal growth must be the number one focus in life. I love this quote a friend of mine recently posted:

Grow so fast that your friends who haven't seen you in
a month have to get to know you all over again.

That sounds like a badass to me.

Personal growth should come before your business, before your relationships, before even your parenting. It's like the oxygen mask on the plane. You've got to fix your own before helping others. If you look at the best entrepreneurs in the world, they put their personal growth first because they know that when they grow, their business takes off. If you look at the best relationships, they are most often between two people who are committed to their own self-evolution.

I believe that by putting my personal growth first, I can better serve my children, my business, and my relationships with others. And so I try to evolve myself in some way every thirty days. One month it might be learning a new meditation program. Another month it might be mastering speed reading.

It's actually a lot easier than you might think. In the span of thirty days, you could easily attend a seminar or a talk that changes your life. Or complete a Mindvalley Quest or another program to go deep and to radically upgrade your life in one area.

You could listen to an entire series of podcasts on any given subject. If you don't think you have the time, think again. The average person spends more than forty-five minutes per day commuting to and from work. Over thirty days that's fifteen hours. Fifteen hours of exploration through podcasts on a given topic will change your life.

You just have to take Rao's advice and make it the MOST important thing in your life. Everything else you touch will then grow and expand like never before.

So how do you set up a personal transformation routine? First, it's not as complex as it sounds. And if you focus on the right, scientifically tested models, you can get amazing results for very little time. And you have to make this a daily routine.

How to Set Up a Personal Transformation Routine

Here's what my highly optimized morning routine looks like. And I want to point something out. This routine does not extract time from my life. That's the wrong way to look at it. With this routine, I actually *add* time because my brain, my mind, my body are optimized. In fact, this routine saves me 15 hours a week. If you add that up, that's 60 hours a month. Or 720 hours a year. This roughly adds up to 30 EXTRA days a year.

Lack of time is not an excuse. As you'll see, the cognitive and energy benefits of this routine actually allow you to do more work in less time. So as you enhance your mind, body, and soul, you also amplify the output of every hour at work.

Now let's take a look at the routine.

1. SLEEP OPTIMIZATION

I've learned to be fastidious about sleep tracking. The goal isn't to sleep less. It's to optimize it. According to Tom Rath in the book *Eat Move Sleep,* depriving yourself of ninety minutes' sleep causes a drop in cognition of 30 percent. That's like showing up to work after having downed a pint of beer!

But the data on sleep is more surprising than that. There was a famous study popularized by writer Malcolm Gladwell showing that it takes 10,000 hours to attain mastery in any field. But what we don't talk about is that the guy behind the study, Swedish psychologist K. Anders Ericsson, discovered something else curious about these maestros. They spent an average of 8 hours and 36 minutes sleeping every night. The average American? 6 hours and 51 minutes a day.

Sleep is essential to high performance. It improves your ability to think, allows you to have better moods and emotions throughout the day, improves your ability to focus and generate ideas, and helps your body heal and recover from the previous day.

The trick, then, is to optimize sleep. I experiment with everything from sleep aids like magnesium supplements, CBD oil, 5-HTP, and more. I test them by tracking my sleep routines on a device such as the Oura ring. For example, I'll use blue-light-blocking glasses before bedtime or I'll practice meditation before bed, then review my stats. I look at how much time I spent in deep versus light sleep and pay attention to things like heart rate variability. By doing so, I've learned to catch more deep rejuvenating sleep while spending less overall time in bed. This means I sleep for 7 to 7.5 hours a day but catch the equivalent of 8 hours of sleep because I go deeper.

As a side note: I also learned that my red wine habit was rubbish. Alcohol helps you fall asleep, but you don't get the same degree of true restful sleep your body requires when you use alcohol. The same is true of sleeping pills. If you have trouble falling asleep, there are many great books and programs on sleep to explore. I recommend looking into the work of Dr. Michael Breus, America's top sleep expert. He also has a sleep optimization program on Mindvalley.

The total time I save per week from optimizing my sleep is 30 minutes a day or 3.5 hours a week. And that's not counting the boost to moods, metabolism, and cognition I get. So as you can see, sleep matters.

Time Saved: 3.5 hours

2. THE 6-PHASE MEDITATION ROUTINE

Meditation has become such a popular performance enhancer that you'd think no one would skip it. Yet many still do. The reason is that we get fooled into believing that meditation is merely about quieting the mind.

I start every day with the 6-Phase Meditation. It's a method I developed that combines science and meditation, ideal for busy people and entrepreneurs who seek to do more in the world. Millions of people now do the same, and so can you (you can find it easily on YouTube by searching "6 Phase").

The 6-Phase Meditation has taken off among the world's most elite performers. Miguel, the R&B artist, told *Billboard* magazine that he does it before his massive concerts. NFL Hall of Famer Tony Gonzalez revealed that he does it to keep his life healthy. And when Bianca Andreescu won the US Open and beat Serena Williams at the young age of nineteen, she told reporters that a key part of her self-improvement regimen was my book *The Code of the Extraordinary Mind,* which introduced the 6-Phase to the world. Bianca is also a graduate of the seminar I created that teaches the method. (See mindvalley.com/be.)

I share this to help you understand just how powerful this technique is. But know that it's not conventional meditation. Rather it's a practice for people who want to merge the Buddha and the badass of their nature. To be at bliss, but to go forth and conquer the world in their own way.

Why do so many top performers use it? Because it creates noticeable boosts in your performance. Sports stars are incredibly aware of how little changes can impact their game. This is why so many sports stars in every major American league use the 6-Phase. So why is it different?

The 6-Phase stacks together six transcendent practices in twenty to thirty minutes that allow you to reap remarkable benefits. Here they are:

1. **Compassion:** I believe that all human beings need love and compassion in their lives. This phase is about helping you be kinder toward others and kinder toward yourself. It's a powerful self-love tool.

2. **Gratitude:** We may have many goals, but it's important to appreciate and be happy about what we've accomplished thus far. Gratitude has a high correlation with well-being and happiness.

3. **Forgiveness:** Being at peace with the world and the people around you is one of the most effective ways to maintain elevated states of being.

4. **Future Dreams:** As you will learn in Chapter 7, it's hugely energizing to have a vision pulling you forward—a picture of how you want your life to unfold in the future.

5. **The Perfect Day:** This phase gives you a sense of control over how

life unfolds every day. It translates your future dreams into action-able steps.

6. **The Blessing:** We need to feel supported, resting in the knowledge that whatever big projects we're setting out to do, things are going to be okay. This phase is about making you feel safe and supported in your mission.

The magic lies in how you're guided through the phases. You can get the 6-Phase Meditation on its official home on the Omvana app by Mind-valley. Just search for Omvana on the App Store.

When you do meditation right you save yourself hours of time. I esti-mate the productivity boost I get from the 6-Phase gives me an extra two to three hours a day. But let's just say you're starting out and are able to get a one-hour boost in productivity each day. A thirty-minute medita-tion routine is thus giving you time and not taking up your time. And this would save you 3.5 hours a week while making you feel more blissed out, happier, and healthier all week.

Total Time Saved per Week: 3.5 hours

3. OPTIMIZED EXERCISE ROUTINES (SUPER SLOW STRENGTH TRAINING)

Following meditation, I exercise. The traditional idea of exercise suggests that you need to go to a gym for two to three hours a week. This is no longer true. Science shows that a few minutes a day of minimum effective dose exercise can work wonders for your body and be equivalent to hours on the treadmill.

And the best kind of exercise to look into is super slow strength training.

Super Slow Strength Training

Strength has a high correlation to longevity. Imagine if you could boost your strength by 25 percent. This means 25 percent more energy to move about throughout the day. Now, what if you could do this in four weeks, spending no more than one hour per week on strength training at the gym?

It sounds impossible, but this is exactly what the practice of super slow strength training promises. Dr. Doug McGuff popularized it in his book *Body by Science.* At Mindvalley we launched a three-year experiment using some one hundred test subjects and found that after one month of super slow strength training we saw a gain in strength of roughly:

20–40 percent for untrained people under forty

50–75 percent for untrained people over forty

I got my father to try it too. He was seventy years old when he did. In four weeks, with only two trips to the gym a week of no more than thirty minutes each, he saw a 70 percent gain in strength. That's how rapidly the protocol works. I got really into it when I started it at the age of forty-one. I saw a 50 percent increase in strength (measured by my ability to lift a rep maximum at the gym) in thirty days. I'm now hooked.

For information on this, read McGuff's book. Or try the 10X program that has been developed by Mindvalley (you can google "10X Mindvalley"). It's based on the experiments on this process we conducted on over one hundred of our employees and users over three years.

I now go to the gym twice a week for twenty minutes each. That's all for my exercise. But the result is that I'm in my best shape ever. My body has never looked this good and I'm able to beat my twenty-five-year-old self on standard fitness tests. Don't believe the hype that you need hours in the gym to stay fit. I estimate that my routine saves me two useless hours in the gym every week.

Total Time Saved Per Week: 2 hours

4. OPTIMIZED EATING, FASTING, AND SUPPLEMENTS

After exercise, it's time to fuel up. We eat breakfast in the morning. It's a time-tested tradition that goes back generations. But what if this tradition was not effective for the healthiest body?

Today we know that we can optimize our performance and our biology by modifying the way we eat breakfast. But to understand this you first have to understand that breakfast can be eaten for ritual or for fuel.

If you're eating breakfast for ritual— the smell of bacon and eggs, the reunion of a family around a common table after a night of good sleep— then keep it up. I love this feeling on weekends.

Weekdays are different. As a single dad, I rush the kids off to school, and then I want to eat breakfast for fuel, not ritual. So I optimize my breakfast. For me this might be a protein shake laden with organic superfoods like powdered kale, wheatgrass, or spirulina.

And once or twice a week I skip breakfast altogether to practice intermittent fasting. This is a way to replenish your biology by giving your body a break from digesting food for a period of twelve to sixteen hours. So if my last meal was at 8:30 p.m. the night before, by skipping breakfast the next day and going straight to lunch at 12:30 I give my body a sixteen-hour fast. This is a powerful way to keep your biology healthy.

Total Time Saved per Week: 1 hour

5. SPEED LEARNING

After breakfast I like to invest twenty minutes of time upgrading myself by embracing learning. But I use methods of learning that are far more effective than just reading a book.

According to the speed learning pioneer Jim Kwik, most people have been trained to read like a six-year-old. "Think about it. The last time you learned to read was when you were just starting school. You were likely six or seven," says Jim.

Since then, we've never bothered to learn to read in a different way.

Jim taught me to speed-read. The tools he shares involved ideas like visual pacers and how to suppress this six-year-old tendency we have to mentally articulate every word we come across. In just a few hours of learning with Jim I was able to increase my reading speed by 50 percent. For most students of Jim they see a 300 percent speed increase. In my case I do twelve hours of reading a week, and this represented a four-hour time saving for me.

Speed-reading is not simply a nice skill to have. Today, it's essential. If you count all the reading we need to do, including emails, Slack messages, memos, reports, social media, news, and books, by some estimates we spend two to four hours a day reading. Imagine what happens when you double this speed!

The techniques of speed-reading are too nuanced to teach in this chapter, but I want to strongly suggest you look into the speed-reading program by Jim Kwik. It's called SuperReading and I helped produce it. Google for "Jim Kwik Mindvalley."

Total Time Saved per Week: 4 hours

IF YOU DO THE math, all of this adds up to 15 hours saved per week. That's 60 hours per month. That's 720 per year. Or exactly 30 days per year.

With an optimized schedule like this you're adding one extra month every year to your life. And as you're doing this you're getting better, fitter, stronger, and healthier. The net result: You feel and look great and accomplish more in less time.

So those were some personal systems you can bring in to embrace growth as a goal, or the concept self-actualization. Now let's look at how you can engineer a workplace to create a total environment for transformation.

For those of you who want to go deeper, I created a video showing how I bring all these ideas together in my morning. You can get it from mind valley.com/badass.

How to Set Up a Transformational Team Environment

One of the conditions for growth is a healthy environment. Here are four structures anyone can initiate to bring growth into the workplace. You can do this for your team, your company, or for your own home office.

1. GIVE MORNING AUTONOMY

When I interviewed Daniel Pink for this book he shared an interesting idea with me on the topic of motivation (you can listen to the original interview on the *Mindvalley Podcast*). Daniel said that people need freedom. But this doesn't necessarily mean freedom at work. It can mean freedom *from* work—during the morning.

The morning is when we need to prioritize ourselves. For me the morning is when I meditate, eat healthy, exercise, and read. Allow people the sovereignty they need to own the mornings. The simplest way to do this is to let them govern their time. Let them come to work when they want and leave when they want. As long as they attend their meetings and do great work on their projects, does it matter when they work?

At Mindvalley, our first meeting of the day is at 11:30 a.m. Because the morning is personal time. No one has to rush into the office. They can wake up and go work out if they choose. Or engage with family. Or do a morning meditation. Maybe read a chapter of a book with their coffee. Morning rituals set the tone for a great day.

And if they want to sleep more, this time gives them the opportunity to do so too. Pink calls this *morning autonomy,* and his research suggests that it leads to more employee engagement and loyalty than the traditional model of demanding people show up at nine or ten.

2. RESPECT SLEEP

So many companies rob their employees of valuable sleep time. Sleep is essential to well-being and high performance. Morning autonomy helps with allowing people to sleep in and get the rest they need. But you can go further. Ban the idea of pulling regular all-nighters. It destroys a person.

If you don't get enough sleep, you see immunity go down by up to 500 percent. That means more sick days. You also see anxiety and stress go up, and that's bad for any culture. Not to mention, cognition drops massively. Remember: Ninety minutes of less sleep than you need equates to a one-third drop in cognition, according to Tom Rath. So let your people sleep.

As a bonus, we give people time to nap at work. In our new office space we have built-in sleep pods where people can go to lie down when they need to. They can use the time to sleep, or read, or meditate.

A power nap of just twenty minutes can do wonders to boost productivity for the subsequent three to four hours of the day.

3. MEDITATION AND MINDFULNESS

These types of practices need to be embraced in the workplace. Meditation, for instance, is a powerful tool. There is ample science to show that meditating daily, even for short periods of time, results in people making better decisions. They are more creative. And they communicate more effectively. There are now fifteen thousand studies that show meditation is beneficial for health, wellness, and enhancing human functioning.

Though remember to respect people's boundaries. Nothing should be enforced. But instead there should be opportunities given for people to learn new personal wellness techniques. It may surprise you how critical a component this is for innovation.

4. ESTABLISH A TRANSFORMATIONAL EDUCATION BUDGET

Does your company have a budget to allow employees to get access to trainings on health, wellness, and personal growth? If not, establish one. It would be one of the greatest productivity tools you can bring in.

At the time of writing, thousands of companies use Mindvalley's Quest Platform to improve the well-being of their employees. For a low fee, people within the company get access to thirty-day programs that take five to twenty minutes a day and allow you to master every aspect of superhuman functioning—from speed-reading to sleep. Imagine being able to master super slow strength training in January. And then in February, tripling your reading speed. In March, learning how to be a better parent to your kids. In April, learning how to be a masterful speaker. That's what the Quest platform delivers.

It gets addictive, because once you get in the habit of upleveling yourself for twenty minutes a day, you start to love the new you that emerges so much that you just won't be able to stop. It's transformation at its best.

When you bring these practices into your life and into your team you've succeeded in creating a truly transformational workplace. A place where people can really thrive and become their best selves.

And so now we come to the next step of Maslow's pyramid: Self-Transcendence. As we become our best selves, the next stage of evolution is to recognize the desire that will start emerging within you to give back to the world. This is the essence of self-transcendence and what you'll learn in the next chapter.

Chapter Summary

MODELS OF REALITY

Transformation is a permanent shift in the way someone sees the world. It is different from learning. There are two types of transformation. Michael Beckwith calls them *kensho* and *satori*. You can grow through pain (kensho) or insight (satori).

To move away from pain and accelerate growth through insight, make personal growth a way of life.

Focus on your rate of self-evolution. Always consider what you need to do next in all areas of life to expand into a better version of yourself. When you do this you naturally can be a positive guide to others. All people are leaders and have the capacity to shape other leaders. Growth has a compounding effect. So embrace transformation and *"Grow so fast that your friends who haven't seen you in a month have to get to know you all over again."*

Systems for Living

EXERCISE 1: HOW TO SET UP A PERSONAL TRANSFORMATION ROUTINE

Refer to the above section on How to Set Up a Personal Transformation Routine to use as a guide to create your own daily routine. Consider practices for:

1. Sleep Optimization
2. The 6-Phase Meditation Routine
3. Optimized Exercise Routines (Tabata and Super Slow Strength Training)
4. Optimized Eating, Fasting, and Supplements
5. Speed Learning

EXERCISE 2: HOW TO SET UP A TRANSFORMATIONAL TEAM ENVIRONMENT

Refer to the above section on How to Set Up a Team Environment to use as a guide to bring new growth structures into a team. Consider practices for:

1. Morning Autonomy
2. Sleep
3. Meditation and Mindfulness
4. A Transformational Education Budget

CHAPTER 6

CHOOSE YOUR MISSION WISELY

Power without love is reckless and abusive, and love without power is sentimental and anemic. Power at its best
is love implementing the demands of justice, and justice
at its best is power correcting everything that stands
against love.

—Martin Luther King Jr., *The Autobiography of
Martin Luther King, Jr.*

A s you self-actualize you gain an edge in life. The next step
is to use this edge to lift others up and enhance the world—
this is self-transcendence. When you live from this plane you
will tap into a level of fulfillment beyond anything you can imagine.
The goal is no longer to just refine yourself or sit in endless introspection. Rather, it's to use your newfound abilities to make the world
better for others, multiple generations down.

It was after midnight, and I was sitting at a formal banquet table, its
feet nestled in the sugary white sands of Turtle Beach on Necker Island.
Around the table were entrepreneurs from across the world attending a
mastermind with Richard Branson as the host. Branson has an incredible
knack for getting conservative business professionals to ditch their suits for
costumes and party until sunrise. Tonight, we were the pirates of Necker

Island. He had an eye patch on, a hook for a hand, and sported a set of flip-flops in classic Branson style. The rest of us were dressed similarly.

As the party started to die down, I found myself sitting next to Branson and decided to ask him an important question—one that had been rolling around in my head since I'd received my invitation.

"Okay, Richard, I'm curious. Virgin Group has some three hundred companies and some three hundred partners. You employ around fifty thousand people. And you've created this incredible life. If you could sum up your success in one paragraph, what would you say is the secret?"

Branson paused for a moment to reflect. He cocked his head to the side. Looked out to the ocean. Then he turned back to me and said this:

It's all about finding and hiring people smarter than you, getting them to join your business and giving them good work, then getting out of the way and trusting them. You have to get out of the way so you can focus on the bigger vision.

But there was one last piece of advice he gave me that night:

That's important, but here is the main thing: You must make them see their work as a mission.

The Power of a Mission

I learned another powerful lesson about visionaries one day in L.A. in 2015. I was invited to visit SpaceX with a group of board members of the XPRIZE Foundation, a technological development nonprofit that funds innovations that benefit humanity. As a member of this group of global changemakers, I was granted behind-the-scenes access to many of the world's leading tech innovation labs. When I walked into the massive industrial building that housed Elon Musk's rockets I was immediately struck by the sheer grandiosity of how badasses like Elon think.

Back then his companies SpaceX and Tesla were the two companies rated most desirable to work for among the Silicon Valley engineers. Their missions are literally out of this world, yet also quite possible to execute and achieve. Both companies have missions so massive they plan to save the human race. SpaceX exists to bring the human race to Mars and create a backup. Likewise, Tesla's vision is to help move us into a new fair market society where we use alternative energy rather than fossil fuels.

But consider this. SpaceX is nothing more than a vertical trucking company. Some companies move goods horizontally, while SpaceX moves goods vertically. It transports satellites to space. In essence it's not exactly sexy work. But that's not how Elon describes it.

That day in a boardroom at SpaceX, Elon flashed a giant picture of Mars on a screen. He told us about colonizing the Red Planet. His transformational purpose was crystal clear. There's a one-in-forty-thousand chance that an asteroid will hit the Earth during our lifetime, wiping us out as a species. Think about it. We could be the next dinosaurs. And so, just as you would back up a hard drive to a different computer in case your computer gets destroyed, we need to back up the human race. One of us asked him, "How long before we get there?"

"I estimate ten years or so," he replied.

"But I've been known to be overoptimistic with deadlines before," he added with a smile.

Elon doesn't speak dryly about sending payloads to space. He talks about his company ten years out into the future. And he speaks as if it's happening right *now*.

He creates a vision so inspiring you can't help but be swept up by it. His purpose and his *why* are so clear that people flock to him. Even if the end point of the vision is still a decade or more away.

People who join SpaceX and Tesla don't expect Elon to know how to solve the problems the companies are confronting or what the timeframe might be. Remember that when you have such a grand mission, you don't have to know the *how*. You start with the *why* and the *what*. You rally the troops. The point is to then figure out the *how* together. A compelling mission is incredibly powerful to attract these troops.

Both Elon Musk and Richard Branson know how to attract talent through the power of a compelling mission. They also know how to keep their teams engaged by giving them inspiring work.

Human beings are goal-driven creatures. We're hardwired to hunt for the next meal. Or to spot the berries on the tree. And in an age where we get our meat and berries from the corner grocery store, we get bored if we aren't using this goal-driven component of our brains.

Some turn to videogames or other hobbies to fulfill this drive, many of which use goal-attainment tactics called gamification to keep you hooked. But most people turn to their work. They are drawn to companies that allow them to work on projects so bold and inspiring, they give their life meaning.

In 2013, Gallup published a poll on men who refused to retire at sixty-five and continued to work until age eighty. Its findings show that 86 percent of these men kept working because they found their work fun, while 93 percent said they kept working because they found their work meaningful.

When work lines up with the legacy a person wants to create in the world, their mission fuels them. This is what it means to work from a place of self-transcendence.

Maslow theorized that self-transcendence is the highest level of living. Living from this plane is achieved when a person focuses beyond the self. A self-transcendent individual sees the world as their responsibility. They work from a place of altruism, spiritual awakening, liberation from egocentricity, and the unity of being. They are the absolute best types of humans, in my opinion, for they make the world better for all of us. This is where their badass meets their Buddha. They mold, shape, and push the world forward because their love for the human race drives them to make us a better species.

Contribution Is the Essence of Self-Transcendence

Contribution is the modus operandi of self-transcendence. Think about a moment where you contributed to another person without expecting anything back. What did you experience? How did you feel? What did you get back from your act of service? That's operating from self-transcendence. What's incredible about contribution with no conditions is that it's also an access point to many other human needs. When a person makes contribution their primary focus, growth, love and belonging (or connection), and significance often get taken care of too. It's the superstructure of fulfillment.

Your Life Is Not About You . . .

In 2017, at Mindvalley University in Barcelona, I was sitting in the audience watching a particularly mesmerizing lecturer. He was Neale Donald Walsch, the author of the world-renowned *Conversations with God* series of books, which have sold in the neighborhood of fifteen million copies and counting.

Neale's books have transformed many lives, including my own. I picked up his first *Conversations with God* book in 1998 when I was in college. Every page of that book soothed me. He wrote about the true nature of all humans and our divine heritage.

At a certain point during a Q&A session, a woman in her forties stood up. She said: "Neale, I wake up every day feeling stress and anxiety and depression. What do you recommend I do?"

Neale smiled, caught her gaze, and said:

Remember this when you wake up every day:
Your life is not about you. Rather, it's about the
lives of every single person you touch.

Neale went on: "Make an effort to remind yourself of this. When you really get this, when you truly shift and make your life about others, you will never wake up depressed, stressed, or fearful ever again. When you walk into a room with the intention to heal the room, when you wake up with the desire to serve the world, your problems, the negative you feel, disappears."

This idea touched me so deeply I made it a way of living. It became a code I use to conduct my life. And a code guiding how we operate at Mindvalley.

This takes practice. But shifting the focus *away* from personal problems to others is a way to immediately see the world through a bigger lens. Living in this way pulls an individual forward in a way that's motivating and thrilling and joyful.

When a company does this in unison—with its team rallied around a particular problem to solve for the world, you've created a powerful band of superheroes. (As you'll learn below, there are two tools for doing this: the Massive Transformational Purpose and Taking a Stand.)

At the end of this chapter, we'll explore these tactics that anyone can apply to make their work tap into the power of self-transcendence. When you start to make your life about other people, it completely changes the context for every action you take.

But first, let's take a step back and shine a light on why we need to transcend ourselves. Thinking bigger is what the world needs today more than anything. Humanity has changed irreversibly. We are more connected than we've ever been. And according to writer-philosopher Tim Urban, we've actually become a new type of species: the Human Colossus.

Meet the Human Colossus

Tim Urban, who writes the *Wait But Why* blog, is a fascinating character. He doesn't write regular blog posts. Instead, they run up to sixty thousand words. That's 80 percent of the length of this book. This gets him some very special fans.

Elon Musk approached Urban in 2017 to write a piece to explain the work of his latest mega-concept company, called Neuralink. It required Urban's explanation expertise, because what the company aims to create is a seamless brain-to-computer connection.

To explain Neuralink, Urban wrote a post called "Neuralink and the Brain's Magical Future" (read the full post here: https://waitbutwhy .com/2017/04/neuralink.html), which takes readers back 3.5 million years and runs them through a timeline of man's evolution. He playfully articulates how the technology we've built has allowed us to grow our species in ways that were once impossible. In this sixty-thousand-word post, Tim suggests a simple thought experiment:

Imagine an alien explorer is visiting a new star and finds three planets circling it, all with life on them. The first happens to be identical to the way Earth was in 10 million BC. The second happens to be identical to Earth in 50,000 BC. And the third happens to be identical to Earth in 2017 AD.

The alien is no expert on primitive biological life but circles around all three planets, peering down at each with his telescope. On the first, he sees lots of water and trees and mountains and some little signs of animal life. He makes out a herd of elephants on an African plain, a group of dolphins skipping along the ocean's surface, and a few other scattered critters living out their Tuesday.

He moves on to the second planet and looks around. More critters, not too much different. He notices one new thing—occasional little points of flickering light dotting the land.

Bored, he moves on to the third planet. Whoa. He sees planes crawling around above the land, vast patches of gray land with towering buildings on them, ships of all kinds sprinkled across the seas, long railways stretching across continents, and he has to jerk his spaceship out of the way when a satellite soars by him.

When he heads home, he reports on what he found: "Two planets with primitive life and one planet with intelligent life."

You can understand why that would be his conclusion—but he'd be wrong.

In fact, it's the first planet that's the odd one out. Both the second and third planets have intelligent life on them—equally intelligent life. So equal that you could kidnap a newborn baby from Planet 2 and swap it with a newborn on Planet 3 and both would grow up as normal people on the other's planet, fitting in seamlessly. Same people.

And yet, how could that be?

The Human Colossus. That's how.

Urban says we're now in an era of the Human Colossus. Here is how he explains it. "Ever wonder why you're so often unimpressed by humans and yet so blown away by the accomplishments of humanity . . . The better we could communicate on a mass scale, the more our species began to function like a single organism, with humanity's collective knowledge tower as its brain and each individual human brain like a nerve or a muscle fiber in its body. With the era of mass communication upon us, the collective human organism—the Human Colossus—rose into existence."

The Internet is like our collective nervous system. It's enhanced our capability to share ideas, and that's made us collectively a smarter species. Collaboration has become easier. Humanity has become more connected, and this has facilitated the invention of superior systems and technologies that continue to advance our species. The systems built by us have made solving major global issues easier. People can more simply team up, combine brainpower, share ideas, and reach new innovative heights.

I once heard Peter Diamandis say: "The average person with a smartphone today has access to more information about the world than the President of the United States did in 1994."

We're increasingly operating as one unified body. We are no longer in the age of the individual, but of humanity. And each of us is merely cells in that collective body. Everything you create, every time you post on social media, or vote, every action you take impacts the other cells. We are more deeply connected to each other than ever before. We are part of one unified entity and body—the Human Colossus.

The implications of this are both negative and positive. For instance, a president's reactionary tweet can spread in moments and cause the world to think negatively about an entire country. Conversely, what's incredible is our ability to collectively solve problems, like the work of *New York Times* columnist Dr. Lisa Sanders, who crowdsources rare illnesses to find cures on the show *Diagnosis.*

So here's the grand question: If we are all cells, are you a healthy cell or a cancer cell? Does your work positively impact humanity? And for business leaders, is the mission of your company making a healthy cellular contribution to the Human Colossus? Or like a cancer cell, are your work and your actions making the Colossus sicker? The funny thing is that cancer cells don't know that they are cancer cells. They think they are regular cells, growing and reproducing. In the mind of the cancer cell, it's just doing its cellular job.

Is the same analogy true for humans? If you're a soldier taking commands from a dictator to bomb a city like Homs in Syria and create millions of refugees, *could you be a cancer cell*? I'm not saying the soldier is evil. But he may be operating under the wrong principles. The soldier analogy is easy. But here's a tougher one.

What if you're an executive for a Big Tobacco or vape company and your mission is to get more people addicted to your product? Tougher yet: What if you're an executive for a large soda company peddling flavored high-fructose corn syrup as happiness in a can? Are you then a healthy cell or a cancer cell?

And this is where the phenomenon gets weirder. Human beings, when operating as cancer cells, choose not to see themselves as cancer cells. They see themselves as doing what is right and needed. But as Stanley Milgram's famous prison experiments show, we don't often do what is right. We follow orders, hierarchies, patterns, and rules—often over heart, mission, and values. We do this out of compliance and our human need to fit into a tribe or community.

But anyone has the power to rise beyond this compliance. Even small actions can make a massive difference. Sometimes it's simply the act of saying no or walking away from a situation.

People who live from a place of making a positive difference for the world in what they do, have a higher bar of integrity. Like my friend Tom Chi. He has always inspired me with his commitment to using business as a vehicle for good in the world. Tom is an inventor, author, speaker, and cofounder of

X Development, sometimes called Google X, Google's semi-secret skunkworks lab (now a subsidiary of Google's parent company Alphabet).

A few years back Tom ran a think tank in Silicon Valley in which I was an investor. Large companies hired him and his team to help solve their tactical problems. At one point, a major beverage manufacturer approached Tom to solve its marketing hurdle. Teenagers were not buying enough of their product.

As the story goes, Tom looked at the executives seated across from him and said, "You do understand that your product has a high correlation with obesity and diabetes, don't you?"

The company executives defended their product by trying to steer the conversation in a different direction. But Tom, being a scientist himself, knew this was bunk. He shared with me:

"They had many layers of denial, saying that there are hundreds of causes of diabetes, and that their product is just part of a balanced set of choices anyone can make food-wise."

The company, said Tom, claimed that they really stood for progressive values. They were one of the first companies, for example, to show mixed-race couples in their ads.

Tom explained to me, "It's a classic example of fooling yourself, that goodness in one area gives you a free pass in others. Really what's true is that we need to stay awake and keep learning in all the areas we can."

In the end, Tom turned down the offer. He walked away from a quarter-million-dollar deal. It conflicted with his values. Tom is a very world-centric leader. He deeply cares about the human race and that the work he does contributes to bring about positive changes.

Personally, what I found interesting about the situation was Tom's observation that many people in this company seemed to be fooling themselves, that there were many layers of denial that went against empirical data, such as the adverse effects of sugar on human biology and the correlation between soda consumption and obesity rates.

Yet we can also empathize with these executives pushing to sell their drink to teens. They are not evil people. As Tom shared with me, "I felt for them as well, because shaking their reality would mean leaving a corporation they enjoy working at, with coworkers they like and the career they'd invested in, and the financial stability that has helped them support their family. This led them to pile on countless layers of denial and misinformation to protect [themselves]."

Yes, the company's product was a major contributor to the obesity epidemic in the world. While the product might have a time and place in moderation, some might call it utterly useless. Much like cigarettes. Did you know that they were once marketed to pregnant women? This of course was long before the adverse health effects were known. But imagine hearing that frequent cigarette breaks could come in handy to quiet pregnancy jitters.

Thus it's the responsibility of all of us to question our actions. To take a stand for the greater good. This starts with asking this question before you take any action: Is the role I'm playing in this world pushing humanity forward or moving us back?

And to do this we have to take a good hard look at the product or service we're pushing and ask the tough questions, because there are two types of businesses you can run or work for: Humanity Minus or Humanity Plus. (You can also apply these questions to your life in general.)

The Buddha nature cannot harm life. When you truly embrace this aspect of yourself, you have to start examining the products or services your work is creating and asking if you're truly benefiting humanity.

Know the difference between a businessperson and a real entrepreneur? Businesspeople do it for the dollars. But real entrepreneurs do it to push the human race forward.

Are You Humanity Plus or Humanity Minus?

This is the question to ask ourselves about our jobs and the companies we serve: Is my product or service Humanity Plus or Humanity Minus?

Humanity Minus companies are businesses that exist solely for a profit motive, without adding value to the world. They sell harmful products like junk food or unsustainable practices like fossil fuels. Many Humanity Minus companies are founded on artificial demand—that is, they sell products we don't truly need and that might even be potentially harmful. But they are marketed as necessities for well-being or happiness.

An example might be the recent controversy over vape companies. While it's great to see Americans ditching cigarettes, vape has become the replacement. Many vape products contain cancer-causing substances, toxic chemicals, and toxic metal nanoparticles. It's created an entirely new hazard as these companies have targeted the teenage market.

Humanity Plus companies, in contrast, push the human race forward. These are the companies focusing on clean, renewable energy sources, or products that promote healthy eating and living. These businesses work on new ways to elevate and improve life on our planet. Ideally, these are the companies we should be working for, supporting, and starting. Their products make the Human Colossus healthier, not sicker. These are the companies that attract the Buddhas of the world. For the Buddha nature will not engage in actions that would harm humanity.

Now, anyone can work for a company in a traditional industry like airlines, insurance, electricity, and more, and that company might still have a powerful mission that inspires you and others. Think of Southwest Airlines, for example—it's a traditional industry, but they are contributing to the world by radically innovating on customer service and customer experiences when they fly. Flying does contribute to global warming, but it's also a necessity until we create planes powered by alternative energy.

I wouldn't lump every company that contributes to global warming as

Humanity Minus. Timing is everything. The technology to replace all our fossil fuel needs is not yet here. But I would certainly suggest that companies and brands that use false marketing to push products we don't need are treading that line.

Whatever your mission turns out to be—whether it's starting your own business, joining a business, pursuing a cause outside of work, letting your creative light shine out to the world, or devoting yourself to raising amazing children, there's really only one thing you need to remember:

> *You don't have to save the world.*
> *Just don't mess it up for the next generation.*

If your company is in the Humanity Minus column, and you are an amazing talent, I hope you see that the contribution you're making does not reflect your values. Move to a company where your gifts can better serve the collective Human Colossus. Make a difference for all of us. It's up to each of us to use our talents for good. Is it time to level-up your game? Think about it: Should the brightest minds in the world be thinking of new ways to make you buy and consume the next soda or vape? Or should they be solving real problems facing humanity?

A Toolkit to Be Mission Oriented

TOOL #1: THE MASSIVE TRANSFORMATIONAL PURPOSE (MTP)

To truly bring a sense of meaning into your life and the lives of everyone you touch, we must get obsessed with goals or problems that go *beyond the self.*

We are operating as if we are cells in a unified being. We depend on each other more than we know. Everything you do, even the smallest act, has a ripple effect. Recall the words of Neale Donald Walsch: *"Your life is not about you. Rather, it's about the lives of every single person you touch."*

Companies that possess a Massive Transformational Purpose (MTP) to better the world have an edge. They attract the best minds, the most passionate problem solvers, and inspire their people to work toward a higher cause. And the science shows that purpose-driven workers perform at their peak.

When you align your company under a greater mission you're moving people from lower to higher degrees of motivation. You give people bigger problems to care about. Not the guy or girl who didn't text them back. Or the little extra bit of flab around their belly. Or that their favorite concert was sold out. Badasses don't concern themselves with these petty issues. You're giving people bigger problems to wrap their mind around.

The Problem with Most People Is that Their Problems Aren't Big Enough.

Make people care about saving the world and changing the course of humanity. Get your people obsessed about real problems. The destruction of the environment, the rise of nationalism, the health and obesity crisis, the fact that millions of people lack basic necessities like water or a decent education. Or even just making people's lives better through good design, great products, and useful services.

There is a famous story that shows how Steve Jobs used this tactic to motivate Apple engineers to speed up the start time of an early Mac. In his article "Saving Lives," published in 1983, Andy Hertzfeld, one of the computer scientists on the original development team during the 1980s, writes:

> *One of the things that bothered Steve Jobs the most was the time that it took to boot when the Mac was first powered on. It could take a couple of minutes,*

or even more, to test memory, initialize the operating system, and load the Finder. One afternoon, Steve came up with an original way to motivate us to make it faster.

Larry Kenyon was the engineer working on the disk driver and file system. Steve came into his cubicle and started to exhort him. "The Macintosh boots too slowly. You've got to make it faster!"

Larry started to explain about some of the places where he thought that he could improve things, but Steve wasn't interested. He continued, "You know, I've been thinking about it. How many people are going to be using the Macintosh? A million? No, more than that. In a few years, I bet five million people will be booting up their Macintoshes at least once a day.

"Well, let's say you can shave 10 seconds off of the boot time. Multiply that by five million users and that's 50 million seconds, every single day. Over a year, that's probably dozens of lifetimes. So if you make it boot ten seconds faster, you've saved a dozen lives. That's really worth it, don't you think?"

His engineers got the job done. And in far less time than they initially anticipated.

When Jobs expanded the mission, he successfully motivated his team to shave more than ten seconds off the boot time over the next couple of months. A Massive Transformational Purpose is simply far more thrilling to work on.

Your MTP is the massive change you want to bring to the world to make it better off. In some business books this is referred to as the BHAG (pronounced B-HAG), or "Big Hairy Audacious Goal." I consider these the same thing. Your MTP is an overriding, empowering goal that your organization is pushing for.

Elon Musk's MTP is to colonize Mars. Bill Gates's MTP back when Microsoft started was to put a computer on every desk in the world. Google's MTP is to organize the world's information and make it universally accessible and useful. Mindvalley's MTP is to create the greatest rise in human consciousness our species has ever experienced.

The MTP has to be something that is challenging and hard to do. You're not meant to know the answers immediately. This is what makes it so intriguing. It's like a puzzle waiting to be solved.

It's okay for your MTP to be fluffy. For now at least. In the next chapter we'll see how to use a concept called OKRs to bring order and tangibility to the MTP.

Now, what if your company isn't working on a bold new project that can change the world? Maybe you're an Instagram model. Or you sell T-shirts. Or you manufacture glassware. Or you run a dry cleaner's.

You may not have an MTP, but you can still bring meaning to your work by taking a stand.

TOOL #2: TAKING A STAND

Srikumar Rao once told me, "Too many leaders try to be inspiring. Stop that. Instead *be inspired.*"

Think about it. If your focus is on being inspired yourself, you're naturally inspiring to others. The state of inspiration is magnetic. Take a moment now to look at the world around you. What inspires you, draws you, uplifts you? What is it that's worth fighting for? This next story might help you get there.

In 2009, a dry cleaner on New York City's Upper East Side named Carlos Vasquez felt a burning desire to help locals who had lost their jobs to the economic downturn. He put up a sign on his business's window that said:

> *If you are unemployed and you need an outfit cleaned*
> *for an interview we will clean it for FREE.*

In an interview, Carlos said: "It's just something I do to give back to the community. It's to thank them for the support that I get around here, for letting my business keep running by bringing me their clothes."

Carlos accidentally started a movement when the national press picked up the story. Soon dry cleaners around the country were cleaning clothes for free for unemployed people preparing for job interviews.

One cleaner, Don Chapman, inspired by Carlos, cleaned two thousand suits altogether. It was beautiful to see. The movement brought communities together and gave Americans a new model to follow of support for one another. And this was all because one man chose to get inspired. Anyone can do this.

The Instagram influencer can choose to take a stand for health and avoid promoting products that are junk food. The T-shirt designer can create a brand around positivity. This actually happened. Brothers Bert and John Jacobs started the Life Is Good T-shirt line with a mission to spread optimism. Before their great epiphany, they were driving a van selling homemade T-shirts. One day they got fed up by the negative news media and decided to create a line to remind people to be grateful and happy. Customers flocked to them when they adopted this stand, and today their company is worth well over nine figures.

Larger companies can do the same. Patagonia is an outdoor clothing and gear company that inspires millions with its stand for the environment. Nike takes a stand for equality. Starbucks takes a stand for supporting refugees worldwide.

And the best part is, taking a stand can actually help profitability. In a recent study, 75 percent of Americans said they want companies and CEOs to take a stand. Perhaps this is why when Nike chose to run an ad campaign supporting Colin Kaepernick, the football star who got into a massive public fight with Trump, its shares closed at all-time highs. People flocked to support Nike.

We live in an extremely polarized world. People are losing faith in government. So they are looking to entrepreneurs to stand up for what is right. They expect brands to take a stand in politics, social issues, the environment, and even issues like gun control, gender equality, and social justice. In 2019, a poll by Sprout Social reported that 66 percent of consumers want brands to take a public stand on social and political issues.

The old way of business was not to push boundaries. Yet taking a no-stand position today might actually be dangerous to your business.

Businesses that take a stand naturally attract incredible alliances with like-minded business partners, employees, and investors. So take a stand and then share it regularly.

As you start doing this you might just evolve into a new version of yourself. The entrepreneur-activist or the CEO-activist or the creator-activist. This happened to me, and quite by accident.

The Era of the Activist

There is a term I use to describe myself that's written on all my social media accounts and business cards: Underneath "Vishen Lakhiani" it says: *Founder-Activist.*

The definition of activist is: *A person who promotes, impedes, directs, or intervenes, in social, political, economic, or environmental reform with the desire to make a societal change.*

I never realized I was actually an activist until I was asked to be on Tom Bilyeu's hit talk show, *Impact Theory.* The show explores the mindsets of the world's highest achievers. Tom interviews them to learn their success secrets. He helped me verbalize a shift inside me that I'd been undergoing for months. And it all started when he asked me a question.

"Do you consider yourself a philosopher or an entrepreneur?" he asked.

I replied: "I used to think I was an entrepreneur. But again, entrepreneur is a means goal. So I don't like that label 'entrepreneur.' There are entrepreneurs who are freelancers who will design a logo for you. Entrepreneur simply means you're earning your own income. Then there are entrepreneurs like you who have built billion-dollar companies. The gap is too wide to put everybody into one label.

"So I define myself not by the label entrepreneur but by what I stand for. I believe it's not our labels that matter. It's your stand. Patrick Gentempo said, 'Your stand is your brand.' I believe what makes us truly unique as an individual is what we stand for. And I stand for ONE thing and it's reflected in everything I do. And that one thing is unity. It's my number one value. So I'm an activist for unity more so than I'm an entrepreneur. I mean, if I lost my business, I wouldn't lose my identity. But if I stopped standing for unity I wouldn't be Vishen . . .There's this big desire in me for unity. That's what makes me, ME. I am a fighter and activist for human unity. That's my number one definition for myself."

From that definition you can see I took the ideas of the foundational values in Chapter 1 of this book to heart. My foundational values came first—the businesses I start simply reflect those values.

Following the interview, I realized I wanted to fully commit to what I said publicly. The first action I took was to add the activist title to my business cards and social media accounts. I also felt like the world around me was going through a shift and, in a way, falling apart, and I wanted to do more.

And so, Mindvalley changed too. We decided to devote a portion of our annual budget to social causes.

The immediate reaction among my peers was What if you alienate customers who disagree with you? Would we lose followers? Perhaps. But that wasn't the case at all.

Instead, what we did notice, however, was in the first six months of changing our status as an activist company, we experienced two remarkable results. First, our sales skyrocketed. We deepened our allegiance with more people who were the right fit for our brand. We receive comments on our social media feeds like "I used to think Mindvalley was all about sales. This company has a heart. Never leaving this brand."

Second, it created an immense drive and pride in our people for the work they did. Employees told me how proud they were that we as a company cared for things that truly mattered.

Of course, taking a stand can be terrifying. It's uncomfortable and lonely at first. But one person has to step out in front first and raise their hands. Martin Luther King Jr. expressed this powerfully:

> *You may be thirty-eight years old, as I happen to be. And one day, some great opportunity stands before you and calls you to stand up for some great principle, some great issue, some great cause. And you refuse to do it because you are afraid . . . You refuse to do it because you want to live longer. . . . You're afraid that you will lose your job, or you are afraid that you will be criticized or that you will lose your popularity, or you're afraid that somebody will stab you, or shoot at you or bomb your house; so you refuse to take the stand.*
> *Well, you may go on and live until you are ninety, but you're just as dead at thirty-eight as you would be at ninety. And the cessation of breathing in your life is but the belated announcement of an earlier death of the spirit.*

Martin Luther King Jr. did not mince words. Be the leader who is willing to get uncomfortable to make a positive change. Don't be a bystander of life.

Let me make this clear: *You are the one.* Just as I am the one. What would the world be like if we all took this stand?

So take a stand in this world. Contribute to a cause. Unite with others and create positive change. Humanity needs you.

And if you don't yet know how you want to change the world, the next chapter will give you some useful tools to create a grand new vision of how you want to make a difference. We'll talk about how to create bold visions to change the world.

Chapter Summary

MODELS OF REALITY

The key to making any mission happen is to find and align with people smarter than you, give them inspiring projects, and then get out of their way so you can focus on the vision. Most important, you must remind yourself and everyone of the mission. This helps a team stay motivated, excited, and focused. Both Elon Musk and Richard Branson are masters of this. They both have a Massive Transformational Purpose.

Humans are biologically hardwired for goal achievement. When missions are massive and inspiring, the mission itself is motivating and pulls people beyond thinking only of themselves. They want to be part of making a massive positive contribution to humanity.

Remember that we are connected more today than ever before. We are the Human Colossus. We are all single cells that are connected and that operate together. The actions of one person impact everyone.

And so, always consider if the work you devote yourself to is Humanity Plus or Humanity Minus. In other words, is your mission adding value to the world or detracting from it?

Implant in your mind the wise wisdom of Neale Donald Walsch and Srikumar Rao. Neale says: *"Your life is not about you. Rather, it's about the lives of every single person you touch."*

Rao says: "Too many leaders try to be inspiring. Stop that. Instead *be inspired.*"

To do this, consider: What are you an activist for? What matters to you? Get excited and then connect and collaborate with like-minded people. There is nothing more powerful today than taking a stand and living for a bold mission.

Systems for Living

EXERCISE 1: MASSIVE TRANSFORMATIONAL PURPOSE (MTP)

Step 1: Reflect on these two quotes and the questions below:

> "Your life is not about you. Rather, it's about the lives of every single person you touch."
>
> —Neale Donald Walsch

> "Too many leaders try to be inspiring. Stop that. Instead *be inspired.*"
>
> —Srikumar Rao

What missions in the world already inspire you?
What causes can you be an activist for?
What topics or fields light you up?
What types of groups do you want to make a difference for?
What brands can you support?

Step 2: Take action. What actions can you take to align yourself with or create positive missions that forward initiatives in the areas that matter to you? Write them down. Then get in action.

EXERCISE 2: TAKING A STAND

There are numerous books and classes you can take on how to align your brand with a stand. But you can start fairly easily. In the age of social media, all of us are media companies of one. If your company has a social media account, speak to your boss or supervisor and see if there's a cause you can support.

Also, if you run Web advertising, know that supporting causes can be great for your ad return. This is NOT the reason to do it—but sharing the data below with your CEO might help convince them. In June 2019 Mindvalley changed its logos on all social media to reflect the rainbow flag to support LGBT pride. That same month we saw a huge increase in ad returns. Over a 20 percent boost in performance. The public was clicking on our ads more and buying more. We couldn't fully explain it, but the data was there. I guessed that we had connected better with our audience by showing how much we cared.

You can follow Mindvalley on Instagram at @mindvalley to see how we regularly take a stand for a cause that matters.

PART III

BECOMING A VISIONARY

MERGING THE BUDDHA AND THE BADASS TO CHANGE THE WORLD

H aving attained the right allies, the right self-esteem, and having embraced self-evolution and self-transcendence, the next step is to lead the way to changing the world.

You shifted into living your values and thus attracted the people you need to turn any vision into a reality (Part I). You've created structures that massively enhance peak performance (Part II). Now it's time to launch into the next gear. Part III gives you the practices for visionary thinking and execution. It's about putting the pieces together so that you can change the world with joy and ease. It's about making a dent in the Universe.

Become the visionary leader you were meant to be. Create inspiring missions that pull you and everyone around you into action. Learn how to collaborate with others as a united front. I call this the Unified Brain model. And then, don't burn out like so many others do. You don't need to sacrifice your health, your love life, or your family.

Here is a breakdown of what you'll learn:

Chapter 7: Activating the Visionary in You. Motivation is a *brule*. When a mission is inspiring enough, it pulls you and everyone it resonates with forth and into action. That's the power of bold visions. Learn how to amplify your visions and to create audacious goals that inspire and move humanity forward.

Chapter 8: The Unified Brain. The world is changing fast. So is the business landscape. And technology accelerates at an exponential rate. It moves faster than any human can. To remain competitive, teams must collaborate at superhuman speeds. In this chapter, you will learn how to break lines of hierarchy in a team so you innovate rapidly and work as a united front. In other words, you become a Unified Brain. You will learn this model and a former military system for streamlining communication called the OODA loop.

Chapter 9: Identity Upgrading and the Beautiful Destruction. Time to go beyond the myth of hard work. Learn how to tap into a higher level of work where you can access heightened states of consciousness that allow you to effortlessly glide through work.

This beautiful state, where you pull on the dual sides of your nature that you've been developing throughout this book, is what I call the merger of the Buddha and the badass. In this chapter, you will learn how to balance the two so you never experience debilitating stress or burnout.

Everyone lives between two worlds, and your inner world gives clues to the identity you desire to become. There's a three-step process for this. So I'll leave you with one final transformational exercise that will allow you to easily become who you authentically want to be and access the life that calls to you.

CHAPTER 7

ACTIVATE YOUR INNER VISIONARY

Good leaders have vision and inspire others to help them turn vision into reality. Great leaders create more leaders, not followers. Great leaders have vision, share vision, and inspire others to create their own.

—Roy T. Bennett, *The Light in the Heart*

T here is no greater experience than to live your life working to achieve a vision so bold that it scares you. Any vision you commit to should be so inspiring that you stay up at night as it pulls you and flirts with you. Now, here is a big secret: The bigger your vision, the easier it gets. When you live this way, you may find that the vision is not coming from you. Instead the Universe is choosing to go through you to realize what the world needs.

IN 2003, AT THE age of twenty-seven, I quit my job as vice president of a promising Silicon Valley start-up so I could dedicate my life to a career that gave me great meaning. I had decided to teach and promote meditation.

My very first site made me a decent living teaching meditation classes around the world. But I quickly realized that teaching meditation was nowhere as lucrative as my previous job. Instead it was a pretty reliable path to going broke. And so to make ends meet, I ran a side digital marketing agency that helped authors with their websites and their tech backends. One of those authors was Bob Proctor.

Proctor, of course, is an American author, speaker, and success coach. When I was fourteen years old I discovered his books on the bookshelves in my dad's library. Proctor is a master of the wealth mindset.

In 2006 Bob Proctor needed a website. He contracted me to build it for him, which was a major break. Proctor was one of my heroes. I mean, come on, he was one of the guys from the most-watched DVD in the world at that time. Bob-fricking-Proctor from *The Secret*! I couldn't believe my luck. And so, we worked together and became friends. His career was blowing up and I was honored to be the guy helping him build his online sites.

So I divided my life between teaching meditation classes and working with my tiny team of around eighteen people. This was early Mindvalley. We were barely breaking even. We specialized mostly in building sites for other personal growth brands.

But that was about to change. My world was about to blow up, and Bob would be a catalyst.

In my first book, *The Code of the Extraordinary Mind,* I coined a term I refer to as *the Beautiful Destruction.* It simply means:

> *Sometimes you have to destroy a part of your life that*
> *is merely* **good,** *to allow what is* **truly great** *to enter.*

My life was merely good then. Not great. And I'd gotten complacent without noticing.

I didn't have much of a vision. I was simply plodding along, year to year. I was focusing on short-term growth and didn't realize how limited my thinking was. That is, until Bob Proctor bluntly pointed out my shortcomings at a restaurant in downtown London.

I had flown to London to conduct a meditation seminar for a small group of thirty people. Proctor was there at the same time, speaking to thousands of people at a nearby hotel. He graciously invited me to join him for lunch.

I showed up in a T-shirt and jeans, and of course, there's Bob Proctor in a crisp classic navy suit, with a slick red tie and a gleaming watch on his wrist. Bob was a man of impeccable taste and style.

So he asks: "So what brings you to London, Vishen?"

In my head, I am thinking: *Bob, you're gonna be so proud of me. I'm teaching meditation now. I don't just build websites.*

So I explain to him that there were thirty people attending my seminar for £300 per ticket. I spoke about how much joy I got teaching my passion. I spoke about the lives I was changing.

Bob pauses and then says: "Wait, wait. You flew from Malaysia to London? What's that, like, fifteen hours? And you left behind your wife and one-year-old son?"

"Erm . . . yes," I replied.

"I hope you're flying business class at least?" he asked.

I wasn't. "Bob, I only make three thousand dollars per seminar. If I flew business class, I would not make a profit," I explained.

Bob looked at me like a wide-eyed cartoon character, then he crinkled his face and let out a deep sigh. I knew something profound and wise was about to be uttered. I also knew it was going to be painful to hear.

"You travel that far and that's all you make? You are wasting your time," he said firmly with a sigh. "I wouldn't do that if I were you," he continued.

In my head a reactionary alarm bell set off a chain of thoughts of me fully justifying my actions. *I mean, I love teaching, plus I'm adding value to the students' lives, I've grown my business internationally, and I don't think I'm wasting my time, and, and . . .*

Thankfully in the presence of Bob I kept my lips shut and didn't let any of that cascade out of my mouth.

"You're so much bigger than this. You're playing way too small, Vishen."

I'm what? You're kidding me!

The internal dialogue was ruder than that. *Breathe, Vishen, breathe.* Bob is one of the sweetest, most compassionate, good-willed human beings on earth. But my mind was thinking . . .

Screw you, Mr. Bob Proctor with your fancy suits, your millions, and your perfect-smelling cologne . . .

Of course, none of this comes out of my mouth. I swallowed it all. Because deep down inside I knew he was right.

His words echoed in my head.

I finished my weekend seminars, then took a fifteen-hour economy-class plane ride home in which I had hours to think. The next day, I quit teaching seminars. I was lying to myself and I was lying to my students. I was telling them to write down their goals and dream big, and I wasn't. I was playing really small. That was the last small-scale seminar I would teach.

When I got home, I posted a Bob Proctor quote on my Facebook bio. This was in 2008. Eleven years later, it's still there, and it says:

> *The question is not: Are you worthy to reach your goals?*
> *The question is: Are your goals worthy enough of you?*

Bob's advice transformed me. Armed with a bolder vision, I went back to teaching personal growth in 2010. But in a widely different sense. And this time on a much larger scale.

I decided to create an event that combined the beauty, music, magic, and scale of a festival with a personal growth event. I called it A-Fest. It was a massive success. Attendees had to apply and be selected to come. The ticket price was $3,000. And the event was set at five-star resorts in spectacular paradise locations. Instead of traveling around training small groups, putting in sixteen-hour days, and working on my own, I was now bringing the world's best teachers together under one roof. Mindvalley still runs A-Fest today, but it's grown so big it's spun off other massive events like Mindvalley University in 2016, which is a thousand-person, three-week event. This new incarnation is one of the biggest transformational festivals in the world. I went from teaching twenty people in a three-star hotel to running a global festival. All in twenty-four months.

A-Fest became one of the most successful business ventures I ever started. But I owe its birth to Bob Proctor getting me to leave my small, simple vision behind and truly dreaming of a goal that was worthy of my own potential.

That conversation with Bob was a turning point. Thanks to his kick in the butt, I learned how critical visions are. They propel us. They give clarity. They are the driving force that allows us to put a larger mark on the Universe. But to get there we have to take a good look at where we are first and question our choices and our decisions. Discomfort is essential. For this reason, I've made envisioning a consistent practice. And my visions continue to grow. With what you learn in this chapter, yours will too.

The Power of the Bold Vision

Envisioning is the act of conceiving an idea. It's how all things start. Especially because while it's the first step in giving the form*less* some form, it can also hold people back. A leader with a small vision will limit their entire team.

To better explain this concept, let's talk about fleas. There's an age-old flea-in-the-jar experiment where a team of scientists placed a flea community in a glass jar with no lid. Since a flea's favorite hobby is high-jumping, with no seal, all of them jumped out. And so, the scientists placed the fleas back in the jar and sealed it with a lid. The fleas continued to jump, but now only up to the height of the lid. After several days, when the scientists took the lid off, they were shocked to find the fleas now only jumped to the height of the lid, even though their ceiling had been uncapped.

Humans are bigger and smarter and much more advanced than fleas, but we are vulnerable to the same type of conditioning. A person's capacity to envision can also have a lid. It's invisible too. It's held in place by their beliefs of what is and isn't possible.

Before my lunch with Bob, I couldn't see that I could be doing far more to expand my business. I was wearing blinders. Thankfully, Bob ripped them off my face.

The practice of envisioning should never stop. It is so critical for leaders, because it requires being in a constant state of learning. The more a person adds to their wisdom and awareness, the more perspectives they can use to enhance their visions.

In 1951, the mountaineer William Hutchison Murray published a book called the *The Scottish Himalayan Expedition*. In it he wrote the following, which has become one of the most quoted discourses on vision:

> *Until one is committed, there is hesitancy, the chance to draw back, always ineffectiveness. Concerning all acts of initiative (and creation), there is one elementary truth, the ignorance of which kills countless ideas and splendid plans: That the moment one definitely commits oneself, then Providence moves too.*
>
> *All sorts of things occur to help one that would never otherwise have occurred. A whole stream of events issues from the decision, raising in one's favor all manner of unforeseen incidents and meetings and material assistance, which no man could have dreamt would have come his way. I have learned a deep respect for one of Goethe's couplets: Whatever you can do, or dream you can, begin it. Boldness has genius, power, and magic in it.*

I love that quote. You might too. But most of us underestimate just how much easier it gets when we seek to go bold. There are four rules I've observed that magnify your ability to be bold with your visions.

Often we hear people talk about the Buddha nature of visions. To go within and practice transcendent practices like creative visualization. I love these. But there is a badass nature to vision as well.

To bring the badass into your vision means to never play small, and to be bold about the mark you want to leave in the world. It has to do with embracing the four tactics of envisioning that I've laid out below.

THE FOUR TACTICS OF ENVISIONING

1. The Bigger Your Vision, the Easier It Gets
2. Always Speak of Your Project Ten Years Ahead
3. Give Yourself Permission to Fail
4. Be Audacious, But Not Fluffy

Let's go deeper in each.

Tactic #1: The Bigger Your Vision, the Easier It Gets

People tend to assume that bigger visions are harder to reach and they have a higher probability of failure. Not always true.

When I was part of the Innovation Board for the XPRIZE Foundation, I got to know many of America's foremost visionaries and billionaires—from Peter Diamandis to Anousheh Ansari to Naveen Jain. Here is what they drilled into me:

The BIGGER the vision, the EASIER it gets.

Let me explain how Naveen Jain trained me on this. Naveen has founded multiple billion-dollar companies. And when we met first met, he had just created Viome, the gut microbiome testing company that is revolutionizing medicine.

While scaling Viome to a $500 million valuation in two years he was also selected to receive $2.7 BILLION from NASA to send robots to the moon via Moon Express, another one of his companies. His prior company Infospace was first to realize the power of mobile phones and achieved market cap of over $35 billion.

This is not a guy with small dreams. Naveen explained it like this and I scribbled down his advice on my notepad. *Note:* I am writing this exactly in Naveen's words. He said this in a very poetic way. Naveen speaks with the intensity of a mad scientist and the wisdom of a Zen monk. He told me . . .

When you do something audacious, it becomes easier.
Because you get the best people to join you.
The problem you're solving is worth solving!
You have the magnets.
And you get the *money*.
Because then investors call.
And then you tell them, you don't need their money.
Now like a bull they charge!
So, sell the benefit to humanity.
Cult leaders say *loyalty lies with me*,
But entrepreneurs say *loyalty lies with the cause*.

This is why great leaders are expert inspirers. Naveen is one of the greatest visionary thinkers I know. And one aspect I appreciate about him is that he started with humble roots as an immigrant from India who came to the United States with nothing.

His book *Moonshots* is about expanding visions so big that the ideas themselves launch people into action. "Impossible ideas become *more* possible," he said.

The fact of the matter is, a big idea is just way more exciting than a small one. People want to take action on it. And if they are constantly reminded about the vision, and regularly induced into a state of inspiration, then hurdles shrink and problems are approached with curiosity and not fear.

There's a thrilling momentum that builds in teams when an outlandish vision is pitched to solve a problem.

"If Viome's mission was to build an app to help find a roommate, no one would care," he explained.

"Instead, Viome's vision is to make illness a choice."

This vision rallied brilliant scientists to his cause. The smartest people in the world want to work on big problems. The United States federal government even licensed technology to Viome. This is because the company has an agenda to solve a huge global issue. This is how Moon Express, his space exploration company, came to team up with NASA too. Naveen decided that it was time America went back to the moon.

Impossible is a state of mind. "When one person believes an outcome is impossible, it's not just impossible for them, it becomes impossible for other people," said Naveen.

Recall the fleas in the jar. Beliefs are self-fulfilling prophecies. If you say something can't be achieved, no action will be taken. And you will prove that it cannot be achieved. You put an invisible lid on your own jar.

As Naveen explains it, to create inspiring visions that pull people, a leader must think from abundance. Surprisingly experts can be quite the Debbie Downers. They tend to use too much of their logical mind. They can come from a place of thinking that they know everything and refuse to consider what they don't know.

Naveen says, "The less you know, the better the chances you have to succeed. When you become an expert, you become an incrementalist."

To conceive a vision, it is important to disengage from logic. This helps you escape any constraints that may already be programmed into you. (Note: This is also why the acceleration and navigation technique you'll learn in Chapter 9 is so effective.)

TACTIC #2: ALWAYS SPEAK OF YOUR PROJECT TEN YEARS AHEAD

I alluded to this in previous chapters. To truly move forward fast and attract the right people, always speak not of what you're working on now, but what you're planning on building in ten years.

In 2014 when I launched Mindvalley Academy, an online website for personal growth courses, I didn't say that we were "an online publisher of personal growth content." That would be too obvious. It was what we were then. Instead I spoke of what we planned to be—that we were *transforming global education*.

Our website in 2014 said this:

> *Mindvalley builds companies that revolutionize education, through mediums that range from digital publishing, online learning, mobile and web apps, content, events and more. We stand for ideas that allow people to unleash their full potential and live healthier and happier lives through innovation in learning and education for all ages.*

The site also listed our current projects. But, most important, it listed what we planned to do. We listed our plans to launch a university in 2017, a new learning technology based on community learning, and even a health division. We also mentioned that we'd be training governments and Fortune 500 companies on health and wellness by 2017 (four years out).

They were mere dreams. Truthfully, I had no idea how to accomplish any of them. But not knowing the *how* is irrelevant. Get your mind focused on the *what* and *why* and speak of your vision as if it's on its way. Thinking like this often becomes a self-fulfilling prophecy. The money, people, and clients who believe in your dreams come to you. People are attracted to boldness.

These crazy people who join you will help expand your mission, and it all amplifies exponentially. But, if you describe what you do, you attract people who just facilitate the functions of their job.

By 2017 we launched our university—Mindvalley University—just as stated. We launched our health division and the next year we received our first corporate clients and trained our first government.

A few of our goals missed the deadline. Our community-based learning platform, called Quest, failed in 2014 and 2015. But in 2016 we pivoted and found a way to make it thrive. It became 90 percent of our revenue.

These were bold goals. And I had no idea if we'd get there. But by thinking bold and speaking of the future as if it's inevitable you move faster than if you choose to play small and be stuck in the present.

The takeaway? Speak not of what you're doing now, but what you plan to do.

Remember, when explaining SpaceX Elon Musk spoke about his future plans of colonizing Mars even though they were a decade or more ahead. This ability to speak boldly and envision the future helped him attract the best minds on the planet to figure out the *how* for him.

To effectively articulate your ten-years-ahead vision, you need to play a little mental game and ask yourself: "If I magnify my company a thousand times, what would it look like?"

If I take Mindvalley where we are today and I magnify it a thousand times we would have one billion people globally studying transformational education, and learning how to be healthier, wiser, and more spiritual. We will likely be used in Fortune 100 companies across the world, and in every schooling system across the planet, teaching young children practices of mindfulness, self-esteem, and teaching adults conscious parenting. That's one billion people living their best life.

Now, after magnifying it, consider the opposite. What would the world be like if your company did not exist? If you didn't do what you seek to do?

What if Mindvalley, for instance, did not exist? Human beings are still stressed out. Kids are learning the same crap they're learning right now. Companies are continuing to operate like factories. And 85 percent of people around the world are continuing to hate their jobs.

When you make the comparison, it's easy to see why *you do what you do* is the difference between you not existing and you existing times 1,000 percent.

> *Remember: Don't describe what you do today. Describe what you're going to do in ten years. Be humble and admit that there's a chance of failure. But talk boldly of what you aim to do.*

Now, how do you balance speaking ten years ahead and also being focused on your goals for the quarter or year, so your team has clarity?

I'm a big fan of the process of OKRs (Objectives and Key Results) used by companies like Google and Intel. My bible is the book *Measure What Matters* by John Doerr. John suggests that when setting goals for your business or team you create TWO distinct types of goals (or as he calls them "objectives"): *committed* and *aspirational*.

At Google, for which John Doerr was an early adviser, he used these objectives, as described in his book:

> *Committed objectives* *are tied to Google's metrics: product releases, bookings, hiring, customers. Management sets them at the company level, employees at the departmental level. In general, these committed objectives—such*

as sales and revenue goals—are to be achieved in full (100 percent) within a set time frame.

***Aspirational objectives** reflect bigger-picture, higher-risk, more future-tilting ideas. They originate from any tier and aim to mobilize the entire organization. By definition, they are challenging to achieve. Failures—at an average rate of 40 percent—are part of Google's territory.*

Now, here is the last part that trips people up. If I told you I knew of a company that fails on 40 percent of all its goals, you'd think it was a mess. Yet this is what happens at Google. It's not a mess, though. It's a unique approach to failure espoused by Google founder Larry Page. And it's an idea I brought into Mindvalley with phenomenal results. This is the essence of Tactic #3.

TACTIC #3: GIVE PERMISSION TO FAIL

Larry Page is a fascinating guy. I looked up to his leadership style because of what he has accomplished at Google. But there's another reason. We graduated from the same university (University of Michigan, with degrees in electrical engineering and computer science) and while there both attended a strange little summer camp called Leadershape whose motto was: "Lead with Integrity. Disregard the Impossible. Do Something Extraordinary."

Page attended Leadershape in 1992 and I attended in 1996. It was an influential part of both our lives. In his 2009 University of Michigan commencement address Page shared what he learned from Leadershape:

When I was here at Michigan, I had actually been taught how to make dreams real! I know it sounds funny, but that is what I learned in a summer camp converted into a training program called Leadershape. Their slogan is to have a "healthy disregard for the impossible." That program encouraged me to pursue a crazy idea at the time.

I think it is often easier to make progress on mega-ambitious dreams. I know that sounds completely nuts. But, since no one else is crazy enough to do it, you have little competition . . . The best people want to work the big challenges. That is what happened with Google . . . What is the one-sentence summary of how you change the world? Always work hard on something uncomfortably exciting!

This idea, "Always work on something uncomfortably exciting," is the essence of this next rule. The key word there is *uncomfortable*. But to do so, you need to give yourself permission to fail.

And so at Google, Larry and his team developed a model for how to balance the fine line between speaking in the future years ahead and being focused on your goals for the quarter or year so you have clarity. Here is what he preaches:

50 percent of your goals should have a 50 percent rate of failure.

Let's break that down. This means that when you set a list of goals (OKRs), half of them should basically be a coin-flip. This means (if you do the math), at any given point you're only attaining 60 to 80 percent of your goals.

At Google the failure rate is 40 percent. Larry Page created this model by design. It allows visionary leaders to experiment and set bold goals, knowing that there is no shame or loss if they don't achieve them. While Google fails often, it also produces incredible hits like Gmail and YouTube and Google Photos.

See, we often get goals wrong. We think it's about attaining them all. And we think failure is a bad thing. We have to change our brains to accept what I now call the 50-50 rule: 50 percent of your goals should have a 50 percent rate of failure. Only then can you truly be bold. Bruce Lee said it best:

> *A goal is not always meant to be reached, it often serves simply as something to aim at.*

So remember, give yourself permission to fail. And structure your goals and your team's goals so that the target accomplishment rate is actually only 60 to 80 percent. It sounds counterintuitive. But it works.

When I see at Mindvalley that we've met 80 percent or more of our goals for the quarter, I know we've been playing too small. And this brings us to Tactic #4. As you set these big goals and give permission to fail, be sure to not set "fluffy" intangible goals.

TACTIC #4: BE AUDACIOUS, BUT NOT FLUFFY

I stood in awe, taking in the dreams posted on a giant vision board in the hallway of a conference I was speaking at. At the top of the board, it said: "My Vision" in large type.

Attendees from over fifty countries had written their visions for the future on sticky notes and tacked them to the board. It was incredible to see how most were focused on serving humanity.

- My vision is to spread happiness around the world.
- My vision is to create a healthier world.
- My vision is to transform parenting.
- My vision is to build a million-dollar business.

I was impressed by the big bold hearts of the people attending.

But I noticed one striking theme. The visions written on the notes were what I would call "fluffy." Their intent was amazing, but none of them were written in a way where the language was actionable. People who write inactionable visions are what author and entrepreneur Peter Thiel calls "Indefinite Optimists." He popularized the label in his brilliant book *Zero to One*. An Indefinite Optimist trusts that the world will get better, but they have no idea how that will happen. They simply keep their fingers crossed. They wait for someone else to step up and do something.

He also defined another term: "Definite Optimist." These people are leaders who think audaciously and follow through. They choose to have a say in how their vision will turn out. They put themselves in charge and help make their vision a reality. They also set amazing multidecade goals to radically transform the world.

An Indefinite Optimist would say: "My dream is to transform education."

But the Definite Optimist would say: "My dream is to transform education. And here are my four OKRs on how I plan to do it."

For any vision to move forward, it must be actionable. First, the conceiver has to really believe in it. They have to be inspired themselves. But there is an element of practicality involved. There must be a measurable end goal. Similar to how we approach sports. When you play a sport and you win, there is an end goal.

So if you were trying to change education, you'd need to take that overriding goal and break it down. I use the concept of OKRs.

How do we get bold with our ideas without getting "fluffy"?

Step 1: It starts with writing down your CORE PURPOSE

An example of this is Mindvalley's Core Purpose: "To create the biggest rise in human consciousness our species has ever experienced by 2038 through the transformation of spirituality, politics, education, work, and parenting."

Step 2: Break Your Core Purpose Down into
Aspirational Objectives
Mindvalley's Four OKRs exemplifies this step:

TO EXECUTE OUR CORE PURPOSE,
TWENTY YEARS FROM NOW WE WILL . . .

1. Create the best experience for human transformation
2. Make Mindvalley the biggest transformational organization globally
3. Make workplaces that make humans better and happier
4. Raise national consciousness through governments and education

But above alone is STILL foggy. You have to go further. Each aspirational OKR above needs to be broken down into *measurable results.* This is Step #3.

Step 3: Create Measurable Key Results for Ten Years,
Three years, One Year, and One Quarter
Let's look at OKR 3 above: "Make workplaces that make humans better and happier."

This is an aspirational objective. It talks about our desire to change the nature of work to make work a place where we can thrive as human beings. In short, taking the ideas in this book and helping them get to billions of people everywhere.

We take that OKR and turn it into a series of Key Results to accomplish for various timelines that are important to us.

I like to start with a ten-year vision, and then break it down to

- three years
- one year
- one quarter

This is what it looks like:

THREE-YEAR VISION: BY JAN 2022

1. Be part of every company in the Fortune 500.
2. Shift the culture of ten thousand companies worldwide.

ONE-YEAR VISION: BY JAN 2020

1. Get into two hundred businesses with under five hundred employees.
2. Sign seven multinationals.

ONE-QUARTER VISION: Q3 2019

1. Complete and submit manuscript of this book
2. Launch new app features for Mindvalley for Business and have one thousand paying customers.

Notice how every item there is precisely measurable. This gives clarity. And it gives focus because we typically only list three to five OKRs per timeframe (it's important to set no more than three to five OKRs per timeframe).

If you find this idea of OKRs interesting, I created a two-hour talk on the subject that will guide you through setting your own OKRs. It's on the "Mindvalley Talks" YouTube channel. Visit mindvalley.com/badass to get the video link.

Once you embrace envisioning at your workplace, many things will change. But one big shift will be the clash between people who naturally think years ahead and people who are focused on what they need to do today. Both types are needed in a healthy team. But only one type, the visionary, should be leading the team. I learned this the hard way.

The Art of Visionary Leadership

In 2017 I realized I was skipping our weekly management meetings. These were important meetings where the key managers of Mindvalley would come together to talk about their teams, their progress, performance issues, and more.

They were important. But I was beginning to find them boring and a waste of my time. I thought I was the only one. Then I noticed many of the most brilliant people on my team were also skipping these meetings.

I stopped several of my managers one day and asked them why. "I'm not getting anything useful from these," one said.

"I have my product to build and my team is kicking ass. I don't want to hear other managers whine about their nonperformers or go in circles debating things I'm fine for HR to just decide. Just let me build my product."

They were right. Innovation at Mindvalley, which had been our lifeblood, had started to slow down, and I was concerned. Some of our teams were creating and pushing the company forward, while other teams were stagnating. There was a drive missing from these teams.

I realized what was going on. We had made a mistake in our company. We had begun to select managers for their ability to *manage* a team. But not for their ability to *lead* a team.

The two are very different. Leadership, you see, is not about management. It's about building a team so inspired by the work they do that they don't need to be managed. Steve Jobs said it best:

"The greatest people are self-managing. They don't need to be managed. Once they know what to do, they'll go figure out how to do it....What they need is a common vision. And that's what leadership is ... leadership is, is having a vision, being able to articulate that so the people around you can understand it and getting a consensus on a common vision."

At Mindvalley, we had made a mistake. We put people who were managers, not visionary thinkers, in charge of teams. And in some cases, when a visionary was in charge of the team, they were so bogged down with the nitty-gritty of management that they hardly had time for the vision.

I realized that many of the team leaders were not focused on innovation, new technologies, or changing the world. Instead they were focused on insignificant, sometimes petty situations that didn't matter in the grand scheme. In August 2017, I decided to do something about that. I flipped the leadership of half the teams at Mindvalley. I made it very clear that the people who run our teams have to be visionary thinkers. It led to a major shuffle. I promoted some people. A number of people left. A few changed roles. In the end, I gained several brilliant visionaries who are now leading our teams.

And if the team was big enough, I didn't want that leader being bogged down by management duties, so I'd give them a manager to take care of the necessary aspects of management. But the leader of the team was the person who pointed the way forward. And for that the quality of visionary leadership was key.

Within one year the company transformed. By August of 2019, we had grown close to 70 percent in revenue year on year. It was our biggest year of growth in a long while. Furthermore, all the indicators of employee well-being shot up. Our eNPS score, which measures employee satisfaction, went up by almost 50 percent. Retention also went up significantly. People were staying longer and thriving more.

Dov Seidman describes it bluntly in his book *HOW*. He calls it "Envisioning the Future Disposition." It's the idea of true leaders being future focused and not short-term focused. Here is what Seidman wrote in his book:

> *Having a leadership disposition means mentally envisioning a better future for yourself, the tasks at hand, and those with whom you labor. Leadership starts with vision, and leaders envision every moment. You could envision a feature in a technological platform, or envision a whole new product, or*

simply envision a way to make someone else's day a little bit better. You can create a new vision or embrace someone else's and make it your own.

If you don't have a vision, then you fall outside the lens of HOW and are a short-term manager: Task-oriented, obedient, and obsessed with and limited to what you can see right under your nose. Short-term managers tend to be reactive by nature and find themselves putting out fires more often than they light the beacons that show the way. It is a defensive posture and worries more about appeasing others than about engaging them.

The short-term manager assumes that people need rules, procedures, oversight, to do well. This is sometimes true. But when you are already choosing great people and have the right values in place, people will self-manage. What they need from you is vision and clarity. And when your vision is bold and aspiring, it's like lighting rocket fuel under your team.

In her book *Powerful,* Patty McCord, who was the chief talent officer at Netflix from 1998 to 2012, writes: "Great teams are not created with incentives, procedures, and perks. They are created by hiring talented people who are adults and want nothing more than to tackle a challenge, and then communicating to them, clearly and continuously, about what the challenge is."

When you practice visionary leadership, the petty detailed stuff becomes less necessary, because people are driven by the vision. Visionaries who guide teams automatically remove obstacles.

And visionary leadership is addictive. It leads to all areas of an organization striving for excellence.

When I visited SpaceX in 2013 I got a glimpse of how visionary thinking extends from the leader across an entire organization. After meeting Elon we were invited to dine at the SpaceX diner for its employees. The diner was right at the entrance of the building, and above us towered the glass chambers that held "Mission Control," the room where Elon and his team watched the progress of the rockets they launched.

I was struck by the mesmerizing tiles on the floor of the diner. One of our hosts, a member of the SpaceX team, explained to us: "See those tiles? When Elon first came here he hated the tiles. They were the wrong color. They did not reflect light right. He made the builders rip out all the tiles and start all over again so he got them just right. He needed the tiles to reflect mission control at just the right angle."

Visionary leaders inspire excellence in every aspect of the company—yes, even kitchen tiles. When we made it a key principle in Mindvalley, other departments jumped in. Our office at that time in 2017 was beautiful. But it had been built in 2009 and was due for an upgrade. I had hired a workspace experience designer by the name of Luke Anthony Myers to fill this role. Luke's job was to ensure that our office was upgraded to feel like a five-star working experience. Because of the ripples of visionary leadership echoing through the company, Luke embraced this concept. He set a goal to build a new workspace so gorgeous it would make *Inc.* magazine's list of Top Ten Most Beautiful Offices in the World.

He was given a budget, a mandate to create a gorgeous award-winning space, and freedom to dream, Luke teamed up with local interior design firms and architects. In December 2018 he unveiled our new office. It was amazing to see. Inspired by the Sagrada Familia, the Gaudí-designed cathedral in Barcelona, it used colored glass and steel to create a modern space called the "Temple of Light."

They innovated on everything from floor space to desk design. And in August 2019 it made the *Inc.* magazine 2019 list of Top Ten Most Beautiful Offices in the World. The day this happened Luke came to me with tears in his eyes. "Did you know that three years ago to this month I was homeless in Melbourne?" he said. "Thanks for letting me dream so big." I'd had no idea that he'd been homeless. And I was so proud of what he achieved.

This is what visionary leadership does to an organization. It allows people to unleash their best selves and provide their greatest work. This is why to this day, my senior leadership team is chosen primarily for their ability to envision the future.

Inspiring Future Leaders

Visionary leaders inspire, engage, and help grow the people they lead. True leaders implant visions in the minds of others. It's a nuanced skill but when done right can be truly transformative. The best visionary leaders get others to dream as boldly as themselves. This was essentially what Bob Proctor did for me. And in 2019 I witnessed how another visionary leader did the same.

If a visionary entrepreneur and well-known stunt man like Richard Branson challenged you to do something insane—would you do it? This happened to me one Thursday night, while attending a mastermind on Necker Island. Branson casually made an announcement at dinner that caught us all off guard. He clinked his fork to his glass three times, stood up, and when the room quieted he declared: "I'll be up on the beach tomorrow at six a.m. I'll be swimming three miles (five kilometers) from Necker Island to Mosquito Island. I'd love to invite anyone interested enough to join me."

At 6 a.m. I was on the beach. Branson had amassed a team of six other loonies. Swimming is not a strength of mine. I figured I'd stay safely on the boat and tag along. I loved photography and thought I'd play photographer. I hadn't swum in years.

But then Richard said, "Look at that, guys."

A gorgeous double rainbow appeared over Mosquito Island. It was as if the Universe was teasing me. I saw it as a sign to get over my bullshit fears. So I jumped into the deep, quite literally.

Three Miles. Five kilometers. Two hours. And I suck at swimming.

I figured I couldn't die. Richard Branson is like a superhero. Nothing kills him. The guy is notorious for death-defying stunts. He has had seventy-six near-death experiences. And Richard, who's sixty-nine, coolly backstroked the whole way when he realized he'd forgotten his goggles. The way in which he approached things gave us no excuse.

Anyway, we made the swim. I managed 1.5 miles and I rested on the boat for part of the way. The final kilometers in the water navigating the rocks approaching Mosquito were the toughest.

The winning swimmer, who was three hundred yards ahead of any man, was my friend Stephanie Farr. Steph crushed it. We eventually reached Mosquito Island, where we were greeted by Richard's family and served a gourmet breakfast. We thought the swim from one island to the other was insane enough, but Richard, like all good leaders, won't let you quit while you're ahead. Richard convinced Stephanie to attempt to swim BACK, against currents, all the way to Necker. No one had done this before. Yet with Richard's "peer pressure," she did it.

What impressed me was just HOW Richard inspired Steph to do it.

Before eating breakfast, Branson toasted to Steph's accomplishment. He congratulated her, thanked her, insisted on taking a picture together. Then he said: "I can't wait to see how you'll do on the way back."

Branson was creating the future before it happened. He was baiting Steph into a challenge that would have her experience what she could really do in a new way. He expanded her concept of what was possible. And he showed he believed in her. Steph agreed to swim back. She went on to become the first human being we know to swim between Necker and Mosquito Islands both ways.

This is the art of envisioning the future for another person, and it's powerful. There's a name for it too: the Presupposed Close.

He presupposed that she would take on the challenge and succeed at it. And by doing this, he made the picture for her of herself completing this challenge so real in her mind that she had no other choice but to say yes.

I know Steph, and I know she was glad she said yes. It was just this small interaction that reminded me of one of the most powerful lessons: Great leaders don't let you get complacent or comfortable. They push you to push yourself. And in their presence you do things you once thought impossible.

In Closing: What Is Your Vision?

As you go on your path to figure out your vision, I'd like to share with you some words from my friend Lisa Nichols. Lisa is one of the most inspiring speakers I've ever seen on stage. She's a brilliant author and was the second black woman founder to take a company public.

At one of my events, Lisa delivered a rousing spoken-word poetry piece on the power of living your vision even when others try to dim your light. It touched me so deeply I got permission from Lisa to share it here. I'll leave this text here as a powerful closing reminder for you to always stay true to your vision.

LISA NICHOLS ON SHINING BRIGHT

So maybe the world didn't give you permission to be here, but you didn't ask for it either. Sometimes you have to stop asking for permission, and instead just give the world notice.

I invite you to give the world notice that you're coming. Give the world notice that you've been here.

Give the world notice that you played polite long enough—now it's time to play full out.

Give the world notice that unapologetic just showed up.

Give the world notice that nonnegotiable just showed up.

Give the world notice that if they can't handle your light— you're no longer going to dim your light.

THEY can put on some shades.

Because when you become that bold, when you become that audacious, when you become that unapologetic, all of a sudden, you become INFECTIOUS.

All of a sudden, just the mere glimmer of you, the mere glimpse of you, just being in your hemisphere, and your atmosphere, and your zip code causes something to happen to me because I'm in proximity to YOU.

And then you become absolutely aware of the true assignment on your life, that you are here to save us.

You are here to inspire us by the way you walk,

by the way you rise above your own uncertainty,

by the way you push past your religious conversation, your cultural conversation, your economic conversation, your gender conversation,

by the way you show up and say, "How can I serve humanity?"

By the way you recognize that your human spirit is unbreakable,

your human spirit is unshakable,

your human spirit is unstoppable.

Your human spirit is simply asking for you to give it a command.

Who will we serve next?

What will we do,

and what mountain will we require to bow down?

And when you get that and you operate with that knowing, all of a sudden, you become contagious, and people just want to be in your space, and share your oxygen.

Because you make them believe again.

So what is YOUR vision?

Chapter Summary

MODELS FOR REALITY

There is a term I coined, a term I refer to as *the Beautiful Destruction*. It simply means: Sometimes you have to destroy a part of your life that is merely *good,* to allow what is *truly great* to enter. Great visionaries adopt this idea.

And remember Bob Proctor's rule: "The question is not: Are you worthy to reach your goals? The question is: Are your goals worthy enough of you?"

Bold visions are inspiring, motivating, and propel people into action. So think big. Envision always. This is the act of conceiving an idea. And it's how all things start. It's the first step in giving the form*less* some form. Also remember that a small vision can limit an entire team. And so, there are four tactics to apply to envisioning:

1. The Bigger Your Vision, the Easier It Gets
2. Always Speak of Your Project Ten Years Ahead
3. Give Yourself Permission to Fail
4. Be Audacious, But Not Fluffy

Naveen Jain says: "When you do something audacious it becomes easier. Because you get the best people to join you. The problem you're solving is worth solving!" So be bold. Be a Definite Optimist, a person who thinks audaciously and follows through.

This includes speaking about what you're building ten years into the future. When you do this, you might find it becomes a self-fulfilling prophecy. Actions line up with what you believe you're going to achieve.

Be committed to the overarching outcome. Failure is inevitable. It's good. Failure is your feedback mechanism. Always use what you learn from failure to your advantage and stay committed to the end goal. You might need to pivot to get there, but embrace failure.

Goals must be achievable, so be audacious but not fluffy. Always reverse-engineer your goals. Start with the fluffy dream that excites you, then bring it back to reality. Ask yourself, What could I do now to move toward that goal? Plan in this way and make sure targets are measurable. The OKR system is one useful method for chunking down big goals into small near-future targets.

Lastly, remember that the best visionaries get others to dream as boldly as them. Use the Presupposed Close for this. Speak to another as if they've already achieved the dream you envision they are bold enough to follow through on. It might surprise you how truly remarkable humans are.

Systems for Living

EXERCISE 1: BRING ANY VISION TO REALITY

Step 1: Go back to the Vivid Vision you created in Chapter 2. Now start considering the bold milestones you want to get to in order to achieve what you envision. Think ten years out. Ask yourself: "If I magnify my company [or project or idea] by one thousand, what would it look like?" Build a list.

Step 2: Reverse-engineer your list. Consider your future, then reflect on your present. *What do you need to do first to move toward what you want?* It may help you to further explore the OKR system so you create a solid action plan. This will help you see a pathway to actually achieve what you dream about. Refer to the above sections Tactic #2–Tactic #4 to understand how OKRs work. For a ninety-minute crash course on OKR, get on YouTube and search for "Vishen OKRs."

Step 3: Share what you plan to achieve everywhere and with everyone. Get obsessed and excited about your goals. Speak to other people with the level of excitement as if you've already achieved your goals. You'll attract the people you need that will help you make your ideas a reality. You'll find your goals are self-fulfilling prophecies.

Step 4: Take action. Actions produce results. No action produces no results. So take action. And remember, failure is inevitable. But it's good. Use failure as a feedback mechanism.

CHAPTER 8

OPERATE AS ONE UNIFIED BRAIN

It's about communication. It's about honesty. It's about treating people in the organization as deserving to know the facts. You don't try to give them half the story. You don't try to hide the story. You treat them as true equals, and you communicate and you communicate and communicate.

—Louis V. Gerstner Jr., former CEO of IBM

To tackle a truly grand vision you need to have many brains; you need a team of people to act as one unified superbrain. For the first time, we have incredible tools for this. Yet most teams work inside of age-old collaboration systems. When you learn to create a unified brain you move with amazing speed and prowess.

In the summer of 2019, I sat with my chief human resources officer. "You know. Kiel, I don't think I want to be a CEO anymore," I said.

Ezekiel, or Kiel as I call him, has an intuitive knack for reading the pulse of an organization. "I've been thinking the same." He smiled.

That was the day I removed that label from my name. I told my team to stop calling me CEO. I tossed away my business cards. I updated my social media accounts. I asked everyone to think of me as the Founder of Mindvalley.

Roles are made up anyway. Humans are information processors; we are "meaning-making machines." Titles are merely useful tools for interpreting, organizing, and sorting information quickly. *Mother. Father. Senator. Colonel. Rabbi. Teacher. Principal.* These are simply words that describe a collection of attributes. They also inform people of how to act. And others on how to behave around them.

When two people work at a human-to-human level, respecting but at the same time disregarding their levels of status, the ceiling of what's possible expands exponentially.

While the CEO label explained my role to the world, it was destructive in my company. Many of my colleagues separated me from the pack. I was perceived as *not like them.* The interpretation of a label affected how people treated me, as well as how I acted in response to them, since relationships are reciprocal.

If a person's general beliefs about CEOs were *"CEOs are too busy to speak to me"* or *"CEOs are jerks"* or *"CEOs care more about business than their people,"* that rationale informed their behavior. In all these cases they would be more inclined to avoid, resent, and distance themselves from me.

So it didn't surprise me that when I changed my title to Founder my relationships transformed. And the level of innovation, joy, and fun at Mindvalley exploded.

Most people perceive Founders as more relatable than CEOs. The name itself implies rags-to-riches stories of surviving years of struggle with dashed dreams and unexpected successes on the rise to the top. Every start-up goes through near-death moments. The title change made me appear more human, though in actuality, my behaviors, values, and beliefs hadn't changed at all.

When I wrote this chapter, I googled the phrases "CEO Story" and

"Founder Story" to compare how the media frames each one. For "CEO Story" this was the top news result:

> *The CEO of NPM, a start-up that provides a crucial service to eleven million developers, has resigned after a year-long tenure marked by controversy.*

It was a story of scandal. A CEO had to resign after being criticized for the dismissal of employees involved in unionization efforts. Now, here's the search result at number one for "Founder Story":

> *Netflix cofounder Marc Randolph on the company's earliest days, the streaming wars, and moving on.*

It was a story of grit and hope. It showed how Netflix went from a scrappy start-up that was barely making it to a company worth $130 million.

So do we have a CEO? Well, I still make the chief decisions, but in actuality we don't have one. Instead what we have is a *Unified Brain*. Each person operates like a neuron sending signals back and forth. But we function as one moving entity. Let me explain why it's such a remarkable way to work.

Idea Sex and Brain Coupling

Ideas have the same effect on the brain as happy drugs. When the brain is in a state of inspiration, it releases a surge of dopamine and serotonin. This is why conceiving brilliant ideas feels incredible. And sharing them is even better. The experience is like being a kid at an ice cream counter. You ask for a chocolate scoop and the clerk asks if you might like to add a second one. So seizing upon the brilliant idea, you ask for strawberry. Now you have a chocolate strawberry combo of deliciousness that's just far better than what you had initially envisioned.

The modern term for this commingling of lightbulb thoughts is *idea sex*. Idea sex is when two thinkers come together with separate ideas and meld them together to form one new superior idea.

When people share ideas and hit on the right idea, they tap into an experience of awe that's difficult to put in words. However, there is a name for this phenomenon and it's *brain coupling*. Here is how the Emmy-nominated host of National Geographic's hit TV series *Brain Games,* Jason Silva, explains it:

> We've all experienced that feeling when we're really connecting with somebody, right? You meet somebody new and they are really exciting and you find yourself hypnotized by their presence. You find them bewitching. And as you start to converse. As you share stories you feel like you come into this kind of synchronized kind of element. You feel connected. You feel like you're meshing. You feel like you're on the same vibe. You feel like you're on the same frequency.

These types of interactions are captivating and challenging to describe. But most of us have had them and would say they are very desirable. Neuroscientific research shows there is a reason for this. When two people get fired up on one idea, their brains do too. One study hooked people up to fMRI machines to uncover what was happening in their brains. It revealed that they sync together. They are literally on the same frequency.

"This is what we should look for when we connect with anybody. Like, 'Hey, you want to brain couple with me . . . you want to put our brains together because that's what I'm interested in?' Skip the small talk and go straight to that inner subjective rapture," Silva says.

This is why the Unified Brain model is so effective. And it's far more enjoyable. It's invigorating to work in an environment like this. Anyone can create a Unified Brain work environment with others. It doesn't even have to be at work. This model can be extended to families, community groups, friends, and nonprofits. So now let me show you how it works and how to build yours.

The Power of the Unified Brain

Technology is evolving fast. Yet in most companies we still operate like we're in the 2000s.

One Sunday morning in 2019, I experienced how rapidly technology is accelerating. I'd just purchased an Apple HomePod for my room. My daughter Eve had learned to ask it to play songs and tell jokes. (Surprisingly, Siri, the HomePod's AI, actually has a pretty good sense of humor.) But then, like all smart five-year-olds, Eve began to teach herself the true power of this technology. Eve learned how to ask Siri to send messages. Imitating Dad, she sent a message to the Mindvalley team.

So a group of my colleagues receive from their CEO at 8 a.m. on a Sunday the following message: "Tell me everything about UNICORNS!! Are they real? Really real?"

Several of my team members now think their CEO spends Sunday mornings high on drugs. I had to release a public statement: "It was Eve. For the record, I am not obsessed with unicorns. And I don't do drugs on Sunday morning. Thank you for your understanding."

But you see, technology is connecting people in mesmerizing ways. And it's completely changed the power we have to make decisions and share ideas.

At any given moment I'm in a conversation on my smartphone with 25 percent of the people at Mindvalley. This includes stakeholders, advisers, contract workers, and authors. In total, that's around four hundred people. I typically have a hundred messages to respond to on my Whats-App app from this network. That may sound crazy, but what happens next is unique.

I don't do phone calls anymore. I limit meetings. Most of my time "at work" is spent brainstorming and removing barriers so decisions get made. My job is to be an *accelerator* for idea flow so the business is always rapidly growing, evolving, and innovating.

Fewer meetings and no calls also means no wasted time. I have time to write, be with my kids, travel the world, and run a business with three hundred people, which grows over 50 percent year to year.

This is the essence of the Unified Brain model. My job is to make sure the experts across the organization get the data, connect, and have the information they need to make the best decisions.

To bring the Unified Brain model to your company, whether it's just you and you're making your first hire, or if you have a business with thousands of people, there are two steps:

1. **Break Hierarchy and Create the Right Beliefs**
2. **Introduce OODA**

Keep in mind that if you work for a larger organization you don't have to apply the Unified Brain model to the entire company. As a stealth leader you can bring this to a smaller team. You can bring these ideas into your relationships, families, and social groups too.

1. BREAK HIERARCHY AND CREATE THE RIGHT BELIEFS

Most of us are trained to operate inside an outdated chain of command where a worker reports to a superior and works in a team of similarly skilled colleagues. The first part of the Unified Brain model is to disrupt how people perceive hierarchy.

Most companies and people in them think that ideas have to flow via the usual chain of command. Sort of like this:

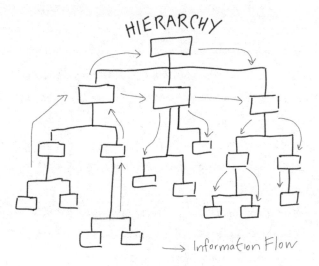

But idea flow needs to be free of company hierarchy. The proper model should look something like this:

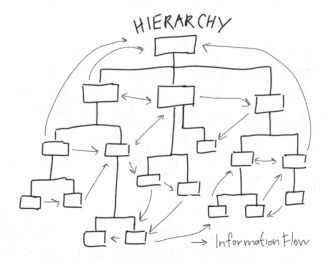

In his book *Creativity, Inc.*, Pixar president Ed Catmull explains how Pixar blurred the traditional lines between workers to unlock a higher level of collaboration, inspiration, and innovation. It involves precisely the act of teaching people that company hierarchy and idea hierarchy don't travel the same way. Catmull writes:

> *Because making a movie involves hundreds of people, a chain of command is essential . . .we had made the mistake of confusing the communication structure with the organizational structure. Of course an animator should be able to talk to a modeler directly, without first talking with his or her manager. So we gathered the company together and said: "Going forward, anyone should be able to talk to anyone else, at any level, at any time, without fear of reprimand."*
>
> *Communication would no longer have to go through hierarchical channels. The exchange of information was key to our business, of course, but I believed that it could—and frequently should—happen out of order, without people getting bent out of shape. People talking directly to one another, then letting the manager find out later, was more efficient than trying to make sure that everything happened in the "right" order and through the "proper" channels.*
>
> *This was a success in itself, but it came with an added and unexpected benefit: The act of thinking about the problem and responding to it was invigorating and rewarding. We realized that our purpose was not merely to build a studio that made hit films but to foster a creative culture that would continually ask questions.*

Just as Ed Catmull had noticed the hierarchy myth at Pixar slowing down idea flow, I noticed it happening at Mindvalley in 2014. In our case we were a smaller company with around one hundred employees. Our problem was that our people came from all across the world and brought with them their own unique cultural perceptions of hierarchy and beliefs about how to operate at work.

In 2014, I wrote a memo to my team on the importance of questioning beliefs. It's a practice I am obsessed with. It's a key element of expansion. Innovation doesn't happen easily when adhering to old ideas.

THE MEMO I WROTE TO MY TEAM

------------------ START OF MEMO --------------------

Sent: Nov 27 2014

Hi Team,

Beliefs are really interesting. We tend to believe ideas based on our assumptions. Or because they come from an authority figure telling what is true about the world.

And we do so, often without actually assessing these beliefs for ourselves.

The scientist Paul Marsden calls this "Memetics and Social Conditioning." It's a fascinating phenomenon which explains why we embrace religion, believe ideas about certain political figures, or take on national identities. Here is what Marsden writes:

> "The evidence shows that we inherit and transmit behaviors, emotions, beliefs and religions not through rational choice but contagion. When we are unsure of how to react to a stimulus or a situation, these theories suggest that we actively look to others for guidance and consciously imitate them."

Think about what Marsden is saying and how it applies to a company like Mindvalley. He's saying that when you're unsure of a situation you adopt *other people's ideas and beliefs.*

Every new hire joining Mindvalley experiences this. They adopt beliefs (true or untrue) about how to work here, how to interact with me, about perceived character traits of their managers or leaders. Problem is, many of their adopted beliefs have no validity in reality. There's no tangible evidence to back it up.

But what we believe to be TRUE, becomes true. All of us are creating our own reality. All the time. There are no exceptions. And here's what I learned recently.

So yesterday I had two coffee break meetings with new hires. We were discussing their experiences, their roles, how to grow in the company and more.

And one of them, Alexandra, said the following:

"When I came here I asked people if I could talk to you and they said, 'Vishen only spends his time with more experienced people because he's busy, he won't have time to talk to new hires.'"

and then

"I asked some people if I could complain to you about my bad experience with our Housing Relocation program and they said, 'Ha Good luck getting his time—he's super busy with bigger things.'"

All of this is kinda funny because it's the exact opposite of true reality.

1. Not only do I regularly meet with new hires, I memorize their 3 Most Important Questions and use this to help craft development programs for them.
2. I'm so concerned about housing I changed our HR policies on

Monday to make sure new hires don't go through bad housing situations while relocating here.

Yet Alexandria had been infected by really disempowering invalid beliefs about me. And if she wasn't more mature she might have acted on these beliefs and never asked me for coffee.

So let's all remember . . .

Human beings are complex entities. Unless you truly know me, you don't know me. Please never assume a behavior or character trait of anyone at Mindvalley that is disempowering to yourself. You won't do anyone any justice.

And worse, please don't infect the mind of others with disempowering beliefs. Assumptions are *dangerous*. When you have disempowered beliefs, challenge them. Ask that person for coffee. Share that idea. Speak up to voice your suggestions (suggestions and even complaints are not negative—they are merely info that help us become better).

A caveat: When you do this, know that you might get a "no" occasionally.

But *try again.*

I once asked a person (let's call her Belle) who had been at Mindvalley for several years why in years she'd never asked me to lunch until I specifically requested one with her. She said that she did once. But I was double booked and chose to have lunch with someone else (let's call him Duke) rather than her. So for TWO years she assumed I didn't care about her.

I had no memory of this. So I went back to my Google Calendar's history. I found out that I got double booked for lunch that day two years ago and chose Duke because he was going through a crisis situation and needed my help.

But for TWO years Belle held back asking me for lunch because she interpreted the situation in a way that was disempowering to herself. And all that time I would have loved to have lunch with her because I thought so highly of her. We finally did that lunch and had a great time. Note: Belle is still with us today after eight years and is one of our most loyal people.

Yet a simple assumption held her back.

Has this happened to you? If so, I don't blame you.

All of us carry insecurities in some way. When I was a teen, I was pimple-faced and legally blind with thick glasses. In my entire life from thirteen to seventeen I only went out with "friends" less than five times. I thought people found me ugly and boring so I never asked people to socialize with me. I had zero social skills and very little confidence. I believed I was unlikable.

And I acted in accordance to these beliefs.

I want you guys to know this because if you've been holding back from speaking your mind, or sharing a concern, or you've been complaining to yourself about a situation that truly matters, or if you just want career advice . . .

I CARE. We CARE. And we're here. And we'll make time.

Mindvalley is strong because we can have frank talks like this and build authentic relationships. Don't underestimate how much you matter or assume your managers won't have time for your concern or question.

And NEVER ever take on the disempowering beliefs of someone else. In fact, when you hear such a thing, correct them. Simply ask a question like: "Have you validated that belief with hard data science and study? Or is that a personal opinion clouded by Fundamental Attribution Error and one's own childhood insecurities projecting a character trait onto someone else?"

You get the idea ;-)

The simple rule to live by is this:

"If the belief makes me feel disempowered, unless it's backed by empirical scientific data, and not just on someone's opinion, I'm going to choose to ignore it and do what will empower me instead."

Your beliefs are your most important asset. Not your skills, nor your brains. But your beliefs. Believe the best things you can about the value of your work and your ideas. And believe the best things you can about your teammates and yourself.

What are you going to choose to believe?

—V

------------------ END OF MEMO ---------------------

I hope that memo helps you understand how important beliefs are in creating an environment of beautiful collaboration.

2. INTRODUCE OODA

OODA is one of the most game-changing ideas I've introduced into my workplace. I learned about it at a class in Singularity University while attending a series of lectures there on artificial intelligence and the brain.

OODA is short for: Observe-Orient-Decide-Act. It was developed by military strategist and United States Air Force colonel John Boyd.

In short, Colonel Boyd noticed that the BEST military pilots were also the ones wasting the most bullets. They missed more. But they also downed more enemy planes.

OODA is about making innovation accelerate and moving fast by optimizing two things:

> **First, it's about increasing the amount and rate of ideas shared.** You create systems where people can easily and quickly communicate to speed up idea flow.
>
> **Second, it's about speeding up decision making.** You act on imperfect ideas. The idea is that while many of those decisions miss, it's better than aiming for 100 percent hits and moving slow.

At Mindvalley we take OODA to another level with our own unique spin. OODA has dramatically simplified my life. I now spend less than half my time in the office. While I'm on the road, or traveling, or writing, I can communicate with my team and coordinate ideas and execution with surprising speed and ease. You can too if you learn these tools. It applies not just to leaders but to anyone in any company who wants to play bold, innovate rapidly, and execute fast.

OODA removed some twenty hours of weekly meetings from my calendar. And it allows me to run my company on my smartphone using nothing else but WhatsApp. I only spend 30 percent of my work time on an actual computer. Seventy percent is done using nothing but my iPhone and WhatsApp. It allows the Unified Brain to function like a charm.

To best understand the OODA loop I want to share another memo that I send to my team every year as a reminder.

MEMO 2: THE POWER OF OODA

------------------ START OF MEMO --------------------

Dear team.

Mindvalley has a unique element that will break some people. And let others shine. This memo is about that.

If you want to win at Mindvalley, please read this and let it sink in. Because we WANT you to win. YOUR win is our collective win.

But first some statistics:

1. Mindvalley revenues will grow between 60 to 75 percent this year from the previous year. For a company that is over ten years old, this is very impressive growth.
2. Much of the businesses we have today did not exist for more than twelve months ago. 80 percent of our revenue today comes from products that did not exist twenty-four months ago.

Now, here is the lesson:

The OODA Loop and Rapid Change

If you understand this concept you will help us move MUCH faster as a team. And make your job more fun because you move into a realm where you are co-creating on projects versus slowly plucking away at them by yourself. What I shared tends to get resistance from new hires who come from traditional workplaces because it disrupts ideas of "work" drilled into many of us by society.

If you don't understand this, you're more likely to:

1. Feel your work got trashed because change made it obsolete.
2. Not know how to suggest ideas and thus feel less important.
3. Wonder why some people get promoted fast and you lag behind.

First some background:

In 2017, I noticed that since we shifted from email to Slack for more of our communication, it's actually freed up around forty-five minutes of my time every day. I attribute this to a reduction in email threads and faster decision making.

Then I started using WhatsApp and in particular, its audio feature. As I began to travel more I shifted solely to WhatsApp as my means of communication. This freed up another hour or so a day.

Then I learned another trick. And this freed up two hours a day. I stopped holding regularly scheduled meetings. And I stopped all scheduled phone calls. I started using the video and audio feature of WhatsApp to communicate with all our three hundred team members and over a hundred authors, clients, and vendors across the world. What would sometimes take a thirty-minute in-person meeting, I could reduce to three minutes of exchanging voicemails, video, or comments on WhatsApp.

But the main reason is not Slack or WhatsApp itself. It's this:

The Speed Up of Decision Making Cycles

I want you to consider the idea that the point of all our emails and meetings and phone calls and Slacks is merely to *make decisions*. If you can speed up the decision-making process, you move faster. But of course, speeding up the decision-making process can lead to occasional *wrong* decisions because not enough time is spent debating or analyzing them. How do you reconcile this?

I learned about this during a session at Singularity University in 2016 (see image below) during a class on artificial intelligence.

It's called the OODA loop.

Here's a pic of a diagram that explains it.

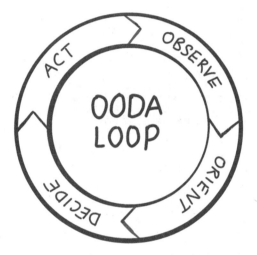

If you notice the image above you'll see that an OODA loop stands for the following:

- Observe
- Orient
- Decide
- Act

OODA was a model created by air force military strategist and USAF colonel John Boyd. Boyd applied the concept to the combat operations process, often at the strategic level in military operations.

Simply put, by following OODA, air force pilots were more likely to shoot down enemy planes.

The idea is simple. **ACT FAST—Even with Imperfect Knowledge.** In air force lingo this would mean:

- **Observe the enemy aircraft.**
- **Orient yourself.**
- **Decide your next move.**
- **ACT and fire!**

The OODA loops suggest that you win by moving fast. Overthinking something can actually be a competitive disadvantage. OODA is designed to avoid paralysis by analysis and to allow those pilots to make as many decisions as possible in a given timeframe.

Now, according to Wikipedia:

The OODA loop has become an important concept in litigation, business and military strategy. According to Boyd, decision-making occurs in a recurring cycle of observe-orient-decide-act. An entity (whether an individual or an organization) that can process this cycle quickly, observing and reacting to unfolding events more rapidly than an opponent, can thereby "get inside" the opponent's decision cycle and gain the advantage.

In summary:

The faster you can make decisions, learn from them, and evolve, the more likely you are to win.

But keep this in mind: The pilot flying the plane with a faster OODA loop will waste more bullets.

He's firing more.

He's missing more.

But he also downs more enemy aircraft.

BUT it's OKAY to waste bullets because this is what WINS the war.

I've heard people say:

"So much wastage happens at Mindvalley, we start something, then kill it."

"We run before planning well. And then the project goes wrong."

They are right. But these are wasting bullets. Wasting bullets is 100 percent correct, according to the OODA philosophy. Because you will *shoot down more enemy planes.*

The <u>pace</u> of innovation is the most important thing.

I don't care if we fail 40 to 50 percent of the time. Google fails that often too. According to Steven Levy in his book *In the Plex* Google fails at 40 percent of everything they start. (Remember the Google Glass or Google Plus?)

But by moving fast we learn, orient, adapt, and innovate faster than the competition.

Failure is completely OKAY. In fact, it's enshrined in our OKRs (50 percent of your OKRs must have a 50 percent rate of failure).

Failing is OKAY. But Being Slow is NOT.

Here's what OODA means to us.

#1. Do everything you can to speed up the Decision-Making Cycle

Eighty percent sure is better than 100 percent if it allows you to move faster. A team that can make five 80 percent sure decisions in a week toward a project is better than a team that can make one 100 percent sure decision.

What I'm noticing is that often we slow down because we cannot make decisions fast enough. Here are some examples:

a. If a split test is 90 percent winning after a week and you need another week to get to 95 percent, scrap the extra week and roll with the 90 percent sure test. Aim for SPEED.

b. Avoid email for important decisions. Use Slack. If you need me looped in, talk to me or use WhatsApp. The purpose of any email or Slack is nothing more than to close a decision loop. I'm not interested in how much you write. So short messages always appreciated. Again SPEED.

c. You'll notice I'm scheduling lots of one-hour brainstorms lately. These are to speed up decision making. We don't have to wait months to figure out how to create mobile optimized sales pages, or the perfect unsubscribe page. We can bring the smartest brains in one room and in one hour hammer out a pretty concrete strategy that's 80 percent there. But this gives us momentum to move faster.

This brings us to point #2 . . .

#2. Move Fast, Pivot, and Learn on the Go

Which diagram below seems to you like a better way to hit the goal?

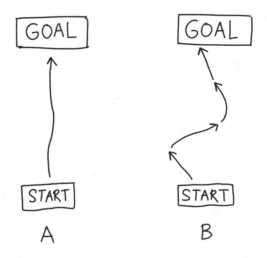

Obviously A, right?

Because with A you go straight for the goal in the shortest path. But in reality, you will never 100 percent know the right path to hit a goal. So in reality you need to MOVE fast and learn as you move. Thus B is the more accurate model of how companies (and the world) work.

A is taking months to launch a podcast because you want it perfect.

B is launching a podcast in one week and tweaking on the go toward perfection.

Always embrace B. It will deliver a better product faster.

To get the perfection of A you may need weeks of planning. B requires more on the groundwork—but you'll likely get there faster because you're *learning as you go*. This is the OODA loop.

So in summary:

Act with Imperfect Knowledge and pivot on the way.
When this happens, you will also create change.
Embrace this.

So how fast can YOU test and tweak ideas? Are you making decisions at 80 percent accuracy and learning fast or are you foolishly waiting for 95 percent accuracy and delaying your ability to deploy, test, and learn?

#3. Fail Fast. Fail Often. Learn from It.

Salim Ismail, the head of Singularity University, came to Malaysia to meet the government. He told me he advised the prime minister to launch a massive nationwide conference and call it something like FailureCon. In it, he said, the prime minister should give an award to the entrepreneur with the biggest failure under his belt. If we're too afraid to fail, we don't try. So Salim suggests we end the stigma on failure.

No one has ever been fired from Mindvalley for failing on an experiment. Failure is wonderful. It makes you smarter. Failing on an innovation will never cost you a promotion at Mindvalley. But not trying to innovate will. Or moving too slow.

#4. Embrace Rapid Innovation and Change

I can tell you that one of my biggest frustrations dealing with some new hires in Mindvalley is the cultural fear of change. Every year we see in our feedback someone saying that "we change too fast," "we're 'always' changing things," etc. etc. But let me ask you this. Are we changing what's working or what's not working?

Are we abandoning winning formulas? Or adjusting them while we toss our losing models. We're not changing . . . we're pivoting. Good companies do that.

Jeff Bezos once wrote a blog post titled "The Smart People Change Their Minds." He wrote: *"The people who are right a lot more often change their minds."*

Bezos went on to say he doesn't think consistency of thought is a particularly positive trait: *"It's better, even healthier in fact, to have an idea that contradicts one you had before. The smart people constantly revise their understandings of a matter. They reconsider problems they thought they had solved. They are open to new points of view, new information, and challenges to their own ways of thinking."*

Mindvalley changes and evolves as much in one month as most computers do in six months. A product owner who is working on core products and is not frequently on WhatsApp and Slack with me will be obsolete in terms of their knowledge and understanding of our needs in thirty days.

Let me emphasize that. If you're not plugged in and connected and communicating you're going to have wrong data and likely make redundant decisions.

#5. Communicate, Communicate, Communicate

> "It's about communication. It's about honesty. It's about treating people in the organization as deserving to know the facts. You don't try to give them half the story. You don't try to hide the story. You treat them as—as true equals, and you communicate and you communicate and communicate."
>
> —Louis V. Gerstner Jr., former CEO of IBM

This is why at Mindvalley ALL OKR docs are open to anyone. All Envisioning docs are equally opened. You can be here for one day and still have the right to edit the Envisioning Doc or OKR doc of a team outside your own. The executive team themselves have no secret folder where we keep visions or plans in isolation from everyone else.

If you understand this—you understand your power here.

—V

------------------ END OF MEMO --------------------

The Unified Brain is truly incredible. When idea flow moves unrestricted and decisions are made fast, a business evolves at an exponential rate. However, there is a dark side to this. It's when you move so fast toward incredible visions that you forget about balance and to take care of yourself. This is what the final chapter of this book is about.

You will learn an entirely new way to work that is about merging the Buddha with the badass to create radical balance in your life.

Chapter Summary

MODELS OF REALITY

Ideas have the same effect on the brain as happy drugs. When the brain is in a state of inspiration it releases a surge of dopamine and serotonin. This is why conceiving brilliant ideas feels incredible. And sharing them is even better. This is called idea sex.

Brain coupling happens when two or more people vibe on the same idea. During these moments their brain frequencies mirror one another. The experience feels thrilling, and joyous, and fun.

When the roles between people are respected but not placed in the foreground of the mind when collaborating on projects, and structures are put in place to speed communication, any group of people can work as a Unified Brain. Working like this is invigorating. Anyone can create a Unified Brain work environment with others. This model can be extended to families, community groups, friends, and nonprofits.

1. **Break Hierarchy and Create the Right Beliefs**
2. **Introduce OODA**

Systems for Living

EXERCISE 1: CONTEXT SHIFTING

Belief to remember and live by:

Human beings are complex entities. Unless you truly know a person, you don't know them. Never assume a behavior or character trait on anyone that is disempowering to yourself. You won't do anyone any justice.

Practice this by questioning how you perceive other people whenever you feel disempowered. Ask yourself:

Why is this person like this?
Based on their actions, is what I believe factually true?
What could be going on in their life?
Am I struggling in this relationship because I am caught up with their title?
What do other people say or believe about this person?
What is an empowering stance I could view this person/situation through?
If I believe that every person is by nature a well-meaning person, what can I see about this person now?

If you work in a group and see that other people are struggling with disempowered beliefs, share these questions. Often we get caught up in our own perceptions of reality. Empowering questions will help you shift context and see an entirely more empowered reality. Practice this and help others do it too.

EXERCISE 2: INTRODUCE OODA

OODA was a model created by an air force military strategist and USAF colonel, John Boyd. Boyd applied the concept to the combat operations process, often at the strategic level in military operations. Simply put, by following OODA, air force pilots were more likely to shoot down enemy planes. The idea is simple: **ACT FAST—Even with Imperfect Knowledge.**

In air force lingo this would mean:

- **Observe the enemy aircraft.**
- **Orient yourself.**

- **Decide your next move.**
- **ACT and fire!**

The OODA loops suggest that you win by moving fast. Overthinking can be a competitive disadvantage. OODA is designed to avoid paralysis by analysis and to allow those pilots to make as many decisions as possible in a given timeframe.

Step 1: Refer back to Memo 2 above to fully understand the process.

Step 2: Consider what messaging systems you can introduce to a team to speed up communication. Then put them in place and see how it optimizes your time and speeds up innovation.

Step 3: Stick to the rule "Don't present, reflect." If people are presenting well-thought-out ideas they are probably overthinking them, not collaborating well, and slowing down innovation. It's okay to be messy when brainstorming back and forth. Innovation is often an iterative process.

CHAPTER 9

UPGRADE YOUR IDENTITY

Life isn't about finding yourself. Life is about creating yourself.

—George Bernard Shaw

The Universe acts as a mirror. It reflects back to you what you are. The miracle of this is that you can shift your identity and the world will obey. But you must shift it so deeply you believe the new identity and live life in accordance with it.

IN *THE CODE OF the Extraordinary Mind,* I share a concept called the Beautiful Destruction. It's when you realize that to evolve into a better version of you, you must first destroy aspects of what you've already built so a new version of you can emerge. I often use this statement to express it:

*Sometimes in life you have to destroy what is
merely good to allow what is truly great to enter.*

Sometimes you choose the Beautiful Destruction. Sometimes it chooses you. Each time it's scary as hell. I'd have to shed old behaviors, relationships, and environments that I'd grown accustomed to. I'd have to confront many unknowns. But every single time I've experienced this, miracles emerge from the ruins of my old life. Visions I once dreamt of became my reality.

The first time was when I left the United States. I packed my bags, left the country I loved, and moved home to Kuala Lumpur. You'll recall this story from Chapter 2. That choice to refuse to let my circumstances dictate my future led to Mindvalley's massive success.

The second beautiful destruction was when Bob Proctor called me to account. I told you that story in Chapter 7. He said I was playing too small, and he was right. I immediately stopped traveling and teaching my seminars. Two years later, I launched A-Fest, which became a major transformational festival. It's now in its tenth year.

My greatest Beautiful Destruction happened when my business almost collapsed, transforming the way I work altogether. It happened in 2008. I'll share the story in a moment. Truthfully, that time, it almost cost me everything. But if it wasn't for that, my life today, and this book, would not exist.

Every single time that I chose to take the inspired path, it was scary. And every single time, I experience a full identity shift. I become a new person.

But it's this new identity that then pulls me into an even greater life. This is because it's your identity that shapes your world. The Universe reflects back who you are. And if you're too stubborn to change, the Beautiful Destruction is the Universe's way of shaking you up to help you evolve into the next version of who you're meant to be.

Identity Shifting

Identity shifting is when we create a massive change in how we see ourselves in relation to the world. I believe it is identity shifting and not the Law of Attraction that really matters.

I once sat down for breakfast with the spiritual teacher Michael Beckwith. We were in Portugal, where Beckwith was taking the stage at A-Fest 2019. And over breakfast we started talking about his philosophies. Beckwith shared with me his concept of the Law of Resonance.

He explained it like this:

> *This "Law of Attraction" thing, you see, the way most people think of it is incomplete. The world doesn't give you what you want or desire. Rather it gives you WHO you ARE. Your identity shapes your experience.*

Beckwith went on to explain that this is why so many people fail at goal-setting, or vision boards, or creative visualization. If what you WANT does not match WHO you ARE, the Universe will resist you.

If the Law of Resonance gives a spiritual dimension to identity shifting, is there science behind it?

In his brilliant book *Atomic Habits,* James Clear talks about the best way to change behavior in a more psychological sense. He advises not to struggle to change a habit. Instead, change your identity. Build an identity that makes you rise above the habit altogether.

For example, let's say you want to be the person who goes to the gym three times a week and loves it. You could focus on the outcome, which might be to lose ten pounds and look great.

Or you could focus on the process, which might be to set an alarm, wake up, drive to the gym every Monday, Wednesday, and Friday and hire the best damn trainer you can find. But both of these methods are tough to maintain.

If you try to motivate yourself by outcomes or processes, you'll find yourself waking up every now and then feeling too sleepy or tired to hit the gym. It's why so many people renege on their expensive gym memberships. It's not enough to keep you motivated.

So instead focus on an identity shift. Focus on gaining a new identity such as: "I am a fit forty-year-old with the body of a sexy athlete."

The habit of going to the gym becomes so much easier. The athlete doesn't want to lie in bed. His body wants to move, train, and get better. Athletes don't skip workouts. It's just what they DO. James Clear suggests that adopting an identity shift is a much more powerful way of changing behavior.

This is what it looks like in a diagram:

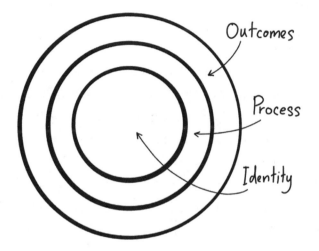

This brings me back to my story. In 2008, I underwent a complete identity shift. Predictably, it caused my old world to disappear and a new expanded world to unfold.

The End of Work as I Knew It

Throughout 2008, I had horrible bouts of insomnia. I'd often wake up in a state of anxiety because my company was in peril; it was bleeding cash daily. I had eighteen employees. Industry shifts had caused our revenue engine to stop working and we were slowly running out of cash.

To raise the stakes even higher, I had become a father. My son Hayden was seven months old. My life was no longer about me. I had a family to provide for. Beyond that, I felt I needed to be a model of success for this little human.

I had tried all the business formulas to fix things, including bringing in amazing experts and even bringing in a partner, a Stanford MBA, to help. Nothing had worked. So I decided to retreat. Not retreat in the give-up sense. I decided to go deep into my study of personal growth to find the answers.

I went to numerous seminars on mindset and wealth. I flew to San Diego to listen to Esther Hicks talk about spirituality. I dived into books written by my favorite teachers, like Neale Donald Walsch. I dedicated a month to deep extensive personal growth while setting an intention to find the answer.

It came one moment when I was sitting at a seminar on the mindset of the wealthy. I uncovered that I was living with an insidious belief that was ruining my life. It was this: Hard work is necessary for success.

I was born into an immigrant family. My mom was a schoolteacher who worked hard. My father started his business when I was thirteen. He worked long hours into the night. Frequently as a teen, I'd have to join him in his warehouse after school. We'd do backbreaking work like load crates of garments onto trucks, or sort and box merchandise. Naturally, the brule "To be successful you must work hard" became part of my identity.

Then I became a dad myself. And because I so respected and loved my father, I wanted to be a damn good one for Hayden. I was determined to come home from work earlier so I could spend more time with him.

My beliefs were clashing. I thought: If I worked less, I could be a better dad. But if I did that, I wouldn't be a success.

At the time, I was doing everything to try and hold my world together. And yet, my business was collapsing. My belief in the power of hard work was so deeply rooted that my identity was tied to it. If I chose to give up some working hours to be a dad, I felt guilty or unworthy of business success. And this belief became true, because reality will reflect to you what you deeply believe.

It was in a seminar by T. Harv Eker that I began to realize how I had blindly adopted that hard-work rule. This awakening immediately caused the rule to lose its power. I realized hard work had little or no relationship to my success.

All of a sudden my identity shifted. An old belief faded into oblivion.

Once I transformed the BS rules that had hijacked me, my outer world changed fast. By August, we doubled the business. By December, the business doubled again. In eight months we grew 800 percent. Our team grew to fifty people and we moved into a gorgeous new office.

One year later, the way I worked had gone through a total flip. While in May 2008 I had nearly lost my business while killing myself at the office, by May 2009, I was on a beach. In fact, it was multiple beaches. I spent twenty-one days beaching it up around the world. I attended a friend's wedding in Cabo. Then a mastermind on Necker Island. I spent nine days at Tony Robbins's resort in Fiji. I only spent six days in the office. During that time we hit new revenue records.

I blew the hard-work rule to smithereens. My new identity had changed the laws of the world for me. You can do that too. In the final half of this chapter I reveal an identity-shifting exercise you can use to do the same. You can create a new identity, and with new tools you can demolish any belief barriers in the way of your claiming that new reality.

And if you also believe that work must be hard, you're simply caught up in society's conditioning. That is just not the case.

The Myths About Work

In Arianna Huffington's book *Thrive*, she shares about a period in her life where she overworked herself so much that she ended up in the hospital. By the second year of running *The Huffington Post* she was working eighteen-hour days. She looked successful, and her business certainly was, but she was exhausted and completely consumed by her work. One day she collapsed in her Los Angeles office, hit her head against a table, and knocked herself out.

"I was successful by all standards, but I was clearly not successful if I was lying in a pool of blood on the floor of my office," she explained in an interview with HuffPost Live.

It took a serious health crisis for Huffington to realize that she was missing the point. She was sacrificing her health, because she had bought into the lie: *Work harder, go farther.* Like me, she learned her lesson the hard way. The good news is, it woke her up.

Yet so many entrepreneurs espouse hard work. If you think hard work is the secret of success, then every sweatshop worker pulling hundred-hour weeks in factories in Asia should be successful. Hard work has no part in the equation.

But there's a blind allegiance to it. And this results in broken humans, damaged relationships, and poor office culture where people are too stressed and overworked to do truly great work or enjoy their life at all.

In 2019, I interviewed Regan Hillyer, who is one of the world's top mindset coaches under thirty. She is one of the many CEOs I know personally who are always joyful, love running multiple businesses, and only work around two hours a day *if they want to*. I admire Regan because she's built multiple successful businesses while under thirty and also leads a life where she gets to travel and enjoy the best the world can offer.

This is what she shared with me:

I see a lot of entrepreneurs who are less successful than me working harder, and when I peel back the layers with them and start asking them some questions, they genuinely believe that business is hard.

I have people come to me who are doing $1 million or $2 million a year and their income won't increase and they can't understand why. It's because they are generating to their max of the hard work they put in. Because their internal structure is wired that way, they find it really difficult to create results.

Instead if we started thinking, What if business was easy? What if making millions of dollars was fun and easy? What if we had a belief that the more money I make, the more money I make automatically?

Regan's point was simple. If you believe work is hard, you'll see hard work as the only way forward. And you'll feel trapped because there are only so many hours you have in a given day.

A better way is to understand that sometimes the way forward is the opposite of work. Sometimes the next big leap will occur when you move from acceleration to navigation.

How to Identity Shift

ACCELERATION VERSUS NAVIGATION

I've realized that to stay in this harmonious place of work one must maintain a subtle balance between two modes of operation. I call them *acceleration* and *navigation*.

So let me explain how that looks in the context of work.

Accelerating happens when a person is executing on the mission. It's when they are in a mode of performance where they are task focused. For me, this is when I'm optimizing the business, meeting with the team, developing new products and systems. But acceleration alone isn't enough.

When the mode is set only to acceleration, it's not possible to see new opportunities, to innovate or to learn from other mentors, or review mistakes even. In this mode, a worker will be so busy hustling, they forget to tune in and ask themselves if what they're doing matters anyway. If too much time is spent in this mode creativity, energy, and fun diminish, which causes a decrease in productivity and fulfillment.

The best workers oscillate between acceleration and navigation.

It's why every now and then, I disappear. I recently traveled around the world for seven weeks straight. This was by design. I was in navigation mode.

Navigation is not about moving fast; rather it's about understanding if you're moving in the right direction, on the right path. It's about concocting new visions for a business, looking for new areas to explore, essentially figuring out where to point your vision.

Spend too much time in navigation and you lose momentum and the ability to execute.

Insight and self-evolution happen best when we shift between these two modes. There's a beautiful integration that happens when you can leave for a while to learn and recalibrate and return with fresh ideas.

My insights of 2008 happened because I stepped back from work for a while and went deep into personal growth. This was me going into navigation. There were times when I questioned if I could really leave my work aside to attend a four-day seminar. But I did it. And amazing insights changed the course of my business.

And there is also a scientific reason why sudden insights come in navigation mode. You may have experienced this: Have you ever wondered why you get great ideas when you're in the shower, while driving, or as you're falling asleep or waking?

Neuroscientists call it the Default Mode Network (DMN). It is a uniquely human brain mode that produces great spikes of creativity, innovation, and problem solving. When the brain is not focused on any task, it goes into a default mode of streaming thoughts. In this state people daydream, imagine, and think about the future. These thoughts are vital for organizing and planning ahead. They help you consider situations and decide on your next action.

Conversely, Task Mode Network (TMN) happens when the mind is focused on a task like typing on a keyboard, playing an instrument, reading a book, anything that requires focus and attention. Many practiced meditators have a highly developed TMN.

In an interview with Big Think, Scott Barry Kaufman, director of the Institute of Imagination at the University of Pennsylvania, said: "There is a unique experience of consciousness when both networks are on even planes of the see-saw."

Many artists, inventors, business leaders talk about times where a brilliant idea came to them, or something clicked. Some say the work of God or the Universe came through them. You may have experienced a time like that. You've got a powerful built-in capacity to envision.

When a person is in navigation it's like having your internal compass that shows you where to go. Acceleration is the rocket fuel that powers your actions, has you achieve outcomes, and gets you where you need to go.

You must be able to step back and give yourself time to gain more awareness. This is the importance of navigation.

And there's an exercise you can do that will help change your identity rapidly.

The Identity Shift Process

There's a process for shifting your identity rapidly toward more empowering beliefs of the world. When you do this, you start to move toward a life where your work is your passion and it feels like life is a playground and you're in full play mode.

When you do this you have truly merged the Buddha and the badass.

Here's the process.

STEP 1: ENVISION YOUR PERFECT LIFE

So how do you go beyond the myth of the hustle or the idea of hard work and truly live a life where work disappears?

First, understand that you are not who you think you are.

The Two Versions of You: Everybody has two versions of themselves. First, there is the identity you walk around with that's made up of roles. You're the office manager. Or the coder. Or the freelance graphic designer. Or the lawyer or CEO. This is, however, *only your shell.* It's the role you're playing in the world around you. And frankly, it's a role you're playing for someone else. It's the role you choose to play so you fit into the grand human collective. That intricate web of human society you belong to.

But this is *not* you. There is a second version of you. It's the person you secretly desire to be. This is your core identity. For example, take a guy working as a lawyer in a law firm, who works seventy-hour weeks and isn't very satisfied. His shell is a stressed-out lawyer. His core identity could be that he's an artist. Or a Casanova. Or a rockstar. That's his core identity. That's who he wants to be.

No matter how satisfied a person is with their life, they always have these two versions of themselves. The core identity (inner version of you) is always trying to inform the outer world of the next evolution for them.

Our deepest core desires are never things such as "make money" or "network." If this is what you think your core desire is, your brain is lying to you. Those are just the surface outcomes. The truth is, the whole point of being a human is to create and to perpetuate experiences. Goals are meaningless unless they come with an experience. As Terence McKenna has said:

> *What is real is you and your friends and your associations, your highs, your orgasms, your hopes, your plans, your fears. And we are told no, we're unimportant, we're peripheral. "Get a degree, get a job, get a this, get a that." And then you're a player, you don't want to even play in that game. You want to reclaim your mind and get it out of the hands of the cultural engineers who want to turn you into a half-baked moron consuming all this trash that's being manufactured out of the bones of a dying world.*

McKenna has a point. Our outdated school systems program us to fit in nicely as a cog in the wheel of modern society to keep the status quo and to keep industries running. So you wake up, get dressed, work your butt off, and buy more crap you don't need.

Yet, if you think about what you want in life, you will probably find that it's not about money or wealth. It's about experiences. Wealth and money are means goals to truly gaining experiences, whether it's the experience of travel, or living in a gorgeous home, or making love to that special someone. Once you start focusing on your real goals, you will effortlessly transform on the inside and find yourself able to influence your outer world, as well. Start by focusing on experiences. Maybe it seems audacious to boil down life to a formula, but if you did, it would look something like this:

Experience + Identity = Life

When you find your core identity, and start living it, you will attract people who match that core identity. The concept of core identity was first introduced to me by a brilliant entrepreneurial coach by the name of Frank Kern. This is an adaptation of Kern's original 2008 exercise.

What you really want to aim for is:

- Experiences (because means goals are meaningless)
- A new identity, and
- The sum of all this is **Life.**

So, the big question is: **If there were no limitations or consequences, what would your perfect, average day look like?**

Let me explain what I mean.

Limitations means you don't have to worry about money, health, geography, nor limiting people.

Consequences means you need to stay safe with your dream for that perfect day. Not anything that would hurt you, get you in trouble, or arrested.

Average means you could do it every day and not get killed (this means your perfect day would not include climbing Mount Everest, for example).

Now create that perfect day. Journal about it. And then take a step back. What does this perfect day tell you about yourself? That perfect day will help you understand yourself and find your core identity.

Ask yourself these questions about your perfect day (and note that these questions are all based on desired experiences—not things):

1. Where would you live?
2. What would your house look like?
3. What time would you wake up?
4. Whom would you wake up with?
5. What would you do first thing in the morning?

6. What would you have for breakfast?

7. What does the mundane stuff look like (for example, taking kids to school)?

8. What would you do in the first half of your day?

9. What would you eat for lunch?

10. Whom would you eat with?

11. What are your body and health like?

12. What would your friends be like?

13. What would you do for personal fulfillment?

14. What purpose would you strive for?

15. What would your business be?

16. What are your clients like?

17. What are your relationships like? What do you like about each other?

18. What would you do for family time?

19. What would you have for dinner? Where would you eat?

20. What would you talk about over dinner?

21. What would you do at night?

22. Whom would you do it with?

23. What would your thoughts be as you go to sleep?

STEP 2: CREATE YOUR NEW IDENTITY

So you have a vision of your perfect day. Maybe you've even gone further and created a vision for your perfect month, year, or life. Even better. Now you want to remember this important nuance about human identity.

The world will reflect to you what you truly, deeply believe you are. Your identity will create resonance with the Universe.

So what makes identity? This is a trickier question. Over the last few years I became fascinated with advanced brain training techniques. I've worked in labs with neuroscientists to map onto my brain the brain-wave states of monks and billionaires. What I experienced was the closest I've been to that idea from *The Matrix* where Neo plugs his brain into a computer.

So what did I find? Different brain-wave states unlock different aspects of being human. There are four states a person can access:

1. **The Alpha State:** When a person works in alpha-level frequencies, they increase their amplitude and coherence. They experience an overall increase in general states of well-being; for example, increased health and vitality, less emotional stress, more bliss.
2. **The Theta Level.** Work at theta-level frequencies increases a person's ability to access intuition and creativity.
3. **The Delta Level.** One of the more curious states is delta. When a person is in delta, they experience increased synchronicity and gain the ability to tackle massive projects with ease.
4. **The Gamma Level.** This is a newer frequency discovered only in 1993, and it seems to correlate to deeper connection and love.

Interestingly, these four brain states suggest that there are four different aspects of a healthy identity.

- Alpha States correlate with Well-being
- Theta States correlate with Creativity and Inspiration
- Delta States correlate with Abundance and Power
- Gamma States correlate with Love and Connection.

Now that you've planned your perfect day, the next step is to ask yourself, *Who* do I have to evolve into to be the man or woman who has this perfect day? (As an aside, do you see how this exercise connects to the Three Most Important Questions exercise from Chapter 4?)

As you explore your new identity in terms of Well-being, Creativity and Inspiration, Abundance and Power, and Love and Connection, journal and write down how you want your life to look in each of these four areas. You only need to spend five minutes or so per category, so about twenty minutes total.

STATE #1: WELL-BEING

The state of well-being means that you take care of your body and mind. We know today that body and mind are connected, so while well-being absolutely means taking care of your exercise, sleep, and nutrition, it also means taking time to care for your mind through practices like meditation and mindfulness.

When you have greater well-being, you do better at work. Lack of sleep and low stamina impact your ability to function at your best at work. Likewise, stress reduces your ability to make good decisions and generate ideas. If you can eliminate stress and learn to relax, expect to see a rise in decision making and thinking ability.

Change your identity to that of a truly healthy person. Someone who meditates daily, eats well, cares for their body, and exercises. You aren't too busy to exercise and meditate; in fact, it's proven that these practices *give* you time.

Now look at the vision of your perfect day and ask yourself, "To be the man or woman who experiences such a day, what levels of well-being would I have?"

Consider these components:

Health and Vitality: Describe your overall health and sense of vitality.

Energy: How energetic do you feel throughout the day?

Emotional States: What are the emotional states you experience on a day-to-day basis?

STATE #2: CREATIVITY AND INSPIRATION

Have you ever noticed how some people tend to burst forth with great ideas? Have you ever experienced states of mind where you are so into your work, you *flow* effortlessly and really crush it on that paper, project, or presentation? These heightened states of inspiration and creativity stem from unique identity traits.

You want to take on the identity of the creative if you're in a field that requires creativity, like graphic design or writing. But if you're in finance or, say, adwords optimization, what you might want to aim for is intensity of focus—the ability to crunch numbers in rapid time and draw smart conclusions. Either sense of identity gives you the ability to crush it at work while working fewer hours of the day.

Now look at the vision of your perfect day and ask yourself, "To be the man or woman who experiences such a day, what levels of creativity and inspiration would I have?"

Consider these components:

Flow: How easy is it for me to access flow states for optimal productivity? What do I experience in these states?

Clarity and Focus: How clear am I on my goals and visions for life and work?

Purpose and Direction: How clear am I on my life purpose? Is what I'm doing on a day-to-day basis consistent with what my true purpose is?

STATE #3: ABUNDANCE AND POWER

When you have the identity trait of abundance or power you see life as being easy and effortless. Recall the Japanese millionaires from Chapter 5 who believed that making money is easy. That's an identity of abundance.

The trait of abundance means that you see abundance everywhere. In your world you have enough money flowing to you for all your dreams, projects, and ventures. You believe the right people, opportunities, and circumstances will come to you when you need them. You also feel in control of your own life and destiny.

Now look at the vision of your perfect day and ask yourself, "To be the man or woman who experiences such a day, what levels of abundance and power would I have?"

Consider these components:

Wealth: Your access to money, connections, home, offices, and assets.

No Overwhelm: Your ability to deal with complex structures, multiple projects and jobs, mastering complexity at everything you try.

Ease and Synchronicity: How easy your life seems. The right answers, connections, and people always show up.

STATE #4: LOVE AND CONNECTION

When you have the identity trait of love and connection, you never feel lonely in life. You have the right partner or partners in your life. You have amazing friends who love you as you are and deeply care about you.

Your business and network, all the way down to your clients and suppliers, are all win-win relationships. You want every act, every pact to be crafted not in competition or win-lose mode but rather as a win-win for all parties.

You deeply care about the people around you, from family to friends to colleagues, and they in turn care about you. In short, you have reverence for all the other human beings you come into connection with. And you have a deep and powerful love for yourself.

Now look at the vision of your perfect day and ask yourself, "To be the man or woman who experiences such a day, what levels of love and connection would I have?"

Consider these components:

Win-Win Relationships: How are your relationships with your team members, colleagues, clients, and customers? Are your relationships honest and about everyone winning?

Surrounded by Love: Do you feel surrounded by love? This love may come from your own heart or from the people around you.

Authenticity: Do you believe in yourself? Are you fearless about standing up, being an original, and living your own life free of the expectations of others?

After you do this exercise, you're now ready for Step 3.

STEP 3: HACK YOUR BELIEF SYSTEM

Once you've completed the two steps above, you're ready to incorporate new beliefs into your being. Hacking your belief system is a form of self-hypnosis to bring these new identities to life.

The technique here is called Lofty Questions. It was taught to me by one of our Mindvalley teachers and a world-class coach of harnessing intuition, Christie Marie Sheldon.

To understand Lofty Questions, you first have to understand that affirmations are quite useless. As early as the 1980s, mind-science pioneer Jose Silva declared that affirmations don't often work for people. Instead, what you want to do is trick your subconscious mind to believe the identity you're placing onto it. And you do this not by making a declarative statement such as "I have a great body," but by asking questions like: "Why do I have such a wonderful body?" Or: "Why am I so kind and gentle to everyone around me?"

Affirmations don't work because you can't reaffirm a belief you don't really believe in. You can tell yourself you're amazing, superb, kind, and genius, but if there is a bit of doubt at the back of your mind, you'll just end up questioning your own statement.

But when you ask a Lofty Question, you're not making a statement. You're posing a question to your brain and asking for evidence. The subconscious mind is wonderful. It will take that question and find a way to resolve it. The more you gather evidence, the more you begin to truly believe.

Lofty Questions are one of the most powerful tools for total human transformation I've ever come across. Let me explain how they work. Let's say you want to gain better mental clarity; here's an example of Lofty Questions you could ask yourself:

- Why am I so creative at work?
- Why am I going to be in flow today as I write my book?
- Why do I have such badass levels of focus?
- Why am I so clear on my vision and goals?
- Why do I operate with such a profound sense of purpose?

You don't have to ask them all. Just asking one is enough. And the rate at which Lofty Questions change your life is truly astounding.

In January of 2016 I started asking myself the Lofty Question "Why do I have such a healthy sexy body?" At that time, I had just turned forty and I was not in the best shape of my life. I had let myself go over the years. But I was determined to have a body I was proud of and a body I felt great about. I would ask myself that question every day during meditation. It took only five seconds to do. You ask the question once. Not repeatedly.

Two weeks later I was at a mastermind for America's top business and personal growth authors called the Transformational Leadership Council and met Eric Edmeades. He was receiving an award for contribution to the community. He built a ninety-day program, WildFit, which teaches people to change their mindset around food. That day Eric announced he would run a ninety-day session of WildFit for free for any of the members attending the event that day who wanted to join.

Spurred by the question I have been asking myself for two weeks, I signed up. I was at 22 percent body fat. Not bad. But it wasn't a body where I felt comfortable taking my shirt off at the beach.

By May 2016, three months later, I had lost twelve pounds of fat. My body weight dropped to 15 percent. I was amazed at how my eating and my health changed in just a few months.

So I kept up with the Lofty Questions. This time I changed it to "Why do I have such a ripped muscular body?"

By then I was eating healthy, but I still hated going to the gym. The results from asking that Lofty Question arrived with ferocity. By July 2016, I bumped into a fitness trainer who was working on a Mindvalley team, and he introduced me to super slow strength training. But spurred by that Lofty Question, I decided to follow through.

Six months later I had packed on some seven pounds of pure muscle. My chest had expanded so much I had to toss away a lot of my old shirts. And I had a body I was proud of.

Now, was it the question that spurred the change? Was the act of asking these questions somehow activating some synchronicity in the world to bring the right people and circumstances to me? Was this the mystical mind-bending reality factor that so many spiritual philosophers talk about? Or was it my brain's reticular activating system (RAS)? That's the part of the brain that helps zero in on objects or ideas you've been thinking about internally that are in your external orbit.

Honestly, to me, it doesn't matter. I'll let spiritual philosophers argue that out. All I know is that it works. Today I start every day with thirty Lofty Questions. I've committed them to memory. They help push me forward in life and allow me to create new realities for myself rapidly. And through this process I attain a beautiful balance between work and well-being and happiness and joy.

Here's how to get started with the Lofty Questions process:

1. Look at the journal entries you made for each of the four aspects of your new identity and start constructing the Lofty Questions that will reinforce the shifts you want to make.
2. Write down five to ten Lofty Questions.
3. Commit them to memory and ask yourself these questions while meditating in the morning or before going to bed at night.
4. As these questions sink in, you can add more questions.
5. As the circumstances of your life change, modify or ask new questions.

Here are some Lofty Questions to get you started. Choose whatever resonates with you.

Lofty Questions for Well-being

Why am I always learning and growing?

Why do I eat only the foods that are best for my body?

Why do I have such a sexy, ripped, muscular body?

Why am I getting younger and younger every year?

Why am I in a perfect state of health?

Why is my body healing itself and getting better and better year after year?

Lofty Questions for Creativity and Inspiration

Why do I have such powerful intuition?

Why are my days always so filled with inspiration?

Why am I so clear on my goals and visions?

Why am I such an amazing writer/producer/filmmaker?

Why is my day-to-day work so inspiring for me?

Lofty Questions for Abundance and Power

Why do I have an avalanche of abundance flowing down on me for all my goals, visions, and inspirations?

Why am I so good at managing, keeping, and multiplying money?

Why do I run a ten-million-dollar business?

Why is my income growing every year with ease?

Why is my work touching one million lives every year?

Why do I have such a beautiful home in (insert location)?

Why am I such a powerful manifester?

Why do I have the Universe on my side?

Lofty Questions for Love and Connection

Why do I have such an exciting and active dating life?

Why do I have such a thrilling and exciting sex life?

Why do people find me so attractive?

Why do I spark love and joy to everyone who comes into my life?

Why am I always surrounded by love?

Why do I have such an amazing relationship with my kids (insert names)?

Why do I have such an amazing relationship with my partner (insert name)?

Why do I have such an amazing team of people working with me?

Use the questions above as a framework to get started or create your own. Congratulations on the new emerging you.

In Closing

At the start of this book, I shared a Rumi poem. I told you that your interpretation of this poem would change as you read this book. *What does it mean to you now?*

> When I run after what I think I want,
> my days are a furnace of distress and anxiety;
> If I sit in my own place of patience, what I need flows to me,
> and without any pain.
> From this I understand that what I want also wants me,
> is looking for me and attracting me.
> There is a great secret in this for anyone who can grasp it.

Look back at the old interpretation of this poem that you wrote down from Chapter 1. Did anything change? These changes reflect shifts in your identity and belief systems. These shifts will likely change your physical experience of life itself. Good luck there.

Final Thoughts

With your Buddha bliss and your badass power, you're going to bring amazing things into this world. I can't wait to see you step into your leadership and be the greatest version you can be for yourself, your family, your community, and the world. I can't wait to see the impact you make.

For now, let's stay connected. I use Instagram to stay in touch with all my readers and I share new insights weekly. Follow me on @vishen.

And I've created a beautiful site where you can get additional videos to support you with many of the ideas I've shared in this book. Visit www .mindvalley.com/badass.

Thank you for going on this adventure with me.

Chapter Summary

MODELS OF REALITY

You *can* create a life where work doesn't feel like work. Break the big fat brule about success: the false belief that you have to work harder than anyone else. Refuse to buy into the lie of hard work. Replace it with this:

The Soul's Experience on Earth Is Not Meant for Hard Work and Toil. It's Meant for Freedom, Ease, and Expansion.

You must merge your inner Buddha with your inner badass.

The Buddha is the archetype for the spiritual master. The person who can live in this world but also move with an ease, grace, and flow to where it seems like the world is beholden to them.

The badass is the changemaker. This is the archetype of the person who is out there creating change, building, coding, writing, inventing, leading. Pushing humanity forward to bring life to new structures in the physical plane.

Now remember this equation. It's your aim in life:

Experiences + Identity = Life

- Experiences (because goals are meaningless)
- A new identity, and
- The sum of all this is **Life**

There are two identities to you. There's the you walking around connecting to the outer world and then there's your core identity; this is the vision you have for the person you want to become. Life is a constant journey of evolving into your core identity. To uncover it there are three steps:

Step 1: Envision Your Perfect Life

Step 2: Create Your New Identity

Step 3: Hack Your Belief System

Systems for Living

EXERCISE 1: ACCELERATION AND NAVIGATION

The best workers oscillate between acceleration and navigation.

Acceleration happens when a person is executing on the mission. It's when they are in a mode of performance where they are task focused.

Navigation is not about moving fast, it's about slowing down and pulling away from the action to understand if you're moving in the right direction.

Remember, there's incredible science on why shifting between both all the time is most effective. When you're in acceleration you're activating a brain mode of connectivity called Task Mode Network (TMN), where the mind locks on to tasks at hand. When you're in navigation you're in Default Mode Network (DMN), where the brain produces great spikes of creativity, innovation, and problem solving.

Step 1: Review your current day-to-day hours of work. Do you cycle between acceleration and navigation enough each day to feel like you are always performing at your peak? If not, consider a new structure of better balance. Institute it and see how your performance is enhanced.

Step 2: Review your monthly or yearly schedules. Are there enough blocks of downtime in between the action to maintain sustainability and peak performance? If not, consider a new structure of better balance. Institute it and see how your performance is enhanced.

EXERCISE 2: CRAFT YOUR CORE IDENTITY

There are three steps to merging your inner world (core identity) with your outer world. They are:

Step 1: Envision Your Perfect Life. This is where you indulge your imagination. Consider your perfect day in your ideal vision for life. Construct it. Go back through the chapter to the questions listed under the section Step 1: Envision Your Perfect Life.

Step 2: Create Your New Identity. Once you understand what you'd like to experience, the question to ask is: Who must I become? Remember Beckwith's Law of Resonance: *"The world doesn't give you what you want or desire. Rather it gives you WHO you ARE."*

Go back to the above section titled Step 2: Create Your New Identity and go through the process.

Step 3: Hack Your Belief System. Once you've created your new identity you must create your Lofty Questions so you can train yourself in new beliefs and behaviors so you become it. Revisit the section Step 3: Hack Your Belief System to do this work.

SOURCES

INTRODUCTION

11 **"Reality is what we take to be true"**: Ricard, Matthieu, and Trinh Xuan Thuan. *The Quantum and the Lotus: A Journey to the Frontiers Where Science and Buddhism Meet.* Vintage Books, a division of Penguin Random House, 2001.

14 **"At the root of his reality distortion was his belief"**: Isaacson, Walter. *Steve Jobs.* Simon & Schuster, 2011.

15 **"I was early taught to work as well as play"**: Chernow, Ron. *The Life of John D. Rockefeller, Sr.* Three Rivers Press, a division of Penguin Random House, 2004.

CHAPTER 1

25 **"Never forget what you are, for surely the world will not"**: Martin, George R. R. *A Game of Thrones (A Song of Ice and Fire, Book 1).* HarperVoyager, an imprint of HarperCollins, 2011.

41 **"You can't connect the dots looking forward"**: *Stanford News,* https://news.stanford.edu/2005/06/14/jobs-061505/ (accessed July 2019).

42 **"Suffering ceases to be suffering at the moment it finds meaning"**: Frankl, Viktor E. *Man's Search for Meaning.* Beacon Press, 2006.

CHAPTER 2

51 **"Find a group of people who challenge and inspire you"**: *Harvard Magazine,* https://harvardmagazine.com/2011/05/you-cant-do-it-alone (accessed January 2020).

55 **"Little ideas that tickled, and nagged, and refused to go away"**: Miller, George (producer) and Chirs Noonan (director). *Babe* [motion picture]. United States: Kennedy Miller Productions, Universal Pictures, August 1995.

59 **"You are a bus driver"**: Collins, Jim. *Good to Great: Why Some Companies Make the Leap . . . and Others Don't.* HarperCollins, 2001.

65 **"People don't buy what you do; they buy why you do it"**: TED (September 2009). *Simon Sinek's talk: How Great Leaders Inspire Action.* Video retrieved from www.ted.com /talks/simon_sinek_how_great_leaders_inspire_action?language=e.

66 **Human beings are biologically hardwired to make decisions**: "The Importance of Feelings," *The MIT Technology Review*, www.technologyreview.com/s/528151/the -importance-of-feelings/ (accessed February 2019).

66 **brain-injured participants could conceptually discuss decisions**: "The Role of the Amygdala in Decision-Making," U.S. National Library of Medicine, www.ncbi.nlm. nih.gov/pubmed/12724171 (accessed February 2019).

70 **"Forget mission and vision"**: Mindvalley (producer), October 21, 2018. *Cameron Herold on How to Create a Vivid Vision for Your Career and Life.* Audio podcast retrieved from https://podcast.mindvalley.com/cameron-herold-vivid-vision/.

CHAPTER 3

81 **"We all are so deeply interconnected"**: Ray, Amit. *Yoga and Vipassana: An Integrated Lifestyle.* Inner Light Publishers, 2010.

84 **experiences of social pain (like loneliness) cause activity**: *Psychology Today*, www .psychologytoday.com/us/blog/the-athletes-way/201403/the-neuroscience-social -pain (accessed January 2020).

84 **One of Harvard's longest, most qualitative studies**: TED (producer), 2015. *Robert Waldinger on What Makes a Good Life? Lessons from the Longest Study on Happiness.* Video retrieved from www.ted.com/talks/robert_waldinger_what_makes_a_good _life_lessons_from_the_longest_study_on_happiness?language=en.

85 **social bonds have a 0.7 correlation**: Deiner, Ed, and Martin Seligman. *Very Happy People* (Volume 13; issue 1, page(s) 81–84), 2002. Retrieved from SAGE Journals, https://doi.org/10.1111/1467-9280.00415.

85 **the four upper levels of Maslow's pyramid**: "Maslow's Hierarchy of Needs." *Simple Psychology*, www.simplypsychology.org/maslow.html (accessed March 2019).

85 **in order for any person to move from one level**: Maslow, Abraham. "A Theory of Human Motivation," *Psychological Review* (1943).

87 **"my employer" (75%) is significantly more trusted than NGOs**: "2019 Edelman Trust Barometer," www.edelman.com/sites/g/files/aatuss191/files/2019-02/2019 _Edelman_Trust_Barometer_Global_Report.pdf (accessed March 2019).

90 **"society's preoccupation with happiness"**: BigThink (producer). *Dr. Susan David on The Tyranny of Positivity: A Harvard Psychologist Details our Unhealthy Obsession with Happiness.* Video retrieved from https://bigthink.com/videos/susan-david-on-our-unhealthy -obsession-with-happiness.

92 **a high PQ means they have a higher ratio of positive feelings:** Chamine, Shirzad. *Positive Intelligence: Why Only 20% of Teams and Individuals Achieve Their True Potential.* Greenleaf Book Group Press, 2012.

95 **Coworkers who report a best friend at work:** "Your Friends and Your Social Well-being," Gallup News, https://news.gallup.com/businessjournal/127043/friends -social-wellbeing.aspx (accessed January 2020).

95 **When the brain is in a positive state, productivity rises:** "How to Use Happiness to Fuel Productivity," training by Shawn Achor with Vishen Lakhiani, Mindvalley Mentoring Program, 2014.

96 **"The people we interviewed from good-to-great companies":** Collins, Jim. *Good to Great: Why Some Companies Make the Leap . . . and Others Don't.* HarperCollins, 2001.

96 **when two people first meet they both make a quick calculation:** Cuddy, Amy. *Presence: Bringing Your Boldest Self to Your Biggest Challenges.* Orion Publishing Co., 2015.

96 **the CEO of Shopify talked about establishing a metric:** "Tobi Lütke of Shopify: Powering a Team With a 'Trust Battery,'" *New York Times,* www.nytimes.com/2016 /04/24/business/tobi-lutke-of-shopify-powering-a-team-with-a-trust-battery.html (accessed April 2019).

102 **"The only true currency in this bankrupt world":** Crowe, Cameron (producer, director, and writer), and Ian Bryce (producer). *Almost Famous* [motion picture], September 2000. United States: Columbia Pictures, DreamWorks Pictures.

106 **Moods go viral, in a similar way as the flu:** *Psychology Today,* www.psychologytoday. com/ca/blog/the-science-work/201410/faster-speeding-text-emotional-contagion -work (accessed March 2019).

106 **when leaders are in a positive mood:** Achor, Shawn. *The Happiness Advantage.* Currency, a division of Penguin Random House, 2010.

CHAPTER 4

122 **the very first task they had to complete:** Mindvalley (producer), 2014. *Shawn Achor on How to Use Happiness to Fuel Productivity.* Video retrieved from https://mindvalley .com/channels/mindvalley-mentoring/media/769-how-to-use-happiness-and-love -to-fuel-productivity.

125 **End goals are the beautiful, exciting rewards:** Lakhiani, Vishen. *The Code of the Extraordinary Mind.* Rodale Books, a division of Penguin Random House, 2016.

CHAPTER 5

146 **"Transformation involves experiencing a deep, structural shift":** O'Sullivan, Edmund, Amish Morrell, and Mary O'Connor. *Expanding the Boundaries of Transformative Learning: Essays on Theory and Praxis.* Palgrave Macmillan, 2004.

149 **a life crisis or a major life transition:** Mezirow, Jack. *Learning as Transformation: Critical Perspectives on a Theory in Progress.* Jossey-Bass, Inc., 2000.

149 **"Google recently demonstrated that its best employees":** Ismail, Salim. *Exponential Organizations.* Diversion Publishing Corp., 2014.

151 **"I've been making a list of the things they don't teach you":** Gaiman, Neil. *The Sandman, Vol. 9: The Kindly Ones.* DC Comics, 2006.

152 **"Human beings are not smartphones":** TED (producer), 2013. *Sugata Mitra on Build a School in the Cloud.* Video retrieved from: https://www.ted.com/talks/sugata_mitra _build_a_school_in_the_cloud?language=en.

158 **depriving yourself of ninety minutes:** Rath, Tom. *Eat, Move, Sleep.* Missionday, 2013.

158 **it takes 10,000 hours to attain mastery in any field:** Gladwell, Malcolm. *Outliers.* Little, Brown and Company, 2008.

158 **They spent an average of 8 hours and 36 minutes sleeping:** Ericsson, Enders K. 1993. "The Role of Deliberate Practice in the Acquisition of Expert Performance" (Vol. 100. No. 3, 363-406). Retrieved from *Psychological Review* http://projects.ict.usc. edu/itw/gel/EricssonDeliberatePracticePR93.pdf.

162 **Imagine if you could boost your strength by 25 percent:** McGuff, Doug. *Body by Science.* Northern River Productions, Inc. 2009.

163 **most people have been trained to read like a six-year-old:** Mindvalley (producer). *Jim Kwik on 10 Powerful Hacks to Unlock Your Super Brain.* Video retrieved from: https://events.blinkwebinars.com/w/5750669740081152/watch-now?_ga=2.163744822 .800747580.1575308463-1706431628.1574210435#5924650399563776.

165 **Daniel said that people need freedom:** Mindvalley (producer), February 1, 2019. *Daniel Pink on the Surprising Truth About Motivation.* Audio podcast retrieved from https://podcast.mindvalley.com/daniel-pink-truth-about-motivation/.

CHAPTER 6

171 **"Power without love is reckless and abusive":** Carson, Clayborne. *The Autobiography of Martin Luther King, Jr.* Warner Books, Inc., 2001.

174 **In 2013, Gallup published a poll on men who refused to retire:** "Most U.S. Employed Adults Plan to Work Past Retirement Age." *Gallup News,* https://news .gallup.com/poll/210044/employed-adults-plan-work-past-retirement-age.aspx (accessed January 2020).

177 **To explain Neuralink, Urban wrote a post:** Urban, Tim. "Neuralink and the Brain's Magical Future," April 20, 2017. Blog post retrieved from https://waitbutwhy .com/2017/04/neuralink.html.

180 **Stanley Milgram's famous prison experiments:** *Simply Psychology,* www.simply psychology.org/milgram.html (accessed January 2020).

185 **One of the things that bothered Steve Jobs:** Hertzfeld, Andy. "Saving Lives," August 1983. Blog post retrieved from www.folklore.org/StoryView.py?story=Saving _Lives.txt.

187 **Carlos Vasquez felt a burning desire:** "East Side Dry Cleaner Helping Jobless with Free Spruce up of Interview Garb," *Daily News,* www.nydailynews.com/news/money /east-side-dry-cleaner-helping-jobless-free-spruceup-interview-garb-article -1.369155 (accessed July 2019).

188 **75 percent of Americans said they want companies:** "Glassdoor Survey Finds 75% of Americans Believe Employers Should Take a Political Stand," Glassdoor, www

.glassdoor.com/employers/blog/glassdoor-survey-finds-75-of-americans-believe -employers-should-take-a-political-stand/ (accessed July 2019).

189 **66 percent of consumers want brands to take a public stand:** "#BrandsGetReal: Championing Change in the Age of Social Media," Sprout Social, https://sprout social.com/insights/data/championing-change-in-the-age-of-social-media/ (accessed July 2019).

189 **"I used to think I was an entrepreneur":** Impact Theory (producer). *Vishen Lakhiani on Breaking all the "Brules."* Video retrieved from www.youtube.com/watch?v =BvpAeRGnkJ4.

190 **"Your stand is your brand":** Gentempo, Patrick. *Your Stand Is Your Brand: How Deciding Who to Be (NOT What to Do) Will Revolutionize Your Business.* Penguin Random House Canada, 2020.

191 **"You may be thirty-eight years old":** Carson, Clayborne. *The Autobiography of Martin Luther King, Jr.* Warner Books, Inc., 2001.

CHAPTER 7

197 **"Good leaders have vision and inspire others":** Bennett, Roy T., *The Light in the Heart.* Roy Bennett, February 2016.

202 **"Until one is committed, there is hesitancy":** William Hutchison. *The Scottish Himalayan Expedition.* Read Books Ltd., 1913.

204 **"When you do something audacious":** Mindvalley (producer), April 5, 2019. *Naveen Jain on How to Dream so Big You Can't Help but to Change the World.* Audio podcast retrieved from https://podcast.mindvalley.com/naveen-jain-dream-big-change-the-world/.

208 **when setting goals for your business or team:** Doerr, John. *Measure What Matters.* Portfolio, a division of Penguin Random House, 2018.

209 **"When I was here at Michigan":** Google (producer). Larry Page University of Michigan Commencement Address, May 2, 2009. Video retrieved from http://googlepress. blogspot.com/2009/05/larry-pages-university-of-michigan.html.

212 **People who write inactionable visions:** Thiel, Peter. *Zero to One.* Currency, a division of Penguin Random House, 2014.

215 **The greatest people are self-managing:** *Inc.*, www.inc.com/marcel-schwantes/a -young-steve-jobs-once-gave-this-priceless-leadership-lesson-here-it-is-in-a-few -sentences.html (accessed January 2020).

216 **Dov Seidman describes it bluntly:** Seidman, Dov. *How: Why How We Do Anything Means Everything.* John Wiley & Sons, 2007.

217 **"Great teams are not created with incentives":** McCord, Patty. *Powerful: Building a Culture of Freedom and Responsibility.* Missionday, 2017.

CHAPTER 8

230 **there is a name for this phenomenon and it's *brain coupling*:** Jason Silva (producer). *Jason Silva on Brain Coupling: The Neuroscience of Romantic Love*, August 1, 2016. Video retrieved from www.facebook.com/watch/?v=1720981828166095.

234 **Pixar blurred the traditional lines between workers:** Catmull, Ed. *Creativity, Inc.: Overcoming the Unseen Forces That Stand in the Way of True Inspiration.* Random House Canada, 2014.

235 **phenomenon which explains why we embrace religion:** "Memetics and Social Contagion: Two Sides of the Same Coin?" *Journal of Memetics—Evolutionary Models of Information Transmission,* http://cfpm.org/jom-emit/1998/vol2/marsden_p.html (accessed December 2019).

245 **Google fails at 40 percent of everything they start:** Levy, Steven. *In the Plex: How Google Thinks, Works, and Shapes Our Lives.* Simon & Schuster, 2011.

248 **"The people who are right a lot more often change their minds":** Bezos, Jeff. "The Smart People Change Their Minds," October 19, 2012. Blog post retrieved from https://techcrunch.com/2012/10/19/jeff-bezos-the-smart-people-change-their-minds/.

CHAPTER 9

255 **"The world doesn't give you what you want or desire":** Mindvalley (producer), 2019. *Michael Beckwith on True Manifesting from the Soul.* Video retrieved from https://events.blinkwebinars.com/w/6246203867791360/watch-now?_ga=2.124996995.800747580.1575308463-1706431628.1574210435#5053427020988416.

255 **Build an identity that makes you rise:** Clear, James. *Atomic Habits: An Easy & Proven Way to Build Good Habits & Break Bad Ones.* Avery, a division of Penguin Random House, 2018.

259 **"I was successful by all standards":** "Arianna Huffington Reveals How Fainting Changed Her Whole Life," HuffPost, www.huffingtonpost.ca/entry/arianna-huffington-fainting_n_5030365?ri18n=true&guccounter=1&guce_referrer=aHR0cHM6Ly93d3cuZ29vZ2xlLmNvbS88&guce_referrer_sig=AQAAAAluVU44dbycY5BJ6TzcEnoiWiRUIqvHliW4c4cFdQWvj1HVsTtpSAV2nqAlU-7H3jTMuTqSBEoqSAuUodgPtEsyv5jz7YGE27twGhQDXbDfrSyPEBF27Dwivxi83LyBX2Ze1bPoDKWf0EwLJGwuRSymDez47Urs_zre9viqHV1Q (accessed December 2019).

260 **"when I peel back the layers with them":** "The Power of Focused Thought" training by Regan Hillyer. Mindvalley Mentoring Program, 2019.

262 **"There is a unique experience of consciousness":** BigThink (producer). *Scott Barry Kaufman on The Science of Creativity: How Imagination and Intelligence Work Together in the Brain.* Video retrieved from https://bigthink.com/videos/scott-barry-kaufman-on-intelligence-and-imagination.

264 **"What is real is you and your friends and your associations":** McKenna, Terence. *Food of the Gods: The Search for the Original Tree of Knowledge.* Tantor Audio, 1992.

ACKNOWLEDGMENTS

My thanks to:

First and foremost to all our Mindvalley authors: Jose Silva, Burt Goldman, Christie Marie Sheldon, Jim Kwik, Eric Edmeades, Jon and Missy Butcher, Steven Kotler, Steve Cotter, Jeffrey Allan, Donna Eden and David Feinstein, Marisa Peer, Barbara Marx Hubbard, Ken Wilber, Neale Donald Walsch, Robin Sharma, Marie Diamond, Emily Fletcher, Srikumar Rao, Denis Waitley, Lisa Nichols, Ben Green Field, Marisa Peer, Anodea Judith, Shefali Tsabary, Michael Breus, Katherine Woodward Thomas, Michael Beckwith, Christine Bullock, Ken Honda, Paul McKenna, Keith Ferrazzi, Geelong Thubten, Naveen Jain, Alan Watts.

To Jeffrey Perlman and Kshitij Minglani, for being such amazing allies. And to Rajesh Shetty and Omesh Sharma for their guidance and advice.

To my team at Mindvalley, especially Ezekiel Vicente, TS Lim, Wu Han, Klemen Struc, Miriam Gubovic, Anita Bodnar, Eni Selfo, Alessio Pieroni, Seerat Bath, Marisha Hassaram, Kathy Tan, Wayne Liew, Agata Bas, Laura Viilep, Kadi Oja, Olla Abbas, Natalia Sloma, Alsu Kashapova, Jason Campbell, Nika Karan, John Wong, Kevin Davis, Riyazi Mohamed, Chee Ling Wong, Shafiu Hussain, and Vykintas Glodenis, and to everyone else at Mindvalley, for ensuring that our company ran smoothly as I stepped away briefly to write this book. I am grateful for your daily efforts, your envisionings, and your commitment to unity, transformation, and love for the planet.

The business partners that I get to play with to bring transformation to the world: Rene Airya and Akira Chan of Little Humans, Ajit Nawalkha of Evercoach, Klemen Struc of Soulvana.

My book collaborator, Kay Walker, for your genius writing and storytelling skills, and your unwavering commitment to bring more transformational training and tools to the world. You were a fierce partner to have in the creation of this book.

My editor, Donna Loffredo, and the team at Penguin Random House, for your belief in this book. You played an instrumental role in shaping every aspect of it, from the content to the cover design to the marketing strategy.

My Director of PR, Allison Waksman, for guiding the PR strategy for this book and for all your expertise as my PR advisor.

Celeste Fine and John Maas, my agents at Park & Fine Literary and Media, who have been major supporters of my work since book one.

The creative minds who contributed their talents to the creation of this book, including the Mindvalley film production team, design team, and learning experience design team, for their work on the online experience. Thank you to Tanya Tesoro, for your gorgeous cover design; Melissa Koay, for leading the Quest creation; and the entire Mindvalley film team and creative design team for bringing your collective talents to this project.

A tremendous thank you to my entire team at Mindvalley, our customers, subscribers, and fans. You are the backbone of what we do. Without you, Mindvalley and this book would simply not exist.

The Mindvalley tribe and students of our Quests, for allowing me to love my job every day and for your commitment to a more conscious planet and inspired lives for you and the rest of the world.

To the teachers who provided wisdom for this book:

Drima Starlight, for being pivotal in the early days of Mindvalley and for your values process that has been key to our continued success and now the success of countless others; Cameron Herold, for your Vivid Visioning technique that took my business to new heights; Srikumar Rao, for your sage wisdom, mentorship, and support through the highs and lows; Lisa Nichols, for believing in me early on, and for your friendship and partnership in the field of personal growth; Reverend Michael Beckwith, for your spiritual guidance, your Life Visioning process, and your commitment to transformation on the planet; Naveen Jain, for blowing me away with your moonshot ideas that have expanded the way I think I run my business; Richard Branson, for suggesting I write the first book that led to this book and for inviting me to mastermind with you on Necker, and being an example of how business and life can flow together with ease; Bob Proctor, for kicking my butt and getting me to think better; Ken Wilber, for being the Father of Integral Theory whose models have shaped me, my work, and many of the ideas in this book; Tim Urban, for your genius blog that tackles the most relevant topics the world needs to know about in a way that's witty and engaging; Tom Chi, for your stand for humanity and for setting an example for how leaders should conduct themselves in business; John Ratcliff, for inspiring other leaders to truly see their people with your Dream Manager program; Daniel Pink, for your commitment to compassionate leadership and teams that thrive; Patty McCord, for reminding the world that people are already leaders the moment they walk in a door; Elon Musk, for being a trailblazer who sets an impeccable standard for how to think ten years ahead; Barack Obama, for your mentorship and inspiration; Larry Page, for sharing the OKR system that's transformed how we work at Mindvalley; Doug McGuff, for your super slow training, and helping me reverse my biological age; Simon Sinek, for emphasizing the importance of sharing your why; Jim Collins for encouraging me to get the right people on my bus.

To the thought leaders who are no longer with us but who have influenced my life and the ideas in this book:

Buckminster Fuller, for showing me how to tackle impossible problems; Terrence McKenna, for your stand for people living self-expressed lives, for your mind-bending wisdom, and for contributing to my worldview; Rumi, for your spiritual guidance and your poems that have stuck with me and shaped the way I work; Martin Luther King Jr., for inspiring us all to live bravely; and Abraham Maslow, for revolutionizing the field of human psychology with your Hierarchy of Needs.

INDEX

ABOUT THE AUTHOR

Vishen Lakhiani is the founder and CEO of Mindvalley, an online learning platform that combines media, filmmaking, tech, and real-world events to build its education empire, with over two million students. He is the author of the *New York Times* bestseller *The Code of the Extraordinary Mind*, which has been translated into more than twenty languages. Vishen is now working to expand Mindvalley's presence globally, with the aim to bring its teachers, tech, and programs into a hundred national schooling systems and every company in the Fortune 500 within the next few years.

Also by

VISHEN LAKHIANI

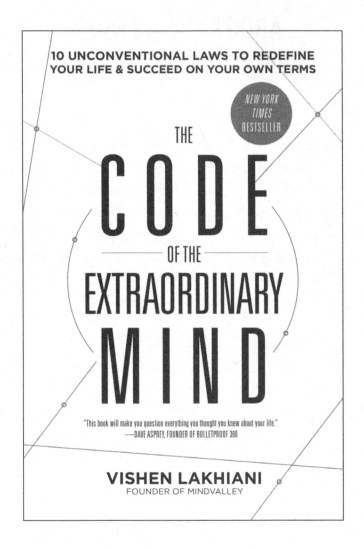

RODALE
BOOKS

Available wherever books are sold